Towards a More General Theory of Value

Towards a More General

Theory of Value

---

by Edward Hastings Chamberlin

NEW YORK OXFORD UNIVERSITY PRESS 1957

© 1957 BY OXFORD UNIVERSITY PRESS, INC.

LIBRARY OF CONGRESS CATALOGUE CARD NUMBER: 57-10390

PRINTED IN THE UNITED STATES OF AMERICA

TO

LUCIENNE

Preface

FOUR of the essays in this volume are new; the other twelve are reprinted. Of these latter, except for a few pages of Essay 8, all have appeared within the last ten years.

Whether new or old, they have without exception evolved out of classroom teaching at Harvard University. Typically, they have been written or adapted from lecture notes or seminar discussions. Thus they have been 'tried out' on hundreds of students, and my first debt of gratitude must be to those from my classes who have contributed directly or indirectly to them. Individually and as a group the essays in this book may be regarded as a small contribution to that further development of the theory of monopolistic competition which was foreshadowed in 1933 by the observation that the theory 'has not been carried in this study beyond its beginnings.' (*Monopolistic Competition*, p. 176).

In addition to pressing forward, the essays also attempt to answer criticisms and to correct misinterpretations. Since this type of theory strikes at the roots of the economist's 'habitual mode of thought,' it is not surprising that it has aroused opposition. It has been rejected by some very simply on the ground that it is 'destructive of traditional theory'—a rather shocking departure from the criterion by which economists usually hold that an innovation should be judged. Beyond this it has been widely misunderstood and misinterpreted, both in itself and through confusion with an alternative theory of similar phenomena, viz. Mrs. Robinson's *Imperfect Competition*. This is an old story. Many of these misinterpretations are now so much a part of the literature that it might seem futile to hope to combat them. However, I continue to believe that the correction of them should also be a part of the literature; and there are encouraging

vii

signs that progress is being made. The documentation on the matter is explicit and conclusive; and surely it is not too much to hope that some freer spirits may be persuaded to behave like scientists and consult evidence, instead of merely repeating a legend.

The reader will find, therefore, that essential distinctions between imperfect and monopolistic competition are frequently insisted upon in the pages to follow, and the key distinction may be summarized here: it rests upon the fact that in Mrs. Robinson's theory the notion of monopoly control is not extended to the individual enterprise at all, but remains firmly attached as always to the industry concept. Competition and monopoly, being industry *alternatives,* are thus as sharply separated from each other as ever. It is not surprising that the association of such a theory with one whose purpose was to destroy this dichotomy has blunted the impact of the latter, and caused endless confusion.

Among the manifold results of this association are: the continued (almost universal) identification of the welfare ideal with perfect competition [1] so that monopolistic competition is made *necessarily* to imply inefficiency in some socially undesirable sense; the (related) widespread belief that the theory holds that labor is exploited; the belief that the theory is concerned simply with applying the 'marginal revenue analysis' to a 'downward sloping demand curve,' so that the 'full cost' principle, oligopoly, advertising and selling costs, and nonprice competition generally are special problems apart from it (or perhaps even opposed to it); and in general the continued use of the industry concept in ways consistent only with the logic of pure competition. These and other matters will not finally be put in order until the full implications of blending monopoly and competition are better understood. It is this which is important for economic science, and which justifies continued insistence that Mrs. Robinson's

1. It is significant that two recent articles designed to summarize the present state of welfare economics (K. E. Boulding, 'Welfare Economics' in Bernard F. Haley, ed., *A Survey of Contemporary Economics,* Vol. II; and F. M. Bator, 'The Simple Analytics of Welfare Maximization,' *American Economic Review,* March 1957, p. 22) do not even mention the problems raised in Essay 5 below.

analysis of *industries* producing *homogeneous* products has only thrown us off the track.

A final word of explanation and apology is in order. Each of the reprinted essays below stands on its own feet, and was directed to a particular occasion or group of readers; so that when all are brought together between two covers, a good many duplications come into evidence. At one point it was my intention to eliminate these duplications, but the surgery involved proved too dangerous to the patient, and it was abandoned, except for two or three small and isolated examples. The essays remain therefore (with only inconsequential changes) as originally published, and the reader is asked to be indulgent if he suspects at some point that what he is reading has already been said. It probably has.

New material, occasionally added to the reprinted essays, has been indicated by inserting [1957]. Original cross references between the articles have in all cases been converted to essay numbers, with pages adjusted to this volume.

Many colleagues and friends have read portions of this book and have either comforted me with their approval or shocked me into making changes. I am especially indebted to Kenneth Galbraith, Alexander Gerschenkron, Gottfried Haberler, Carl Kaysen, Hans Staehle, and Jan Tinbergen. Needless to say, these and all others are absolved from further responsibilities.

I am indebted to various publishers and editors who have granted the necessary permission to reprint these articles. I am especially grateful to the Harvard University Press for their generous co-operation, including permission to use some materials which had previously appeared in book form.

EDWARD H. CHAMBERLIN

Cambridge, Massachusetts
August 1957

Contents

* New essays.

xi

Part

I

_____

GENERAL

1

Towards a More General Theory of Value

*'The book deals, not with a special
and narrow problem, but with the
whole of value theory.'* [1]

THE title to this essay is designed to recognize that there are
many meanings and aspects of the word general. It is not held
that the theory of monopolistic competition, because it is in a
number of respects more general than that of 'perfect' competition, is *the* general theory. It is, however, more general in the
sense that it offers a completer coverage of the economic system
than does the theory of perfect competition, with or without the
allowance for an occasional monopoly. In so far as all economic
theory involves markets, the categories of competition and of monopoly, ordinarily applied, are themselves very general. Monopolistic competition is more general. And just as theory, whether
static or dynamic, micro or macro, short run or long run, must be
written with reference to *some* assumption as to competition, it
will be most general in this respect if it is written under the
assumption of monopolistic competition.

This was and is my own fundamental conception of the theory,
as indicated in the quotation which heads this essay. Yet it is a
fact that it has been widely interpreted as having to do merely
with certain special and narrow problems, such as branded mer-
chandise, for instance,[2] or with certain limited phases of value

1. *The Theory of Monopolistic Competition*, Preface to the 1st edition, 1933.
2. This frequent interpretation may well be explained by the prominence

3

theory, such as the short run, micro theory, etc., etc. It is my present purpose to set forth in some detail the various respects in which it does in fact constitute a truly comprehensive basis for the analysis of the economic system.

A part of my argument is that it is comprehensive in just the same sense and degree that the two theories of competition and of monopoly together have been comprehensive in the past. A second part is that in a number of ways it is more comprehensive than these, embracing the many new types of problems which come into being when competition and monopoly are recognized, not as mutually exclusive categories which 'divide the field' between them, but as contributing elements to a total situation in which they are both involved and interact upon each other. The scope of economic analysis is extended into areas hitherto unrecognized. One writer of the Chicago school, which I shall discuss further below,[3] argues that these changes should be quashed forthwith, apparently for the reason that they are 'foreign to conventional economics.' [4] '. . . the economics of Alfred Marshall and the classical tradition are still useful,' he says (I agree), and follows with the dire prediction that if (in effect) any new life is breathed into them, '. . . economic theory in the traditional sense must depart. A revolution in analysis is called for—a new set of questions, a new philosophical foundation.' [5] This horrible possibility is, in fact, exactly what I have proposed.

I must begin by making clear that I am using the term monopolistic competition in its broad sense to include all situations where elements of both monopoly and competition are present— both product heterogeneity and oligopoly, and of course all combinations of the two. In this general schema, pure competition and pure monopoly appear as limiting cases where one or the

given in the introductory discussion of product differentiation in Chapter IV to a comparison between trade-marks and patents, designed to show that both are *both* (1) monopolistic and (2) competitive.

3. Essay 15, p. 296.

4. Alfred Sherrard, 'Advertising, Product Variation, and the Limits of Economics,' *Journal of Political Economy*, April 1951, p. 127.

5. Ibid. p. 142.

other of the ingredients is zero.[6] The purpose of the theory is to do a better job of explanation by presenting a continuum between two extremes rather than two sharply distinguished and mutually exclusive categories. It seems to be generally agreed, even by most of those who have been most active in criticizing the theory, that the actual economic system is such a continuum. There would seem to be a strong presumption that a theory which recognizes this must be more successful in explaining the system than one which does not.

Let us look first at some of the various ways in which the theory of monopolistic competition is general in the same sense and degree that the theory of pure competition (with occasional monopoly) has been taken to be in the past.

One way is with respect to its applicability to the long list of so-called applied or specialized fields of economics. It is perhaps only natural that the theory should be associated primarily with the field of industry, where examples of 'differentiated' products, of oligopoly, of selling costs, etc. seem to abound. It is strongly associated too in the minds of many, and for the same reasons, with retail markets, and has I believe played some part in the development in recent years (really for the first time in the history of economics) of a substantial interest in the analysis and empirical study of this segment of the economy.

Let us look beyond these, however. Economists have, for as far back as I can remember, tended to treat the whole range of problems identified with 'marketing'—the distribution of commodities as distinguished from their 'production'—not as a part of general economic theory, but as the peculiar province of the 'business

6. Pure monopoly certainly does not, and hardly could, exist in the real world (cf. *Monopolistic Competition*, pp. 63, 64) and the terminology was designed to bring this out. All *actual* monopoly, even 'isolated' monopoly, is subject to more or less competition (ibid. Chap. IV, also pp. 74, 111, and *passim*), and thus is a part of the theory in a very vital sense and not to be regarded as one of its limits. This has been clear from the first, yet it is hard to think of anyone today who does not use pure monopoly as simply another term for monopoly.

economist'; and I should doubt if very many courses in economic theory even today will pay any attention to the analysis of such an unorthodox subject as advertising. The ice has been broken, however, and students of marketing are at last able to use more of the tools of economic theory, and to integrate their own studies of this important segment of the economy with those of the general economist. Indeed, some of the most significant articles on economic theory in recent years have appeared in the various journals of business economics, unknown, I am sure, to most economists beyond this special group.

Agriculture has been by tradition the field which yields most readily a few examples of pure competition (wheat!), and perhaps for this reason is not often associated with monopolistic competition—except by agricultural economists themselves. Indeed I have been reproached a number of times by these latter for not having drawn more illustrative material from the agricultural area. In so far, of course, as agricultural economics embraces the marketing phase of its products, monopoly elements abound. In consumer economics too, closely affiliated historically with agriculture, product differentiation in its many aspects, problems of quality and in general of the product as a *variable,* advertising, etc., come into their own. It is also evident that many agricultural producers have local markets for their products in any of several senses, that many products are branded, advertised, and marketed by co-operative associations acting as single units for this purpose, and that many of those products not so marketed are sold under monopolistic conditions created and administered by governments.

Location is a highly special subject to most economists, although it is beginning to be appreciated that economic activity happens in space as well as in time, and that the subject has been held in undue isolation from the rest of economics. One force arguing powerfully for the importance of spatial problems is the realization that not only are purely competitive *markets* spatially separated, but also that space intervenes more typically between *individual* sellers and buyers, so that 'spatial differentiation' is the general rule. The impact of this analysis upon the theory of location has been worked out especially by Lösch [7] and Isard,[8] although a number of others have contributed to it. The main point is that, space being a major phase of product differentiation and also of location theory, it is not surprising that the generality of monopolistic competition theory should be manifested again in this area.

It seems gratuitous to point out that differentiated products cross international boundaries, and that oligopolistic forces are present internationally as well as within national economies. Indeed, there is no reason to suppose that the influence of these forces, including nonprice competition, on exports and imports is any less important in international than in domestic trade. Also business cycles and economic fluctuations have their being in an economy which is monopolistically competitive. Indeed even in the monetary area it has been shown that the typical banker sells a differentiated service and that oligopoly power is very general, both in local and in wider areas. To this may be added that no better example of oligopoly power could be found than that which the government exerts in the bond market and on the interest rate. It is equally evident that taxes are levied on products and on incomes earned under conditions of monopolistic competition, and a substantial literature on tax incidence under these conditions testifies to the growing generality of the theory in its application to the field of taxation and public finance.

In the field of incomes, the discovery that productive services are paid their marginal *revenue* products instead of their marginal products as defined under pure competition is sweeping in its generality, and (properly interpreted) would seem to the writer to be one of the truly revolutionary features of the new analysis. Specifically, in the labor field, the question of whether and to what extent labor unions possess monopoly power has long been a subject of debate, and its answer can hardly be given without recognizing the monopolistically competitive nature of

7. August Lösch, *Die Räumliche Ordnung der Wirtschaft,* Jena, 1940. Translated: *The Economics of Location,* New Haven, 1954.

8. Walter Isard, *Location and Space-Economy,* Cambridge, Mass., and New York, 1956; and numerous earlier journal articles.

the economy. There is involved, of course, not only the matter of monopolistic and competitive elements in the market for labor services, but also that of the position of labor as a claimant to a share of the total gross income of firms whose products are sold in monopolistically competitive markets. Although the subject has a substantial and growing literature, it would seem likely that its development has only begun. Apart from the matter of collective bargaining, individuals and hence their services are, of course, like products, strikingly heterogeneous, and the impact of this factor on wages (at all levels including salaries and professional services) is of the utmost importance. As to the rent income, it seems clear that if pure competition is seldom to be found, purely competitive rent theory must be quite inadequate. The old issue of whether rents are monopoly incomes, which seems to me to have an easy answer under the old dichotomy, is again to the fore, together with the reverse question of whether monopoly incomes may be treated as rents; and now the answers are not easy at all. As to profits, if monopoly elements are everywhere, the possibility is suggested that so also are monopoly profits (having, of course, their competitive aspects as well). Surely it is no longer possible to explain profits in terms of purely (though imperfectly) competitive markets; and monopoly forces have in fact played an important part in a revived interest in the theory of profits.

To summarize, in all the applied fields or special subjects mentioned, and in the explanation of which competitive theory has typically played the central role, the recognition that the economy is actually one of monopolistic competition would naturally give to the theory of this latter an equally central role. In this sense the theory is general at least in the same degree that pure competition has been general in the past. In support of this thesis, one may refer to the fact that a substantial application and development of the theory has in fact taken place in most of the areas mentioned, as is easily seen by consulting a bibliography on the subject.[9] No doubt its application has been developed

9. See *Monopolistic Competition*, 7th ed. The sixth edition lists almost 700 items up to 1948. A recent supplement, of about 800 more, covering the period

furthest in the area of industry; elsewhere it has been taken up usually by a relatively small number of innovating spirits and against the always powerful current of tradition. But enough has been done to leave no doubt that the theory is one of the broadest applicability in the sense that it is not directed in a special way to any particular sector of the economy.

Other ways in which monopolistic competition theory is general in the same sense that pure competition has traditionally been, are with respect to the issues of (1) static versus dynamic, (2) partial versus general equilibrium, and (3) micro versus macro analysis. Potentially, at least, it embraces them all. It is true that it is mostly associated with static, with partial, and with micro analysis, for the very good reason that it has had its first statement and development in these terms. But it is also true that it has made some invasion of the dynamic and macro fields,[10] and that its potentialities have at least been recognized with respect to general equilibrium theory.

Without lingering long on this set of issues, the point can be made that the fundamental question is the nature of the economy. If its structure is one of monopolistic competition, this must be true whether it is being studied as a system of static equilibrium or as one of dynamic movement, or perhaps of 'development'; whether segments of it are being studied in isolation or whether the whole of it is being studied as a single system; whether the focus is upon the parts or upon their aggregates.

With respect to the dynamic problem, it is interesting to note that the position stated above is different in important respects

1948-56, appeared in the *Quarterly Journal of Economics*, November 1956, and is added to the seventh edition.

10. Professor J. Tinbergen has suggested in a letter to me a reason why monopolistic competition 'is often disregarded in macro economics or in quantitative studies.' He says, 'It is, I think, mainly because monopolistic competition theory, in order to be applied, requires the use of more parameters of conduct, most of which have not yet been measured. In the cases where they have been estimated—as e.g. for substitution elasticities—there is no difficulty, and much advantage by way of realism, in applying the theory. The difficulty therefore seems to be that there is a lag of measurement behind theory, which forces the users of applied economic theory to stick to the older and simpler theories.'

from that involved in the system of Schumpeter, whose influence
has been so great in this area. The Schumpeterian static state, or
'circular flow,' is one of pure competition; 'development' takes
place through (temporary) monopolies in the form of innovations. The explanation of this sharp contrast is, I think, that
Schumpeter's system was evolved in a period when 'economic
theory,' especially static theory, was purely competitive theory. It
is a fact that he was greatly troubled by the impact of monopolistic competition theory; but he was able to integrate it into his
own system only as a part of the dynamic, disturbing forces to
which he finally gave such sweeping importance.[11] Yet this must
surely be no more than an historical anachronism. We may accept enthusiastically the great support of Schumpeter as to the
role of monopolistic competition in economic dynamics, and still
ask: what is there, after all, about product heterogeneity that is
incompatible with the idea of a static state?

As for general equilibrium theory, one may refer to the per-
suasive case made by Triffin that monopolistic competition theory
indicates a comprehensive rewriting of it, and shows the way towards an integration of the Marshallian tradition with that of
Lausanne.[12] It must be granted at once that the actual construction of *any* general equilibrium system involves simplifying assumptions which would leave any but the most dedicated mathematician gasping for breath. But if this degree of simplification is
accepted, what remains so difficult to understand is why anyone
should think that the only or the best simplifying assumptions
are those ordinarily identified with pure and perfect competition.
To consider only one alternative, it would be quite possible to
apply to the entire economy the 'uniformity assumption' [13] as to
the demand and cost curves of firms for certain broad classes of
products, take the products themselves as given, add uniform advertising expenditures, and either assume all firms 'isolated' with
regard to oligopoly problems or assume them all subject to such
forces according to some uniform coefficient. I am sure that this
will seem to many to be an utterly fantastic and unwarranted set

11. See below, Essay 10, esp. pp. 216, 224-5.
12. R. Triffin, *Monopolistic Competition and General Equilibrium Theory.*
13. *Monopolistic Competition*, p. 82.

of assumptions. But it is less fantastic by far than pure competition, which would treat the automobile market as if it were the Chicago wheat pit. No doubt the work of developing general equilibrium models in terms of monopolistic competition is yet to be done. Here pure competition is firmly entrenched, as if it were truly *de rerum natura*.

I confine myself to one observation with respect to aggregative economics. It is of course typically true and of overwhelming importance that an aggregate may behave in a different way from any of its parts taken individually. But a major pitfall is the propensity to regard an aggregate as a kind of mush which loses all the characteristics of its component parts. It is true that increasing the number of sellers of a *homogeneous* product, if carried far enough, will give an aggregate which may be manipulated mathematically as if the price (either for the product itself or for the factors producing it) were a parameter for any individual seller. But it is not true if the products are *heterogeneous*. There is a 'large number' of laborers (and even of unions) in the employment aggregate, but this does not mean that labor services are sold in a purely competitive market. Similarly there is a large number of retail grocers in the United States, or in any good-sized city; but this does not mean that the aggregate of grocery sales may be treated as a function of a price index in any way which would convert the process of price formation into one of pure competition. Prices are still not parameters for individual sellers, and the function itself must be defined to embrace some 'aggregate' of the policy decisions, not their absence. In other words, aggregates of nonhomogeneous items do not become homogeneous merely by the process of aggregation. 'Large numbers' do not give a purely competitive aggregate unless the additional requirement of homogeneity is actually met. I have argued elsewhere against a strange and widespread belief that product differentiation is reducible to deficiency of numbers,[14] so that if only numbers were large enough it would disappear. Aggregates in themselves are no more purely competitive than are the micro elements of which they are composed.

A final way in which monopolistic competition is general in

14. *Monopolistic Competition* (5th or later ed.), pp. 196-9.

the same sense as the purely competitive tradition calls for special comment. It is with respect to the question of time. The short-run versus long-run issue calls for special comment because (1) the theory has been widely interpreted as merely a short-run theory, and because (2) the evidence for such an interpretation is literally nonexistent. In fact, very little is said specifically about time in *Monopolistic Competition,* since it was taken for granted that the proposition that monopoly and competition are blended is logically independent of time. But on page 139 it is stated that 'the interaction of monopolistic and competitive forces is present in both short-time and long-time market situations. The curve of selling costs, like the curve of production costs, must include such outlays and results as are relevant to the period of time taken into account by the businessman when he decides upon his policies, and must be interpreted with reference to such a period.' [15] In at least two other places, in both of which the fundamental timelessness of the analysis is again affirmed, especial concern is expressed for the *long* run: 'Here, and elsewhere, it is usually the long-run [cost] curve which is in mind . . .' (p. 21n.) and 'Our main concern . . . is with those [variations] which persist over a long period of time' (p. 81). One may conclude therefore that the idea that the theory is short-run has gained currency entirely through the activities of its numerous misinterpreters.

Passing over for a moment the misinterpreters, let us note a further stage, corresponding to what the *New Yorker* magazine would call the 'Department of Utter Confusion,' where the theory, now identified with the misinterpretation of it, is criticized and 'corrected' by simply reversing the misinterpretation. Thus M. Bronfenbrenner describes the 'basic ingredient' of the theory as 'a maximization of *short-run* profits by an equalization of *short-run* marginal revenues and costs,' and proceeds to correct this supposed deficiency by offering a long-run solution.[16] Mr.

15. Mrs. Robinson's *Imperfect Competition* seems also to be timeless in the same sense. For instance, on page 50 she says, '. . . our analysis can be applied equally to quasi-long or to short-period cases provided that for each problem those curves are drawn which are relevant to the period under discussion.'

16. M. Bronfenbrenner, 'Imperfect Competition on a Long-run Basis,' *Journal of Business of the University of Chicago,* April 1950, p. 81. (Italics his.)

Harrod's case is more complicated and will be discussed further below; [17] but, in brief, he describes what he calls the 'accepted doctrine' of imperfect competition as implying 'that the entrepreneur pays attention only to the *short-period* marginal revenue,' and proceeds to refute the 'doctrine of excess capacity' mainly by insisting that it is *long-period* marginal revenue which is relevant.[18]

Let us return to the misinterpretation itself. Since it is without basis in the theory, how is it to be explained? I believe that the chief explanation lies in a twist of thought which derives ultimately from ordinary human inertia. Awareness of the revolutionary character of monopolistic competition theory has been so general that it is not necessary to argue this issue.[19] And in view of the intellectual investment which both the subject of economics and particular economists have made in purely competitive theory it is not surprising that efforts, both conscious and unconscious, should be made to discredit such a threat to the *status quo*. These efforts are both intellectual and emotional, but in view of the heavy preponderance of false bases among those used to attack the theory, one is driven to the conclusion that the latter predominate. Thus it has been asserted that the theory is based wholly on 'buyer ignorance,' or on 'imperfectly economic behavior,' or on irrationality, or on indivisibilities—to mention only a few. The conclusion (often explicitly stated) is

17. Essay 14, p. 280.

18. 'The Theory of Imperfect Competition Revised,' *Economic Essays*, p. 150 (italics his) and *passim*. It is of interest that in the extensive discussion which this article has provoked, not once has the issue of Mr. Harrod's interpretation of 'accepted doctrine' been raised! Indeed, quite the contrary. H. F. Lydall ('Conditions of New Entry and the Theory of Price,' *Oxford Economic Papers*, October 1955, p. 300) states that 'the traditional deductive system of the Chamberlin-Robinson type is founded on short-term assumptions, both on the demand and supply sides,' and credits Mr. Harrod with having 'brought forward' the long-period demand curve as a needed corrective.

19. Two prominent examples are: Hicks, cited below, p. 62; and Stigler, who, although opposing the theory for a jumble of reasons—some of which will be discussed below in Essay 15 on 'The Chicago School,'—states forcefully its revolutionary character and performs the service of sharply distinguishing it from Mrs. Robinson's *Imperfect Competition* in this respect. ('Monopolistic Competition in Retrospect,' in *Five Lectures on Economic Problems*, pp. 12-13.)

that monopolistic competition theory merely elaborates the consequences of violating certain methodological assumptions, widely accepted by economic theorists; and that if these assumptions were only adhered to, it would go away. The issues are all magnificently irrelevant, but in the cloud of dust created by raising them, *perfect* knowledge, *perfect* rationality, and *perfect* divisibility, end up by being equated to *perfect* competition. Our present point is that this same unwillingness to accept the idea that anything very important could really be wrong with pure competition, as the economist's 'habitual mode of thought,' [20] contributes heavily (and I am sure often unconsciously) to the interpretation of monopolistic competition as merely a short-run theory. The concession that 'there may be something to it in the short run' is easily made if the psychologically important proposition is retained, that in the long run, it cannot be so. Hence this latter position is rationalized and fortified: in the long run, it is said, the disturbing monopoly elements are washed out, demand curves become highly elastic [21] (evidence?), economies of scale disappear because with no fixed factors there is an approximation to perfect divisibility,[22] and pure competition is saved.

20. See the longer quotation from Keynes below, p. 139.

21. Much has been made of the argument that demand curves become more elastic with time, a generalization which is certainly true in some cases and clearly the opposite of the truth in others (as when oligopolistic forces are involved, for instance). But even where it is true, nothing whatever follows as to the *actual* elasticity of the long-run curve. The money wages of the average college professor also tend to increase in the long run (i.e. over a lifetime up to retirement) but they do not approach infinity—nor even a very high finite value.

The belief that demand curves under monopolistic competition become highly elastic in the long run is made easier by the common and false identification of the theory with situations where they are already very elastic in the first place. Here we touch a vital (and decisively documented) distinction between imperfect and monopolistic competition: the former is a theory of 'highly competitive' situations, whereas the latter envisages no particular degree of competition, but embraces all degrees from high to low, or alternatively all degrees of monopoly from low to high. (Cf. below, p. 277n.19, esp. the second paragraph.)

22. On this particular matter see Essay 9 below; or *Monopolistic Competition,* 6th or later ed., App. B.

But these are mere tricks to bolster up what is at bottom an emotional position.[23] In the 'long run' do two shops a half mile apart move to the same point? And do the *Atlantic Monthly* and *Popular Mechanics,* both magazines, become a single homogeneous commodity?

But apart from these attempted explanations of how the short-run thesis could have gained such currency, our chief point must be that the theory itself by its very nature is not to be identified with any particular time period, short or long. The conclusion on this issue is parallel to that with respect to the issues of static versus dynamic, partial versus general, and micro versus macro. In all these respects monopolistic competition is general roughly in the same sense and degree as is pure competition.

At this point the reader may be thinking, "This is all very well to say that the theory is general in these respects, but most of them are merely potential. Actually the theory as first presented was not applied thus broadly; and its flavor was strongly static, partial, and micro' (let us pass over the time issue). 'What theory, then are we talking about—the actual one, or an expansion of it which developed later and is still largely potential?' Some of this interpretation could be disputed, since none of the issues mentioned was actually raised in 1933. But without arguing the matter, perspective may be had on the point of view expressed above by adding to the quotation at the head of this essay the following, which is the last paragraph in Chapter VII, and there-

23. Another trick is to put a horizontal 'plateau' in the demand curve. This was proposed as early as 1934 by A. J. Nichol ('The Influence of Marginal Buyers on Monopolistic Competition,' *Quarterly Journal of Economics,* November 1934, p. 121; see also *American Economic Review,* May 1934, p. 30), and has been suggested again more recently by G. Warren Nutter ('The Plateau Demand Curve and Utility Theory,' *Journal of Political Economy,* December 1955, p. 512; see also *American Economic Review,* May 1954, p. 73). The fundamental difficulty is to explain why, apart from some possible qualification for short-run inertia, such 'marginal buyers' should be any more numerous at any one price rather than at another. There is also, of course, the question of fact: is the typical businessman able to sell substantially more than he does without lowering his price or without incurring advertising or other selling expense? If he is, why doesn't he?

fore the last paragraph in the first (1933) edition, of *Monopolistic Competition:*

> The theory of monopolistic competition has not been carried in this study beyond its beginnings. The theory of value has been considered only in its most general terms, and the theory of distribution has been ignored altogether [later remedied in Chapter VIII and elsewhere]. Furthermore, no applications to particular economic problems have been attempted or even suggested. Economic thinking has been completely dominated by the idea of an equilbrium defined by the equation of supply and demand in competitive theory. A reworking of its various fields of interest in terms of monopolistic competition is in order.

We pass now to another phase of our subject: in what respects may monopolistic competition lay claim to being an even more general theory than pure competition? This phase will be taken up under six headings. Most of the issues raised are discussed at length elsewhere in this book or in *The Theory of Monopolistic Competition* itself, and so may be dealt with briefly here. Our present interest is in relating them to the theme of this chapter, viz. the generality of the theory.

(1) Monopolistic competition is more general than pure competition in that it includes monopoly as well as competition, and combines both in all degrees, with the aim of giving a complete 'coverage' of the economic system with respect to these categories.[24] It is this complete coverage which is more general. Instead of regarding monopoly as an 'imperfection' to be excluded from the theory of the subject, except in a few cases

24. The case for such a theory could hardly be better stated than by Milton Friedman, who says, 'It would be highly desirable to have a more general theory than Marshall's, one that would cover at the same time both those cases in which differentiation of product or fewness of numbers makes an essential difference and those in which it does not. Such a theory would enable us to handle problems we now cannot and, in addition, facilitate determination of the range of circumstances under which the simpler theory can be regarded as a good enough approximation.' (*Essays in Positive Economics,* p. 38.) But when such a more general theory actually appears, he is sweeping in his condemnation of it. It 'possesses none of the attributes which would make it a truly useful general theory,' it is 'logically meaningless,' it 'offers no tools for the analysis of an industry,' etc. etc. (loc. cit.) . Is it that Marshall really cannot be improved upon? Friedman's position is further discussed in Essay 15 below.

where it is so strong that it takes over completely and excludes competition, each element is recognized and given its true value in a continuum which extends from one extreme to the other. Marshall's motto, *natura non facit saltum,* could never be better applied than here; and argument for the adequacy of a theory of pure competition with an occasional monopoly, and nothing in between, would be quite analogous to defending an economic theory which on the time scale was restricted almost entirely to instantaneous markets with the exception of a few cases in which only the longest run forces were present. The important problems in Marshall's time analysis lie mostly in between and so do they here.

Just as nature has drawn no sharp lines on the time scale, so 'nature' has made no sharp distinction between monopoly and competition. The chief target of monopolistic competition theory therefore is the traditional sharp dichotomy between them in economic theory. The evolution of Stigler's position is of interest in this connection. Having begun by following Knight in the proposition that monopolistic competition is explained entirely by 'consumer ignorance,' [25] but nevertheless giving it substantial importance, he dropped this explanation when he later argued on other grounds that it was a 'failure.' [26] More recently he seems to have reverted completely to the traditional sharp dichotomy. In the latest revision of his *Theory of Price* (1952) he defines a monopolist as 'a single seller of a commodity that does not have a highly elastic demand' (p. 206). We are given no clue as to just where the line is to be drawn, but he avoids including all elasticities short of infinity on the ground that 'then we should be embracing almost all the firms in the economy' (Exactly!—and without denying that most of them are highly competitive), 'and what is more serious treating as similar an elasticity of -100 and of -2.' But there are important similarities between elasticities of -100 and -2.[27] Granted that there may be also some signifi-

25. See below, p. 299n.7.

26. 'Monopolistic Competition in Retrospect,' in *Five Lectures on Economic Problems.*

27. Among them that they are both on the same side of infinity, so that this latter is revealed not as an approximation but as a limiting case.

cant differences between the two figures, Stigler's position necessarily involves him in finding a significant difference between, say, −5 and −5.1; for his conception of the problem requires that a line beyond which we have monopoly be drawn *somewhere* in the continuum. In order then to avoid treating −100 and −2 as 'similar' we are asked to treat −5 as monopoly and −5.1 as competition.[28]

In maintaining that the theory embraces the intermediate area between pure competition and pure monopoly it should be made clear in particular that the later extreme is *not* the monopoly of traditional economics. The line of least resistance is, of course, to identify the two concepts of pure competition and pure monopoly respectively with the familiar categories of perfect competition and monopoly, and this is commonly done; but neither is correct. Pure and perfect competition are carefully distinguished from each other in *Monopolistic Competition,* pages 6 and 25; [29] and it is made very clear in Chapter IV that ordinary monopoly will not do at all as a limit, for the reason that it is *always* more or less competitive.[30] 'Ordinary monopoly' refers not merely to control over the supply of something—a definition which is adhered to throughout *Monopolistic Competition*—but also to the absence of oligopoly forces in the sense that the monopolist's demand curve is a *datum* and not itself a function of movements along it. The term isolated monopoly seems to describe this condition very well, and it is, of course, consistent with competition from substitutes. The point here is that isolated monopoly, which is what most people think of when the word monopoly is used without any qualifying adjective, is actually a *part* of the theory; and in this sense too the theory is more general than pure competition.

The classification of pure competition, monopolistic compe-

28. Further argument on this matter is given in *Monopolistic Competition,* Chap. IV, esp. p. 57.

29. Cf. the comment by R. G. D. Allen on the way in which this distinction has been lost, *Quarterly Journal of Economics,* February 1949, p. 117n.7.

30. The requirements for a definition of monopoly which is pure in the sense that it contains no competition, and which is therefore at the opposite pole from pure competition, which contains no monopoly, are given on pp. 63-4.

tition, and pure monopoly appears to me by its nature exhaustive.[31] It thus includes, for instance, such categories as 'workable' competition. I recently heard the observation, 'What we want is workable competition, not monopolistic competition.' But this is a complete misunderstanding of both the categories in question. Workable competition is simply that variety of monopolistic competition which, from the point of view of public policy, 'works' reasonably well. This is not merely my own interpretation; it is made abundantly clear by Professor Clark himself. He points out (1940) that the 'important beginnings' which have been made in the formulation of 'theories of imperfect and "monopolistic" competition' have shown the limited usefulness of perfect competition as an ideal, and he therefore seeks a 'working approximation' in accord with 'actual conditions.' 'It would,' he says, 'be a truism to say that the most effective forms of competition we have, or can have, are imperfect forms, since there are no others . . . And it will be useful if we can learn something about the kinds and degrees of "imperfection" which are positively serviceable under particular conditions.' [32]

The exhaustive character of the classification mentioned above is also relevant generally to the problems of welfare economics, since whatever welfare measures are advocated (including, of course, myriad issues which are unrelated directly to the categories of monopoly and competition) the outcome must fall somewhere within the classification. The key role of perfect competition in welfare norms is well known, and to many, the significance of monopolistic competition in this field is principally to indicate certain aberrations from this competitive 'ideal' which are to be corrected. But it is argued in one of the essays below that in a world in which products are actually heterogeneous, partly by their nature and partly in response to a demand for variety from buyers, the welfare ideal too must fall within the area of monopolistic competition.[33]

31. The term monopoly must be taken to embrace both sides of the market, buyers as well as sellers.

32. J. M. Clark, 'Toward a Concept of Workable Competition,' *American Economic Review*, June 1940. Quotations are from pp. 241-2.

33. See Essay 5 below; also *Monopolistic Competition* (5th or later ed.), pp. 214-15.

(2) Monopolistic competition is more general than pure competition in that it embraces heterogeneity of the product in all degrees, and not merely in the lowest, or zero, degree to which the theory of pure competition is restricted. It will be said in defense of pure competition that in a world of diversity, some simplification, and hence an assumption of homogeneity, is necessary, and this is true. By an absurd and literal interpretation of heterogeneity, the economist would be obliged to inquire into the price of each individual orange or each individual egg as a separate problem. But it is perfectly clear that nothing of this sort is proposed, and that simplification in this respect is in fact duly allowed for under monopolistic competition—to exactly the same degree that the market allows for it. Heterogeneity is to be recognized in the theory to the extent that it is recognized by buyers,[34] since it is precisely to this extent that it is a force in the market. Thus if eggs or oranges are graded as to size or classified with respect to other characteristics, they are recognized by the theory too as homogeneous within such classifications.[35] It is only to this extent that the assumption of homogeneity can be accepted, and the reason is that where heterogeneity exists, even in small degree, it may radically alter the functioning of the market which it is the business of the economist to explain.[36] In theorizing about the functioning of markets under

34. Cf. *Monopolistic Competition*, p. 56 and (5th or later ed.), p. 204n.

35. It is of interest to note that pure competition rests largely upon legislation or collective action which establishes such grades, and is to this extent not in the 'nature of things' at all, but an artificial creation. Furthermore, in many cases in which the market superficially treats units as homogeneous, their actual heterogeneity emerges nonetheless. An excellent example is in the labor market where workers who by nature vary in efficiency (or desirability on other grounds) are paid the same wage. J. R. Hicks has given an illuminating and detailed discussion of this problem, pointing out that the less efficient may be discriminated against in other ways, receive lower annual wages by being laid off first, etc. etc. (*Theory of Wages*, esp. Chap. 3).

36. The theory has, in most of its development until recently, involved a major simplification in identifying product and firm, thus in many cases treating as single figures (price or output, for instance) what should more properly be interpreted as index numbers. More recently the important problems of intra-firm product and price relationships are beginning to receive the attention they deserve.

monopolistic competition, nothing from the theory of pure competition that is relevant and important need be omitted. The chief difference is in the recognition of important new forces, including of course their impact upon and modification of the old, to the end that our understanding of the economic phenomena involved may be improved.

(3) Monopolistic competition is more general than pure competition in that it ranges in the field of numbers over the one, the few, and the many, thus embracing oligopoly wherever it is present, instead of assuming it away.

Since oligopoly has come to be recognized rather generally in recent years as a subject of importance,[37] it seems unnecessary to argue for the greater generality of a theory which includes it. As with product heterogeneity, it may be said here too that the forces at work when numbers are few may be totally different from those when numbers are large; and pure competition 'simplifies' only in the sense of simply leaving them out.

(4) Monopolistic competition is more general than pure competition in that it embraces selling activity, instead of assuming that goods are sold automatically and costlessly, as does the theory of pure competition.

It may be said that the theory does not *necessarily* include selling costs, since certain assumptions may be made consistent with product differentiation which would exclude them; and this is true.[38] But the answer is that their inclusion is possible and clearly indicated by monopolistic competition theory, whereas it is decisively ruled out by purely competitive theory. That selling costs are logically inconsistent with pure competition is, so far as I know, noncontroversial.[39] With the recognition of monopoly elements, they are at once revealed as one of the leading ways in which monopolists compete with one another, and their

37. In the transformation of 'oligopoly' from its earlier status as a mere theoretical curiosity to this position of importance, one wonders what part may have been played by its being given for the first time (see Essay 2) a 'marketable' *name*, which helped to 'sell' it after the manner of a successful trade-mark.

38. My own Chapter v, in which selling costs are 'postponed' (p. 72), is an example.

39. The argument is summarized, *Monopolistic Competition*, p. 127-8.

exclusion would be arbitrary indeed. Finally they are in fact included in the actual development of the theory.

Selling costs illustrate again how pure competition simplifies, not by approximating but by eliminating. The quantitative importance of what is left out can only be estimated. But it is necessary to mention only one such estimate, 29.5 per cent of the total value of goods sold to final buyers (in 1929),[40] to indicate at least roughly the magnitude of what is involved. Why should an item of this order—almost one-third of the total of economic activity—be omitted from economic theory?

(5) The expansion of monopolistic competition beyond the range of problems envisaged by pure competition is perhaps nowhere so dramatically in evidence as in its admission of the product itself as a variable in the problem. It must be remembered that 'product' is always broadly defined to include not merely a physical product or service itself but also all circumstances associated with its sale which are of significance and therefore play a part in the 'contract.' The factor of spatial location should be mentioned specifically as an important branch of this phase of the theory.

The importance of nonprice competition in the real economic world has become a commonplace in recent years, and one wonders how anyone could seriously maintain that the economist should have none of it. The almost endless ways in which economics opens out when this factor is admitted are discussed at length in Essay 6 below, and no attempt will be made here even to summarize them. They are so much and so vital a part of actual competition that it would seem that any arbitrary attempt to exclude them by a ruling that the economists' province is price only would be on a par with limiting a surveyor to north and south distances, to the exclusion of east and west and up and

40. *Does Distribution Cost Too Much?* Twentieth Century Fund, New York, 1939. Costs of distribution were estimated at 59 per cent of the total cost of producing and distributing commodities in the United States in 1929 (pp. 117ff.), and 'selling and promotional activities, in contrast to the physical task of handling, storing, and delivering goods' were estimated as 'at least 50 per cent of the total costs of distribution' (p. 298), or 29.5 per cent. Since there is no allowance for selling costs in the manufacturing stages, the figure is understated to this extent.

down. No doubt the scope of economics is greatly widened by releasing products from their status as data and recognizing them as variables crying out for analysis. But so many narrowing influences have been at work in economics in recent years that if the 'science' is not to lose complete touch with reality, and even vanish into the blue as a pure exercise in logic, the discovery of some new worlds to conquer should be welcomed.

Without indulging in any rulings myself as to the scope of economics, I should like merely to point out that some of the standard conceptions of the scope of the subject are unsuccessful in excluding from it analysis of the product itself.

The conception of the subject as dealing with the allocation of scarce resources among given demands raises the question of why, when products are so volatile in fact, the given demands must be for some particular, arbitrarily chosen set of products. In the now familiar problem of buyers distributed along a line, or over space, their demands are not only in terms of different prices but also in terms of different spatial locations. An essential part of the whole problem, with given demands interpreted to include demands both at different prices *and at different places,* is how many sellers, and how located in the spatial area. No one to my knowledge has objected to this problem. If the analysis is now made more general by extending the spatial problem by analogy to other aspects of product variation,[41] it is clear that the question of how many and what kinds of products falls into place along with what prices and outputs, as an essential and integral part of the economic problem of scarcity.[42] An interpretation of given demands which would take the 'locations' of sellers as data and thus debar the economist from looking into them is of course possible, but quite arbitrary. Furthermore, one may argue alternatively that if the allocation of scarce resources includes more or less of particular products, the 'less' may well include a reduction to zero, and the 'more' an increase from zero, so that the question of 'what products?' is already posed as a part of the problem of scarcity.

41. Cf. Essay 3, esp. pp. 46ff., and Essay 6, esp. pp. 117, 124ff.
42. Alfred Sherrard, op. cit. p. 127, has argued the contrary view.

Again, if economics deals with the 'measurable,' this will evidently include not only prices and outputs, but also space, time, speed, acceleration, size, durability, horsepower, butterfat content, and endless quantitative attributes of products, any one of which is often more important than price in economic decisions. But one wonders why measurability is so necessary. The 'discovery' that utility is not measurable and therefore that ordinal indifference curves must be substituted for cardinal utility curves has actually been hailed by some as one of the great advances of modern economics. Perhaps the analysis of some of the similarly nonmeasurable aspects of products would not be so unthinkable after all.

Furthermore, if economics deals with 'maximizing,' there is clearly as much of this activity in the product area as in the price area.[43]

Thus, by several of the familiar conceptions of the nature of economics, nonprice competition, and in particular the product as a variable, falls readily enough into place as a part of the subject. It already has more than a foot inside the door and is even on the way to becoming respectable. Monopolistic competition is more general than pure competition in that it called forth and now embraces this development, which could hardly be a part of a theory in which products are taken to be homogeneous.

(6) Finally, monopolistic competition is more general than pure competition in that it embraces policy objectives other than profit maximization; and specifically the 'full cost' principle. This matter is discussed at length in Essay 13 below. There simply can be no questions of price policy at all under pure competition, where a seller had only the single possibility of conforming to the market price. But when more than one price possibility exists, then policy enters, and among alternative policies may well be found the setting of prices in conformity to cost in some sense, or to other criteria, as well as that of profit maximization, or the equating of marginal revenue and marginal cost. Although most of monopolistic competition theory is in terms of the traditional assumption of profit maximization, it has in-

43. See below, pp. 124ff.

cluded the full cost principle from the first as an important element in the explanation of 'excess capacity,' so that the greater generality to the theory which is here involved is not merely possible, but actual.

The present point (of alternatives to profit maximization) can and must be extended from the price area to that of the product as a variable, discussed immediately before. If, in the price field, economics is legitimately concerned, not merely with profit maximization but also with such other forces and objectives as may enter in, why should the same not be true for its concern with the explanation of products? The conformity of price to full cost may be taken to represent a 'standard,' and the matter may be illustrated by reference to standards in an even more general sense. The *prices* of medical services and of education are examples of prices which no economist would think of seeking to explain without some reference to standards or objectives other than that of maximum profits. And, although maximum profits certainly play some part also in determining the *products* in each of these fields,[44] if the economist is to study nonprice competition at all in terms of profit maximizing, why should he not also include some of the problems of 'standards' as they play a part in the determination of *products?* [45] This is of course already recognized in many fields, such as labor, population, and consumption, for example, where any economist who pretended to be competent in the field would be laughed at if he passed over the nonprice and non-income-maximizing phases of its problems.

'Sterile problems of what is economics,' some will say. But the only point it is sought to make here is that whatever the difficulties of defining the limits of economics they become much greater under monopolistic than under pure competition. The objective, dear to so many, of an 'autonomous science' [46] seems

44. 'Minimum losses' would be a better way of saying it for education.

45. The nature of some of these is sketched below, pp. 124ff. A recent article by Harvey J. Levin, 'Standards of Welfare in Economic Thought,' *Quarterly Journal of Economics*, February 1956, p. 117, is also of interest in this connection.

46. Cf. below, p. 121ff.

further away than ever, and the lines called for in order to define it more than ever arbitrary. If this is not so, let some apostle of 'autonomy,' (and one who will not simply parrot 'pure competition') tell us what they are with respect to the issues here raised. In fact, is not the greater generality of monopolistic competition in some of the senses discussed above a leading reason (both consciously and unconsciously) for the extremely critical attitude towards the theory on the part of right wing orthodoxy? One is reminded of the three monkeys who will see no evil, speak no evil, and hear no evil. Such insulation from 'evil' is of course one way to keep out of trouble.

Addendum

The essay above has discussed only monopolistic competition, and has avoided the issues between this and 'imperfect' competition. This addendum has the limited purpose of pointing out in summary form why each of the six reasons given above for holding monopolistic competition to be more general than pure competition is without applicability to Mrs. Robinson's theory.

(1) The blend of competition and monopoly. This was considered by Mrs. Robinson and specifically rejected because it involved too narrow a definition of a commodity.[47] Her commodity is therefore defined with reference not to a firm but to an industry, and her system is a classification not of interfirm relationships but of industries, each in every case producing a (homogeneous) commodity. Industries may be *either* monopolistic *or* competitive, and if the latter, either perfectly or imperfectly. The traditional dichotomy is complete, and monopoly is, as it has always been, an *industry* concept.[48] The greater gen-

47. *Imperfect Competition,* p. 5. See my more extended comment, *Monopolistic Competition* (5th or later ed.), pp. 208-12; and below, pp. 65ff.

48. It is, of course, monopoly in the sense of control over supply which is here meant. Mrs. Robinson uses the term in this sense, but 'bases' her book (p. 9) upon another: a monopoly is simply a firm. This definitional innovation has in fact been followed by no one to my knowledge, and has only caused endless confusion.

erality of monopolistic competition in picturing a continuum between the extremes of pure competition and pure monopoly, although often credited to the two of us jointly, simply does not exist in Mrs. Robinson's *Imperfect Competition.*

Additional recent evidence that no break was intended with the dichotomy between monopoly and competition has been given by Professor Austin Robinson and is discussed below, page 277, note 19. The dichotomy is found also in Mrs. Robinson's *Essay on Marxian Economics,* in which she contrasts 'the general run of more or less competitive industry' with something called 'outright monopoly' (p. 78); and in her article 'Imperfect Competition Revisited,' [49] in which she continues (p. 592) to use the terms competition and monopoly simply as *industry* alternatives.

(2) Product heterogeneity. It should never be forgotten that when the term product differentiation appeared in *Monopolistic Competition,* Mrs. Robinson's first reaction was to reject it as not to the point for 'market imperfection.' [50] Nothing could serve better to indicate the fundamental differences between us.

It is of course true that, in her own concept of 'preferences,' she had in mind some similar market phenomena. But her actual assumption of product homogeneity was highly significant, for it could never have been made unless it had been thought that (as in 'competitive' theory) the differences within any particular 'commodity' really do not matter very much, and hence could be assumed away. Further consequences of this assumption are discussed in this addendum under headings (1), (4), and (5) and below, pp. 95-6, 141ff., 309ff.

(3) Oligopoly. Mrs. Robinson's recent disclaimer to have said anything at all about oligopoly [51] should provide helpful clarification in a situation where the two of us have been jointly (always jointly) both praised for bringing the subject to life [52] and

49. *Economic Journal,* September 1953.
50. See *Monopolistic Competition* (5th or later ed.), p. 202, for references and further discussion.
51. 'Imperfect Competition Revisited,' p. 584.
52. Cf., for instance, J. K. Galbraith, *American Capitalism, the Concept of Countervailing Power,* pp. 44-5.

criticized for neglecting it.[53] Actually the contrast between us could not be sharper.

In this connection it is of prime significance that Mrs. Robinson *defined* perfect competition and hence imperfect competition, in terms of elasticity of the demand curve.[54] In contrast to this, pure competition in my own case is *defined* as large numbers plus product homogeneity; and the perfectly elastic demand curve is a *derivation* from this more general definition.[55] Here such a perfectly elastic curve is not necessarily *restricted* to pure competition. The demand curve under product heterogeneity is similarly a *derivation* from nonrandom pairings of buyers with sellers; [56] it will typically yield curves of less than perfect elasticity, but may not in the full sense.[57] What is more important in our present connection is that in my own case, oligopoly (Chap. iii) is simply small numbers, without any generalizations whatever as to demand elasticities. Under certain oligopoly assumptions, demand curves, as in the case of pure competition, are perfectly elastic (pp. 34ff.); under others they may be not only quite inelastic, but also of the same elasticity over a range of sellers from one to a substantial number (pp. 46-50). Furthermore, different types, or definitions, of demand curves are required for different parts of the oligopoly problem; and under certain assumptions demand curves simply cannot be drawn at all. In sum, my own definitions were not in terms of elasticity; and in particular, the oligopoly problem by its very nature defies definition in such terms.

Returning to Mrs. Robinson, the point here is not merely that she neglected oligopoly. (There is in fact some limited discussion of the problem of numbers in her article 'What Is Perfect Competition?',[58] highly confused, in part because of its attempt to conceive the problem as one of demand elasticity.) The point is that 'imperfect' competition, *defined* as less than perfect demand

53. See below, p. 67n.22.

54. *Imperfect Competition*, p. 18; also 'What Is Perfect Competition?' *Quarterly Journal of Economics*, November 1934, p. 104.

55. *Monopolistic Competition*, pp. 7, 16.

56. Ibid. p. 56; see also p. 8.

57. Ibid. pp. 66-7, esp. p. 67n.1.   58. Op. cit. pp. 114ff.

elasticity, *could* not logically include more than certain limited phases of oligopoly theory. In other words, such a conception really cannot be made to embrace oligopoly theory at all. The latter naturally becomes 'a certain difficulty' in the way of analyzing the demand curve and marginal revenue, and is omitted significantly as 'not to our purpose' (*Imperfect Competition*, p. 21).

I believe it is fair to say that the literature of the late 'twenties on 'increasing returns,' out of which Mrs. Robinson's *Imperfect Competition* evolved, did not conceive oligopoly as a part of its problem. It may be noted that Mr. Harrod's 1934 article, setting forth 'the principal points of significance for economic theory in the doctrines relating to Imperfect Competition that have been recently evolved,' [59] continues this approach, of which he himself was a part: oligopoly is not one of the 'principal points,' or even a minor point; like Mrs. Robinson he is concerned with a 'downward sloping demand curve.'

(4) Selling costs, and (5) The product as a variable. Neither of these two phases of nonprice competition plays any part in Mrs. Robinson's *Imperfect Competition*. The first, like oligopoly, is specifically ignored because it introduces *complications* into the all-important demand curve (p. 21)—in order to get on with this latter it *may be assumed* that advertising expenditure can be treated like a price reduction.[60] The second could hardly have been envisaged in view of the assumption of product homogeneity.[61]

In a theory in which the 'downward sloping demand curve' (and marginal revenue curve) is so much to the fore, it is not surprising that nonprice competition should be absent. A demand curve envisages only *price* competition; and especially when the subject is *defined* in terms of this curve there is no room for anything else. It is clearer than ever why monopolistic competition cannot be *defined* in such terms; and even to conceive the subject principally as a matter of demand elasticity

59. 'Doctrines of Imperfect Competition,' *Quarterly Journal of Economics*, May 1934, see p. 442; reprinted in his *Economic Essays*, see p. 111.

60. For some of the consequences, and for further discussion, of this procedure, see Essay 8 below, esp. pp. 155-6, 161ff.

61. Cf. below, p. 106n.3.

would be to narrow it down, like 'imperfect' competition, to the price variable.

(6) 'Full cost' and, in general, nonprofit-maximization. In Essay 13 below, it is explained at length why the only price policy possible under 'imperfect' competition is that of profit maximization, and not even a summary will be attempted here. Imperfect competition is not, like monopolistic competition, a more general theory in this respect.

On the Origin of 'Oligopoly' [1]

SEVERAL years ago at a meeting of businessmen and academic economists, the president of a (very) large corporation delivered himself without restraint on his opinion of the fellow, whoever he was, who was responsible for having introduced the word oligopoly into the language of economics. Impressed with the blackness of my offense, I rose after he had finished to acknowledge my guilt, and to assure him that, in spite of the severity of his language, there were no hard feelings on my part for his having unwittingly let me know what he really thought of me, by contrast with his very amiable conversation of earlier in the afternoon. After all, there was no reason why a prominent industrialist should not resent being called by such a horrible name; and no reason at all why he should have any knowledge as to its origin, since most professional economists for some reason appear to be equally in the dark about it.

It is true that the word came into general usage so quickly with the increased development in the early 'thirties of interest in the subject, that it was naturally applied at once to earlier writers. The result was that references such as to 'Cournot's theory of oligopoly,' etc. became frequent, and it was easy for the general economist to suppose that the word had been in common use for a long time. But many of those with a special interest in economic theory or in the monopoly problem, who therefore are aware that it is of recent origin, seem to have only

1. Reprinted from the *Economic Journal*, June, 1957.

the vaguest notions, if any, as to where it came from.[2] The matter is of some interest, not only for the word itself but also for its subject matter as a segment of economics. It may therefore be in order to set down a few facts and even to include a reminiscence or two.

My own development of a theory designed to challenge the conventional dichotomy between competition and monopoly raised difficult problems of terminology, especially since there appeared to be not one, but two, leading phases of such an intermediate theory, viz. (1) numbers and (2) substitution.[3] The word in most common use at the time for the numbers phase— 'duopoly,' denoting two sellers—was evidently too narrow, and 'oligopoly' was coined to indicate explicitly the greater generality of the problem.[4]

There was no word in use at all at that time for the substitution phase of the problem, since it hardly existed as a theoretical

2. Fritz Machlup, after referring to a 'probably first,' earlier use of the word (mentioned in the second edition of *Monopolistic Competition*, p. 8n., and to be discussed shortly), continues: 'It was, however, only the appearance of the books by Edward H. Chamberlin, Joan Robinson, and Heinrich von Stackelberg in 1932 [sic] and 1934 respectively, which firmly established the word oligopoly in economic terminology.' (*The Economics of Seller's Competition*, p. 349n.6). There was no need, however, for the familiar grapeshot with respect to the books in question. Mrs. Robinson could hardly have contributed to 'establishing' the word, since she never used it, and did not even say anything about the problem, describing it (correctly) as 'not to her purpose' (*Imperfect Competition*, p. 21); and Stackelberg, who later used its German equivalent in his *Marktform und Gleichgewicht*, 1934, explicitly acknowledges (p. 2n.1) its origin in *Monopolistic Competition*.

3. Actually the problem of small numbers was investigated first, and 'product differentation' was discovered as a complication of the oligopoly problem. Vestiges of this bit of history can be found in the early part of Chapter 1; as for instance, in the third paragraph. The strange accusation has been made that the theory 'neglects' oligopoly (K. W. Rothschild, 'Price Theory and Oligopoly,' *Economic Journal*, September 1947, pp. 301-2). The fact is that it was *born* out of oligopoly.

4. *Monopolistic Competition*, p. 8. 'Duopoly' as a term for the general problem has now almost disappeared from use, as has the notion that the treatment of this important though highly special case is adequate to the general problem. R. F. Kahn, however, preferred it not only 'for the sake of brevity and of simplicity' but also (very rightly), of 'euphony' ('The Problem of Duopoly,' *Economic Journal*, March 1937, p. 1n.)

category. In the first edition, it was called both product differentiation and monopolistic competition, with strong emphasis on the latter phrase, although this latter had been used by Pigou (1924) specifically to describe the small numbers problem.[5] But beginning with the second edition (1937) the more general sense of the phrase monopolistic competition was stressed, to include *both* product differentiation *and* oligopoly, as in the general thesis of the book, which aimed to blend monopoly and competition in their *two* phases, and of course in its title.

In the real world the most common case is certainly 'differentiated oligopoly,' or small numbers *plus* a differentiated product; and it would seem that this would be monopolistic competition *par excellence,* since it qualifies by both the broad and the narrower use of the phrase. Yet the very success of 'oligopoly,' together with what seems to be a strong human penchant for mutually exclusive categories, has led many to say that since differentiated oligopoly is oligopoly *ergo* it is not monopolistic competition. Thus is monopolistic competition converted from an almost universal phenomenon, which it surely is (in either sense), to the relatively unimportant one of differentiated products in the restricted case of 'large numbers.' [6]

It is at least an amusing story to recount why it was that my own use of oligopoly in print did not date from 1929 (instead of 1933), when Chapter III of *Monopolistic Competition,* entitled 'Duopoly and Oligopoly,' appeared as an article in the *Quarterly Journal of Economics.* The reason is that it was vetoed by F. W. Taussig, then editor of the *Journal,* who thought the word a monstrosity and crossed it out. Since my own bargaining power was weak at the time, protests were of no avail, and the article bore the title: 'Duopoly: Value Where Sellers Are Few.' [7]

When, freed from the Taussigian veto, the word did finally appear in *The Theory of Monopolistic Competition,* in February 1933, I was unaware of any prior use of it in print. However,

5. Cf. *Monopolistic Competition,* Preface, first sentence.
6. And usually under still more restricted assumptions which yield the 'tangency solution.'
7. *Quarterly Journal of Economics,* November 1929.

two earlier uses have since been pointed out to me. In 1936, Arthur W. Marget wrote me that he had run across it in the literature of money and banking, viz. in Karl Schlesinger's *Theorie der Geld- und Kreditwirtschaft* (1914), where in the German text the adjective *oligopolistische* is used several times (but no theory of the subject developed). This information was added in the second edition of *Monopolistic Competition* (1937).[8] Schlesinger's use of the word had gone unnoticed until then, and was clearly without influence. It was, for instance, unknown to Schumpeter (see *Journal of Political Economy*, 1934, p. 250) and to Stackelberg, writing (in German) a major treatise on the subject in 1934 (see note 2 above, p. 32).

A much earlier use of it has since come to my attention, viz. in the original Latin of St. Thomas More's *Utopia* (1518). It is mentioned in Eli Heckscher, *Mercantilism*, Vol. I, on page 273, where the following quotation from More is given: '*Quod si maxime increscat ouium numerus, precio nihil descrescit tamen; quod earum, si monopolium appellari non potest, quod non unus uendit, certe oligopolium est.*' Heckscher comments that 'the English translation omits this statement.'

The first English translation of the *Utopia* was by Ralph Robynson in 1551, and the standard edition, edited by J. H. Lupton (Oxford, 1895), gives both the original Latin and the Robynson translation, as follows: 'And though the numbre of shepe increase neuer so fast, yet the pryce falleth not one myte, because there be so fewe sellers.' (The Robynson text continues: 'For they be almoste all commen into a fewe rich mens handes, whome no neade driueth to sell before they lust; and they luste not before they may sell as deare as they lust.') Lupton's comment is as follows: 'Here again Robynson curtails his rendering of the Latin. More makes an antithesis between *monopolium* and *oligopolium*. We have "monopoly," but not "oligopoly" (the sale by a few), and so cannot preserve the point of the sentence. Burnet renders: "Tho they [the sheep] cannot be called a Monopoly, because they are not engrossed by one Person, yet they are in so few Hands, and these are so rich, that" &c.'

Other English editions in the main follow Robynson, yet even

8. P. 8n.

where the translation varies, I have never found 'oligopoly,' but always 'sale by few persons,' 'a few rich men,' or variations on these. Perhaps the explanation is to be found in an editorial comment in the edition by J. Churton Collins (Oxford, Clarendon Press, 1904). The translation (p. 17) follows Robynson, and Collins comments (p. 163): 'More's antithesis between *monopolium* and *oligopolium*—a word coined by himself—cannot be rendered in English.'(!) At any rate, it wasn't.

I have searched through a number of French, German, Spanish, Italian, and Dutch translations of the *Utopia* in the Harvard University Library, but found only the equivalents of 'few sellers,' with great stress on 'the rich.' The search was not exhaustive, however, because of an irrepressible feeling after a time that diminishing returns had more than set in. In a French edition of 1643 (printed in Amsterdam), we find '*les riches*'; but in another of 1789, we find '*oligopole*' with the following footnote of explanation: '*oligopole, commerce dont s'emparent un petit nombre d'hommes. L'oligopole comprend encore les privilèges exclusifs, dont on n'a pas assez démontré l'abus.*' [9] It may be noted that, although the earlier Italian editions which I saw spoke only of the few and of the rich, a very recent one (edited by Tommaso Fiore, Bari, Guis. Laterza & Figli, 1942, p. 26) translates '*un oligopolio.*' Perhaps the untranslatable *oligopolium* will now return to *Utopia* in other languages than Latin with the help of modern economics.[10]

9. Paris chez Blanchon, 1789, pp. 34-5. (In the library of Professor Léon Dupriez of the University of Louvain, Belgium, and shown to me by him.)

10. Although the word is now common in the technical economic literature of various languages, I have not found it in any general dictionary of a language other than English, nor have I found it in any dictionary published in England. Its first appearance that I know of is in *Webster's New Collegiate Dictionary*, G. & C. Merriam Co., Springfield, Mass., 1949, where it is defined as 'virtually exclusive control of an industry by a few corporations *covertly allied.*' (Italics added.) This, I fear, does represent a widely current conception of the term. A decided improvement has been made in the 1951 edition, in which the definition is: 'control by a few competing sellers of the amount and price of a given product or service to a large number of buyers.'

So far as I know, no other of the great proliferation of new terms which has been proposed in this area: monopsony, polypoly, heteropoly, pliopoly, etc., etc., has advanced beyond the stage of technical jargon.

Oligopoly is certainly not a difficult word to coin, and after the belated discovery of these two earlier uses, in Schlesinger and in More's *Utopia*, one may well expect it to turn up again, perhaps in an antique poem or a Greek play. But even if other casual examples are found, it seems certain that there will be none which bore any fruit in economic literature. The reason is that, although oligopolistic forces have certainly been of great importance throughout history (they must surely have been more important in past centuries than in the present one), they have been recognized by economists as important only in recent years.

I should like to reminisce for a moment and recall the state of 'duopoly' theory as it appeared to me when I began to look into it in 1924-26. At that time not more than a very small number of economists had even noticed the problem; and I believe it is not an exaggeration to say that, to the extent that it was recognized at all, it was regarded as a mere theoretical curiosity. The 'literature' consisted of a chapter by Cournot, an article by Edgeworth, a few pages [11] or paragraphs or even lines here and there, and a few footnotes, including the inevitable one by Marshall. Both Cournot and Edgeworth had written much earlier (1838 and 1897); each had his followers, and on the whole Cournot was either accepted blindly or considered as having been 'refuted' by any of several people, notably by Edgeworth. Everyone sought *the* solution, and I can recall no hint of my own general position that the problem is a manifold one with a large number of different answers depending on which of many possible assumptions are made.[12] And I remember that the discovery that this was so seemed a major step forward in my own

11. Three pages in Pigou's *Economics of Welfare*, 2nd ed., 1924, form a chapter.

12. Pareto's 'refutation' of Cournot, and his position that the problem is 'overdeterminate' should receive specific mention. Although he was perhaps 'on the right track,' his conception of the problem seems to me to go completely astray (Cf. *Monopolistic Competition*, second page of Appendix A). Were it not for this fact, overdeterminateness might be interpreted as implying that the problem was a manifold one.

progress with the problem.[13] Although this view (for which I believe I may claim some responsibility) has gained a substantial following in recent years, it by no means prevails, and many today are still looking for *the* answer. I have even heard it seriously proposed by one of our newer crop of mathematical economists that what we must do is to '*define* the problem in such a way that the answer will *be* determinate.'

Certainly two major subdivisions of this manifold problem must turn on whether the fact of mutual dependence is (1) ignored or (2) recognized. Both of these categories are very general. With respect to the latter in particular, 'what each seller thinks the other is likely to do' has many different aspects and involves a variety of uncertainties and hence of *conjectures,* including conjectures, not as to what the other will *do,* but as to what his conjecture will be, and so on indefinitely. It invites maneuvers for positions of advantage, including those of the leader-follower relationship (in the ordinary sense of price leadership, and also in the totally different Stackelberg sense, which excludes this). In itself it raises special problems of the short and long run, including time lags; of perfect and imperfect knowledge; of 'rational' and 'irrational' conduct; of security or risk; and in general, of 'warfare,' including tactics and game theory. Like the broader subject of oligopoly, of which it is a part, it is not a problem but a family of problems, with a family of different solutions depending on how it is conceived, i.e. on what assumptions are made. It has in fact received extensive development in the indicated directions in recent years, and from a variety of different sources.[14]

13. *Monopolistic Competition*, Chap. III *passim,* but esp. pp. 30, 37. Stackelberg, who traces the history of the subject in exhaustive detail, classifies me, together with Zeuthen, as an 'eclectic,' and mentions no one earlier in that category (op. cit. p. 83).

14. Among these sources—and also as a part of the state of 'duopoly' theory in the middle 'twenties—should be mentioned the solution given by Bowley in 1924 (*Mathematical Groundwork of Economics*, p. 38). With essentially Cournotian equations, but differentiating without the Cournot assumption that for each seller the supply of the other is fixed, he came out with an equation for each seller containing the derivative of the output of the other with respect

Another feature of 'duopoly' theory in the mid-'twenties was that it ignored almost entirely the 'mutual dependence recognized' solutions—that phase of the subject which is now thought by many to be the essence, or even the very definition, of the oligopoly problem. Such recognition is of course foreign to both the Cournot and Edgeworth solutions, which, as has been pointed out above, dominated the scene.[15] Irving Fisher, advancing the game analogy (chess) for the first time to my knowledge (1898), and H. L. Moore (1906) had both criticized Cournot on this score, but neither one carried the matter further. Pigou (1924) again presented the chess analogy, but seemed to think that it led to Edgeworthian oscillation (although proposing a new set of limits which has always been completely mysterious to me); and three years later (1927) Wicksell, arguing also for the recognition of mutual dependence, rejected Edgeworth *because* he had ignored it, and favored Cournot (who had equally ignored it!). To me at that time, the real problem seemed to be to develop 'mutual dependence recognized' as a separate category, and to make clear that it had nothing to do with either Cournot or Edgeworth, both of whom had on the contrary assumed that mutual dependence was ignored.

The solutions to which 'mutual dependence recognized' led in my own case were multifarious, involving time lags, frictions, and a variety of uncertainties.[16] They all took, however, as their point of departure, a conception of the fundamental nature of the problem on which I should like finally to comment, since it has been much misunderstood, and has even been rejected

to his own. His conclusion was that the problem cannot be solved without evaluating these derivatives. (See my Appendix A for a résumé of Bowley and some further discussion.)

15. A possible ambiguity should be guarded against. The emphasis must be on the word mutual: each seller recognized his own dependence on the other, but not the other's dependence on him.

16. *Monopolistic Competition*, pp. 50-53. It has seemed to me over the past 20 years that, although there is good cause for concern about oligopoly, the alarm felt by students of policy problems in the United States is excessive, being based erroneously on the *identification* of oligopoly, first of all with 'mutual dependence recognized,' and secondly, with this under a particular set of highly simplified assumptions.

as 'incorrect' by Stackelberg.[17] It involves the distinction between (1) the direct effect which a seller has upon price and (2) the indirect effect, which includes the moves his rival makes as a consequence of his own; and holds that for a seller to take the second as well as the first into account is fully consistent with independent action.[18] Although the solution if each seller thus takes account of his *total* influence on the price may be the same in terms of prices, outputs, and profits as if there were an agreement, there are excellent reasons for making clear that no agreement is involved—not even 'tacit' agreement, quasi-agreement, or 'spontaneous co-operation.' In other words, this is a *legitimate* solution of *oligopoly,* consistent with complete independence of the sellers, and not to be excluded from the subject on the false ground that there is an agreement in *some* sense, and hence monopoly.

In defense of this view, an appeal to the analogy of chess may be useful. Clearly if a chess player decides against a particular move because the responses to it which his rival would make would be damaging to him, he cannot be accused of 'spontaneous co-operation'; and he should hardly be *required* by the rules to make the move on the ground that otherwise he would be entering into a 'conspiracy in restraint of chess,' or into an agreement with his rival. Why, then, should a businessman who acts with equal (and rather ordinary) intelligence in deciding not to make a price cut, be accused (either by economists or by attorneys general) of collusion, or of *tacitly* co-operating with someone? The point is that the idea of co-operation in *any* sense is *unnecessary* to the result.[19]

The chief difficulty (and it appears to be very great) in recognizing a distinction between (1) independent action on the part of each competitor with regard to the *full* effect of his acts, and (2) nonindependent action, or collusion (actual or tacit), is that

17. Op. cit. p. 85. It is also rejected as the 'first degree of collusion,' by R. F. Kahn (op. cit. p. 8).

18. Cf. *Monopolistic Competition,* p. 31.

19. Of course agreements, both actual and tacit, are extremely common in reality, and there is certainly no intention to deny them where they are in fact present.

(under certain simplified conditions of symmetry) the quantitative, or mathematical, 'solutions' are the same.[20] It is a familiar case of where mathematics, if its limitations are not recognized, may easily obscure or cover up economic distinctions of the greatest importance for a truthful theoretical explanation of a phenomenon, and hence also for policy. If, in order to prevent certain undesirable economic results, 'agreements in restraint of trade' are prohibited, and if it appears that the same results may follow when there are no such agreements, the means are not effective to achieve the end. And if it is sought in practice to achieve the end by arbitrarily treating as collusion all cases of 'mutual dependence recognized' in the sense here meant,[21] or even all cases of 'price rigidity,' the falsity of the explanation is not likely to be without consequences. One can well imagine, for instance, that businessmen who would like to be independent, when legally harassed for 'spontaneous collusion,' might in desperation actually engage in collusion for the purpose of moving their prices about from time to time in inconsequential ways, so as to give the appearance of not colluding!

To return to the theory, it seems impossible to handle this idea of the indirect effects of independent action by the use of the technique of 'conjectural variations'—the derivative, $\frac{dx_2}{dx_1}$,[22] of one output (price) with respect to the other—which Hicks once

20. An element of paradox in the argument must also be partly responsible: it is *because* the individual seller has *no* (appreciable) influence on the price in the case of large numbers that the price falls, and it is *because* the individual seller *has* an appreciable influence in the case of small numbers that it does *not* fall. (Cf. *Monopolistic Competition*, p. 49 and top of p. 53.) The difficulty is illustrated by a letter I once received pointing out very politely that there was evidently a 'typographical error' at the top of page 53! It is also illustrated by a criticism on the part of Stigler, in which he dismisses the argument as 'equally applicable if there are a million producers,' thus merely revealing that he did not understand it. ('Notes on the Theory of Oligopoly,' *Journal of Political Economy*, June 1940, p. 525.)

21. Joint maximization, although technically unobjectionable as a description (under special assumptions) of the *result*, unfortunately is heavy with the connotation of joint *action*, which may or may not be present.

22. See the reference to Bowley above, p. 37n.14.

described as 'opening a path towards a general theory.'[23] The reason is that there are no conjectural variations,[24] since each seller simply adopts the (joint) optimum figure, being confident that the other(s) will do the same. Likewise there are no reaction curves, for there are no reactions.[25] In the simple case of two sellers (under symmetrical conditions) the attempt to plot a reaction curve for each will simply show that each is independent of the other—in other words that the concept of a reaction does not apply.[26] A general theory in terms of conjectural variations, in addition to many other objections to it, would automatically rule out the recognition of indirect effects as a part of the oligopoly problem.

23. 'Annual Survey of Economic Theory: the Theory of Monopoly,' *Econometrica*, January 1935, p. 13. His sketch of the path, however, brings out its limitations. It is confined to *quantity* variations (which are described at one point as 'similar' to price-cutting!), and progresses from the Cournot case through successive assumptions that first one, and then both, of the sellers 'takes as his conjectural variation the reaction curve of his rival' (p. 15), and it follows the case of both with the observation that 'there does not seem to be any reason why we should stop here.' But there is a very good reason, and it is that we should have stopped much earlier. To illustrate what is happening: under the simple conditions of a straight line demand curve and no cost curve (see my page 32), if one seller behaves this way he will produce ½ and the other ¼, leaving ¼ unproduced; if both behave in this way, each will produce ⅖, leaving ⅕ unproduced. But, although the mathematics are undoubtedly correct, what possible reason could there be for two sellers in the real world actually choosing such outputs? Is this not another illustration of the *substitution* of mathematics for economics?

24. To say that there are no conjectural variations (derivatives) is, of course, not at all the same thing as to say that the derivatives are zero. For instance, if it is quantities that are being adjusted, this latter gives the Cournot solution.

25. It is true that decisions are taken on the basis of reactions which *would take place if the decisions were different*. But the key is that they are not themselves reactions to decisions actually taken by rivals.

26. The logical (and mathematical) distinction between this and market sharing, or between this and 'price leadership,' should be made clear. In the symmetrical case (for simplicity), under market sharing each puts on the same output as the other, and under price leadership each charges the same price. The conjectural variations, whether in quantities or prices, therefore = 1, since any change by either party will be imitated by the other. Reaction curves exist in this case—although the answer cannot be obtained, without added information, merely by solving them—since the curves are identical for both sellers, and therefore coincide throughout.

The Stackelberg approach is an example of this. His basic conception of the problem in terms of the reaction of each seller to a decision of the other taken as a datum, excludes indirect effects by definition; and these latter, rejected by the theory, naturally come to be interpreted as 'co-operation.' [27] In effect, the reasoning is that if A is charging one dollar, the best price for B is evidently 99 cents, with no ifs, ands, or buts about it. The fact that B may, *consistent with independence*, decide to charge one dollar and divide the market with A at that figure, rather than oblige A to lower his price to 99 cents where he will again share the market with him, and less profitably, is not regarded as 'legitimate.' [28]

These final comments on conjectural variations seem to lead us again not only to the conclusion that oligopoly has no single solution, but beyond this to an appreciation of the pitfalls which beset any attempt to bring its multifarious solutions within the embrace of any single formula. It is a disturbing and recalcitrant problem, especially to the mathematically minded theorist who insists upon having *the* answer.

27. The theory also admits only quantity adjustments in the case of a homogeneous product. Price adjustments are excluded on the ground that price differences are inconsistent with a homogeneous product. This seems to be a case where Cournot 'refutes' Edgeworth, instead of the reverse, as was thought for so long. At any rate, this purist logical position taken by Stackelberg cuts off a substantial part of the real problem and thus allows only solutions of the unrealistic Cournot type for homogeneous oligopoly. (Cf. my own treatment of this issue in *Monopolistic Competition*, Chapter III, esp. pp. 35-43, 50-3.)

28. Fellner has also recognized this limitation on the Stackelberg approach (*Competition Among the Few*, pp. 116ff.), and himself gives great importance to the part played by regard for the 'indirect consequences of individual policies.' But he does not draw the sharp distinction between this and co-operation which is here insisted upon—not even in describing my own position (see page 40, for instance, where 'indirect consequences' slips over into 'co-operation').

3

Monopolistic Competition Revisited[1]

THE main part of this paper will be devoted to a reformulation of the theory of monopolistic competition. It might be regarded as an indication of how I should develop and present the theory if I were doing it all over again today—in 1951. The underlying principles remain the same; but the order of development in building up the structure is different, and there are a number of shifts in emphasis designed to avoid the many errors in interpretation which have grown up and which have become current in the literature. A second brief part will be devoted to a statement of the difference between the theories of monopolistic and imperfect competition.

The theory which I propose does *not* deal with a particular

1. Most of the material in this essay was given in lectures in English and European universities in the spring of 1951, and it was originally put together in several different ways, both in the English and French languages. The basis for the essay as here given is the article by the same title in *Economica*, November 1951, but substantial material has been retranslated and added here and there from 'Une Formulation nouvelle de la théorie de la concurrence monopolistique,' in *Economie Appliquée*, April-September 1952. In integrating this material so many small changes were necessary that it did not seem possible (or worth while) to indicate in the final text the precise origin of each part of the whole. However, this much may be said: that most of the discussion of oligopoly (pp. 57-62) appeared only in *Economie Appliquée*, and that the portion of the essay from page 64 to the end appeared only in *Economica*. I do hope that the essay will be more useful in its present form than in either of its original printed versions. The article from *Economie Appliquée* was translated into Italian and appeared in the *Revista Internazionale di Scienze Sociale* in 1954.

43

market form, as has been supposed. Its subject matter is very broad. It *includes* all monopolies and monopoly elements in the economic system. It likewise includes all competition, if those rare cases of pure competition in the market structure may be regarded as special cases where the monopoly elements are zero. It is a blending of two theories, *each* of which has been developed in economic analysis under certain perfected conditions. It is thus not a theory of 'imperfections' in any sense, but a *general* theory, designed to replace that of generalized pure competition (of Marshall or of Walras, for instance) as a point of departure and as a basis for the analysis of the entire economy. It has no particular relation to micro economics as compared to macro economics, since it deals with the entire economic system in which both of these types of theory have their being.

Let us begin our analysis of the structure of the economy by looking briefly at the essential unit of which the structure is composed, namely the firm. It has received a great deal of attention in recent years—Professor Hicks has commented *ad nauseam* —but I think a great deal of attention was needed in order to restore the balance as against an earlier long period during which it received hardly any at all. In any event, it is our economic atom—often a rather big one—and, like the atom in physics, it is fundamental and we shall always need to know more about it. For our purposes two aspects are particularly important—the conditions of cost under which it operates, and the conditions of demand for its product which it faces.

The firm may be as small as a single person or a family. Or it may be a giant corporation, highly articulated, with many and scattered physical plants. Whatever its size, the firm has overhead costs in the short period during which some of its factors are fixed, and because of these fixed factors its short-period cost curve is U-shaped, by reasoning with which we are all familiar.

For long-run problems all factors can be varied; and particularly in planning an enterprise, before any commitment has been made at all, it may be set up on any scale whatever. Here is where economies of scale properly speaking appear, and since an economic structure is mainly the product of long-run forces, the matters here considered are particularly important for our purpose. Again, for any existing set of technical possibilities, the curve of average unit cost as a function of output appears to be U-shaped. Greater aggregates of inputs (including plant along with labor and other variable items) in general make possible greater specialization and in particular the use of superior technical equipment and methods. During this phase unit costs are falling, and the phase may go on for a long time. But it seems certain that sooner or later increased complexity and cumbersomeness of organization, with controls mounting geometrically as size increases, will turn the cost curve up again.

It is of the utmost importance to recognize that efficiency is thus a function of *aggregate* resources, and in the same sense that utility is a function of *aggregate* supply. The assumption that resources are infinitely divisible no more destroys this functional relationship than does the assumption that a consumers' good is infinitely divisible destroy the law of diminishing utility. I have dealt at great length with this matter elsewhere,[2] and in particular have pointed out the purely tautological character of the prevailing definition of divisibility to include, as it generally does, the negation of economies and diseconomies of scale. The importance of the issue for our immediate purpose lies in deciding upon the answer which is to be given to the question: 'What kind of an economic system would result under the theoretical assumption of perfect divisibility?' Mr. Kaldor is fond of saying that 'Where everything is perfectly divisible, and consequently economies of scale completely absent, "perfect competition" must necessarily establish itself solely as a result of the "free play of economic forces," ' [3] and this proposition (or some similar one) is widely held. It is probably the basis, consciously or unconsciously, of the view which lingers on in many quarters that economic theory itself is simply the theory of perfect competition. But the conclusion is contained in the tautological definition of divisibility by which the firm is eliminated from the picture. We are merely being told that if there are no economies of scale there will be no economies of scale; and hence perfect

2. Essay 9 below.

3. 'Market Imperfection and Excess Capacity," *Economica,* February 1935, p. 42 (and elsewhere).

competition, whereas what we want to know is: what kind of an economic structure will result if there *are* economies of scale? It is quite impossible to show (without assuming it) that perfect divisibility of factors eliminates economies of scale. The correct statement is therefore that 'where everything is perfectly divisible, economies of scale remain, and, in a world of human beings having diversified tastes, the free play of economic forces would necessarily establish monopolistic competition.' This, and not perfect competition, is the true underlying structure of theory.

There will, of course, be the greatest variety between different firms in the system as to the details of their U-shaped cost curves, and in particular as to their most efficient outputs. All that I have said so far is that there *is* a most efficient size for the production of any particular product with any given set of technical possibilities. This variety (ruled out by the tautological definition of perfect divisibility) is of the utmost importance, as will appear presently, in defining the structure of the economy which it is our task as economists to analyze.

Let us turn to the conditions of demand facing the firm. Under the picture of the economy given by the theory of pure competition, with theoretically homogeneous products and large numbers in each market, these conditions were so simple that they did not require analysis: the demand was perfectly elastic at the going price. Under such conditions, of course, there would be no advertising or selling effort, since if any amount could be sold freely and automatically at the going price there would be no point in spending money to persuade people to buy it.

But we have now to take into account that there is actually a great diversity of products, with each seller producing a product or products of his own, different in some degree from those of others. Such differences are embodied in technical, chemical, or other qualitative aspects of the product itself (in the narrow sense), including even its name, and also of the conditions under which it is sold, such as the personality of the proprietor and salespeople, and convenience of location, which last-named involves time and trouble in retail problems, and money outlays on freight charges in manufacturing.

In trying to get this type of problem clearly in mind a good first approximation is to think of an abstract 'model' in which a population of buyers is distributed fairly uniformly over a spatial area, and the sellers of a product—homogeneous except for the spatial aspects to be considered, and offered initially by all at the same price—distribute themselves about the area in an attempt to make sales by appealing solely to the convenience of as many buyers as possible. The result would evidently be a fairly uniform distribution of sellers over the same spatial area, each one with a 'market' consisting of those buyers located nearest to his place of business.

Buyers, we have assumed, prefer to buy conveniently; but any seller may, by lowering his price, enlarge his market area by drawing in buyers who are willing to go a little further in order to make the saving involved. Similarly, if a seller raises his price he will lose some customers on the edge of his market but will still retain those nearest to him who would rather pay the higher price than make the trip to a more distant seller. Each product in our example is differentiated spatially, and we see at once that one result of differentiation is that the elasticity of the demand curve is (not inevitably, but generally) finite instead of infinite. Each seller has a local monopoly based upon his location, yet he is surrounded by competitors. Hence the paradoxical expression 'monopolistic competition.' His demand curve has a downward slope the steepness of which will depend upon how highly people value the unique elements of his own product (in our example, his convenient location) as compared with the available substitutes.

If we now recognize that the population, instead of being distributed uniformly, will be most unevenly scattered about, and heavily concentrated in some areas, we have a much closer approach to reality. Since their locations must include not only their homes but their travels as well, there will be heavy concentrations where people work, or travel on the way to work, where they shop, at the intersections of important streets, etc. In such places, shops will be larger, or more numerous, or both. Of course in all this there is mutual adaptation, action and interaction, and the picture could be developed much further in terms of different types of activity, different types of concentrations, etc., if space permitted.

Let us now make use of our spatial example in order to approach still closer to reality by admitting all other types of differentiation. We may speak of economic space instead of literal space, and conceive of buyers distributed symbolically throughout a multidimensional area containing all the various aspects of products (in addition to convenience) which have already been mentioned. In the same way as with literal space, producers are distributed throughout such an area, and although their products may be alike in some respects, they remain different in others. Thus two restaurants located next door to each other in literal space will serve very different food; a particular branded product, in itself identical in all shops, will be differentiated by the surrounding conditions in the shops themselves, by spatial separation, etc. Concentrations of buyers will now include not only their proximity in literal space, but in all other relevant aspects as well.

Tastes exist or are developed for particular products; thus we have 'concentrations of population' around the Digest type of magazine, around automobiles with 360° of window glass, and around movies (cinemas) with happy endings. Any successful product is likely to be imitated at once because its success indicates a following, in other words, a concentration of buyers. Mass-produced goods must be on a price, *and hence a quality*, level to appeal to low income groups, because it is here that the population is concentrated on the income scale. And so we could multiply examples.

A final step in this development is to introduce the advertising and sales effort for which monopoly is a necessary, though not a sufficient, condition. To return to our spatial example, let us imagine that people for some reason were not sure of where the shops were located, or even of where they themselves were located. They would then be receptive to all kinds of information, and of course, misinformation, as to how these matters stood, and markets could be expanded or contracted through the efforts of each seller to inform, to misinform, or otherwise to persuade buyers that the distance involved in trading with him was the shortest. This seems to be pretty close to what happens in the more complicated reality of multidimensional product diversity. If people knew exactly what products were available, at what prices, what they were like and what wants they would satisfy (in other words where they were located in economic space), and if they knew where they themselves were located, in the sense of what they wanted and how badly (in other words, if they knew their own minds), there could be no advertising. Such conditions would rule out selling effort, but their absence would not admit it unless monopoly too were present. In other words, the utilization of economic resources to influence demand, necessarily excluded from a theory of pure competition, finds its place at last in the more general theory of monopolistic competition. Selling costs have always been an integral part of the theory.[4]

To sum up, the demand for a firm's product under monopolistic competition is a function of at least three variables: (1) the nature of the product itself, which might be conceived as its location in economic space, (2) the price, and (3) the selling outlay.

Much has been said in defense of the assumption of generalized pure competition by reason of its simplicity, determinateness, etc. It is of interest therefore to note that it is simple in good part because it rides roughshod over the firm, either assuming it away entirely or arbitrarily assuming it to be small [5] in order that there may be a large number of sellers for each product. Yet if we are to have any respect as scientists for the economic system which it is our duty to explain, the correct procedure would seem to be not to assume pure competition and then to bring the firm into line by Procrustean methods, but rather to

4. Professor Stigler, in his recent visit to the bier of monopolistic competition, has stated: 'I pass over selling costs, since my subject is monopolistic competition, not the economics of Professor Chamberlin.' ('Monopolistic Competition in Retrospect' in *Five Lectures on Economic Problems*, p. 19n.3). Yet he also holds the peculiar view that the phenomena of our subject are to be attributed entirely to 'consumer ignorance' (cf. my review of *The Theory of Price* in the *American Economic Review*, June 1947, p. 414), which makes one wonder why he (of all people) should rule that the analysis of advertising does not belong here.

5. As does Professor Knight, *Risk, Uncertainty and Profit*, p. 98.

build up the system from the firms which compose it, discovering from the facts what assumptions are appropriate as to competition and monopoly, and therefore as to structure. It is possible, of course, that even though, for some particular product, the most efficient size for the firm is large, the aggregate demand for the product in question will be so much larger that the requirement for pure competition—a large number of sellers for a homogeneous product—may be realized. But this appears rarely if ever to be the case in fact. In general the economies of scale for individual firms, combined with a demand for diversity in the output of the system, result in one producer for each product, with often a complicated set of oligopolistic relations between them. This is a far cry from pure competition; and even to define what pure competition would be like in such a situation for purposes of comparison becomes so highly arbitrary as to be meaningless.[6]

Some obvious cases in which superiority of large size (together with other considerations) combined with a limited demand results in a single producer have come to be classified as 'natural' monopolies. These are the public utilities: water, gas, electricity, street railway companies, etc.; but here it is instructive to note that what we really have is a rather neat case of product differentiation, again in terms of space. There is a large aggregate demand for electricity in the United States, for example, but the population is widely dispersed over the country, and furthermore, it is highly concentrated in numerous urban centers. The result

6. I must plead guilty myself to having done what is here held to be 'meaningless,' but in partial extenuation may point out that the brief comparisons in *Monopolistic Competition* between monopolistic and pure competition are entirely polemical, having for their purpose only to demonstrate that the theory of pure competition *may not be applied* where monopoly elements are present (cf., for instance, p. 116, last paragraph, and p. 174, top). It should be pointed out that Mrs. Robinson's comparisons between monopoly and competitive output and between monopoly and competitive demand for labor (*Imperfect Competition*, Books IV, VIII), although open to a similar objection in so far as they involve 'perfect competition,' are not the same thing at all. They are comparisons between a monopolized *industry* and a perfectly competitive industry, preparing the way for welfare conclusions in Books IX and X.

is very generally 'local monopoly,' with the size of the producing unit adjusted to that of the concentration it serves.

But natural monopolies in this sense are everywhere. Cement, for instance, although not perfectly homogeneous in our sense, is very close to it, with the conspicuous exception of the same spatial factor, given a peculiar importance in this case by the great weight of the product and the relatively high cost of its transport. Here again we have local monopolies by spatial differentiation, and each seller in close competition with a comparatively small number of others—a situation which no amount of legislation or antitrust prosecution can change. It is not meant to infer that nothing whatever can be done about price practices in a case like this—only that whatever is done must fully recognize the elements of monopoly which are built into the economic structure of the industry.

As a final example, we have seen that each retailer has some element of spatial monopoly apart from the other individual aspects of his product; and the recent development of the supermarket in the United States is a striking instance of the invasion of this area by a conspicuously large unit. We have here another case of where the large unit makes its way into the picture because of its superiority for a certain type of activity over the small, and because of a sufficient concentration of population to make it possible. In this case the development must clearly be associated with improvements in transportation, particularly the automobile, and the greatly increased mobility of the population which makes it possible to draw customers from a wide area at small cost per unit of distance.

With no limitations from the demand side—that is, with perfectly elastic demand curves to firms—there would be a strong tendency for the most efficient conditions of production to be established everywhere. But even with a limitation in the form of a demand curve of finite elasticity, clearly economies of scale remain a powerful force working to establish large firms. In summary we may say that the technological and economic factors which explain the cost curve are one important force working on the size of the unit which emerges in the economic structure.

A second major force is the demand, and enough has already been said so that it may be dealt with briefly. The location and the elasticity of the demand curve for the individual firm are both the product in good part of the effectiveness of substitutes —i.e. of how near its rivals may approach to its product and of how many such near rivals there are. Evidently, the fewer the rivals the stronger the demand for the product of any one firm; and the better the substitutes offered, in the minds of the buyers who have to choose, the more elastic will be the demand curve facing the firm and therefore the more likely will it be to charge a low price and expand nearer to its most efficient size. In cases where the seller, if left alone, would charge a higher price and make unreasonable profits, public regulation, as in the case of the utilities, has the particular function of enforcing a lower price and correspondingly larger output and size of the producing unit.

Two further special factors affecting the size of the firm are suggested by this discussion of the demand curve.

(1) The possibility of 'entry.' Monopolistic competition implies lack of free entry in the full sense of freedom for another firm to produce the identical product, since the output of each firm has at least a minimum of individuality of its own. But the possibility of producing *similar* products can be such that the multiplication of firms in any momentarily profitable area of economic activity will reduce profits to the minimum necessary to attract and maintain entrepreneurs in the field in question. In this case it appears not to matter whether entry is assumed free or not. But it does matter, because, although the situation can be thus, often it is not. The reason may be put technically in terms of concentrations of preferences for the products of particular sellers in spite of the efforts of others to come close to them. Such factors are universal, but seem to be especially conspicuous in the whole field of trade-marked products, as well as in the areas where personal qualities or peculiarities count heavily, as with lawyers, artists, athletes, textbook writers, etc. Every seller will as a matter of course attempt to maintain his own demand by preventing others so far as possible from locating economically near him, and the 'prevention

of such prevention' is one of the most important elements in a public policy designed to keep monopoly under control. In some cases, notably that of the public utilities, exclusive franchises serve to pre-empt an area of activity for a particular company, whose prices and profits are then subjected to control. Such pre-emption has often been necessary either without control or with only a minimum of control, as an inducement to secure the development of some particular industry or natural resource. This policy has been important notably in the development of the world's railroads and in colonial exploitation. The granting of patents for a limited period is a familiar example of a policy designed to promote general technical advance by such methods. From these examples it seems clear that it is not a self-evident principle of public policy to eliminate all such impediments to entry. Indeed they could not be completely eliminated, any more than all men could be made equal in ability or merit by legislation. Wherever restricted entry raises the profits of some firms it probably lowers them for others and gives a little of the flavor of a lottery to business activity. There are prizes for some and blanks for others. And, like the prizes in the lottery, the high profits of a few draw others into providing a part of what society needs, although the earnings of these latter may be zero or even negative. Restriction of entry has both its pros and its cons; but our main point here is that it has its effects on the size of firms.

(2) Advertising or, more generally, selling activity is the second factor. Such activity has always been important, from the shrewd techniques of the Oriental bazaar to the highly scientific and calculated advertising output of the large corporation with its battery of psychological experts. Advertising today is certainly more brazen and dehumanized, but one may doubt if it is quantitatively any more important than it has been in the past, and is even today in less-developed economies. It is evident that whether it succeeds spectacularly, moderately, or negatively, it is a major factor in the size of firms. The cigarette industry in the United States is an example of where the emergence of a very few large producers seems to be closely linked to high-powered advertising and to the great difficulty of entry arising from

the necessity for any new producer to spend enormous sums to wrest a market from those already in possession of the field.

Let us pass on to the question of relationships between firms—external interdependence, as Triffin has called it.

The recognition of interdependence in the sense here meant immensely complicates the picture so far drawn. What is at issue is whether or not a seller, by his policies, has any effect upon the policies of others which in turn might react upon his own situation. In general he has, because in general he is in close competition with only a few others, as must be clear from our earlier spatial example. Where he is in competition with only a few others, any move he makes will have an appreciable effect upon them, and perhaps cause them to make a move which in turn will affect him.

What is perhaps the simplest example of this type of mutual dependence may be briefly called to mind. Suppose that a seller makes a price cut and gains thereby a substantial amount of business. If his gains come mostly from a few others, this means that they are suffering substantial losses and that they in turn may cut prices in order to keep their customers or to get them back. And the fact that they will do this may be decisive in the calculations of the first seller, who will reason that, since his move will be met by countermoves which will in the end leave everyone worse off, including himself, he might as well stay put in the first place. Or he may decide to go ahead anyway and run the risk.

But these uncertainties do not exist for what I have called an isolated monopolist, and let us look first at this simplest case of all, where there is no mutual dependence whatever. The isolated monopolist, by definition, is not subject to repercussions. The reason he is not is that when he, say, cuts his price, he makes his gains (perhaps substantial) in small degree from a large number of others, so that no *one* of them is appreciably affected by what he does. In such a case he determines his policies in isolation, in the sense that he need not think of repercussions, but can take the prices, products, and selling outlays of others as data.

This is the traditional monopoly problem, with a *given* demand curve (although we must now add to it an analysis of the product itself as a variable, and of advertising), a demand curve drawn on the assumption that the prices of other products are unaffected by what the monopolist does. It has in recent years frequently been described as a 'pure' monopoly, and thus the whole nature of monopolistic competition has been falsified by a misunderstanding of one of its limits. Since the concept of purity in relation both to monopoly and to competition was introduced into economics as a part of the definition of monopolistic competition, I think I have a special right of protest. Just as pure competition must mean the absence of monopoly, so pure monopoly at the other extreme must mean the absence of competition. And since competition is always a matter of substitutes, and since substitutes are always a matter of degree, so that in the last analysis everything is a substitute for everything else as we weigh alternative avenues of expenditure for our incomes, there would be pure monopoly only when a single authority controlled every economic good,[7] as conceivably would be the case under state socialism. No such monopoly exists, of course, in a nonsocialist society, but that is precisely the point that needs to be made: *every* monopolist in real life is subject to competition in greater or less degree, and it is very important for clear thinking to realize that monopoly is after all *only* a matter of degree. An isolated monopolist, as described above, is not a pure monopolist. He is clearly subject to competition; it has an important effect upon both the position and the shape of his demand curve. But his competitors are dispersed, and since he cannot appreciably affect them, he does the sensible thing and ignores them. Any producer who has either no close substitutes, or a very great many, for his product, may be an isolated monopolist, for in either case his moves will have no very substantial effect upon any other single firm.

The isolated monopolist is, like anyone else, beset by the competition of others locating as near him as they can in economic space. It is quite possible that, even though he has no *close* sub-

7. Cf. *Monopolistic Competition*, pp. 63-4.

stitute for his product to worry about, the demand for it will still be adequate to yield him only minimum profits. Such may be the case, for instance, with a retail enterprise in a small or isolated village, with a street railway company in a large city, etc. Evidently the demand for his product may also be greater than this, yielding him profits in excess of the minimum—the familiar monopoly profits. A technically isolated monopolist may also find his profits reduced to a minimum by the fact that there are *many* producers of close substitutes; or again, in spite of the many close substitutes, the demand for his own product may remain strong enough to yield him profits in excess of the minimum. In these particular matters, two misinterpretations of monopolistic competition theory have been especially prevalent from the first: (1) 'tangency' has been associated only with the 'group problem,' and indeed has often been considered as coextensive with it, and (2) the isolated monopolist (wrongly defined as a pure monopolist) has been held strictly apart from the theory. The argument above is designed to show the falsity of both of these views.

It is of interest to note that the single seller under pure competition is isolated in the same sense that we have been discussing. Since he is one of a very large number, the effect of any adjustment he makes in his affairs upon any other individual seller is negligible, and he simply decides upon the best output for himself at the 'going' price, meaning by this the price he expects to prevail at the time he will sell his product.

Returning to monopolistic competition, in a system of isolated monopolists, wherever demand is such as to yield only minimum profits, production must take place (under conditions of tangency) on a scale less than that corresponding to the most efficient conditions of production for any particular product, i.e. to the left of the minimum point on its U-shaped cost curve. Even where sellers are not as hard-pressed as this, the chances are great (although not to the point of certainty) that they will also be producing at less than the most efficient output. Since the minimum point on the cost curve is widely associated with 'ideal' conditions, monopolistic competition has been widely associated with a departure from this ideal, and a large literature advocating corrective measures has come into being. Such a program, to my mind, indicates nothing so much as a complete misunderstanding of the problem. When the output of an *industry* is defined as homogeneous, as in Mrs. Robinson's *Imperfect Competition,* there is every reason to associate its production under 'ideal' conditions with an adjustment of output for each firm in the industry which will make its costs a minimum. But when the product is recognized to be heterogeneous, as in *Monopolistic Competition,* it is the demand curves for the individual products, not those of industries, which must enter into the definition of the ideal. The general system of consumers' preferences now embodies sloping demand curves for the individual firms as an expression of the general desire for diversity which must now be recognized as co-ordinate with efficiency in production in defining the welfare ideal.

Let us now turn to the nonisolated seller, or to the problem commonly known as oligopoly. The literature of this subject has expanded rapidly in recent years. The problem is a highly complex one and for our purposes we must reduce it to fairly simple terms. Indeed, one of the major oligopoly solutions has already been indicated in making clear what was meant by isolation, and we may begin by taking up this particular solution again.

When any seller is so situated that he knows that what he does will have a substantial influence on others and therefore may lead them to alter their present policies, he would be very short-sighted indeed not to take all of this into account. If it is a matter of a price cut, he may very well decide that the most sensible thing to do is to charge the same price as everyone else, since if he tries to sell for less the others will be obliged to come down to his level and all will be worse off than before. I have always been at a loss to see why any blame should attach to a seller if he reasons this way, even though the result of such reasoning may well be the same price as would result from an outright agreement. Herein lies a dilemma which has been for quite some time a number one nightmare for those concerned with antitrust policy.

It is easy to construct a theoretical 'model' in which the result of the reasoning described is identical with a monopolistic agreement. But it is a rarefied model, unlikely to be met with in real life. For one thing, if the resulting price yielded profits which were conspicuously large, competitors would be invited to install themselves near by and make a bid for a share of them. For this reason the desire not to make the field of activity in question so attractive that others will enter it may be and often is a major force holding prices at a level where only minimum or little more than minimum profits are earned.

Other forces, and I believe very real ones, may be conceptions of 'good' or 'reasonable' profits rather than maximum profits, perhaps because of a genuine desire not to 'profiteer,' or perhaps through a fear of adverse publicity or of inviting public regulation. There can be no doubt, however, that the strongest force working against the maintenance of prices at an unduly high level through the oligopolistic influence described above is a fear of attracting competitors.

Let us suppose that prices for some group of sellers are held for a time at such a level that all are enjoying in some degree profits in excess of the minimum, and that no one cuts from this level because he knows that his cut will be matched by the others. The extra profits may still be reduced by a multiplication of firms, each one getting less business at the established price, until profits generally are reduced by the rising unit costs which accompany the smaller scale of operations. Where such a situation obtains, I believe that there is genuine waste. And there is good reason to think that it is not uncommon wherever price competition fails to work or works only sluggishly.

It has been pointed out earlier that the result of 'mutual dependence recognized' may be the same as if there were actually an agreement; and so the possibility of an agreement may now be brought into the picture. In fact, it seems obvious that one of the most likely results when there is a small number of sellers is the formation of a price agreement, or some kind of rough equivalent in the form of a division of territory or other device arising out of common action on the part of the group, perhaps organized into an association or cartel.

One may throw into this general class of problem the case of price leadership, where one seller, either tacitly or openly, sets a price which others then follow. One may also add to the list the possibility of a customary or traditional price, more important perhaps in earlier periods of history, but certainly far from unimportant today, even in advanced economies such as that of the United States. In all these cases the price may be in greater or less degree above the level at which it would be established by active price competition, depending upon circumstances.

It does not follow because a situation is characterized by price leadership that the leader can do anything he pleases. If the general sentiment is for a price which will not attract newcomers into the field, the leader may be able to lead effectively only within rather narrow limits. But it is a common characteristic of all the factors mentioned above that they are forces tending to maintain prices at a level in some degree above that to which they would be adjusted if each seller sought his maximum profits under conditions of isolation as described earlier. Hence all these forces open the way to a multiplication of producers in the area where they occur, with consequent excess capacity and inefficiency.

Closely related to the foregoing is the setting of prices according to what has come to be known as the full cost principle.[8] It is well known that, especially in large areas of the retail field but also in manufacturing and other areas, prices are set as a matter of policy at a figure equal to cost plus a conventional distribution of overhead, including a conventional margin of profit. Here again an adequate treatment of the subject would involve refinements, but roughly that is what happens. In this case we may get results similar to those just discussed, but via a different route: the influx of sellers may come first, simply through a larger number of people trying to extract a living from some particular kind of activity. As a result each one gets less business and his unit costs are higher; hence also his prices.

This case differs from the others in that the larger number

8. This principle has always been an integral part of the theory of monopolistic competition, in spite of its being presented by Hall and Hitch in their famous article as a correction. Cf. *Monopolistic Competition*, pp. 105-6, and Hall and Hitch, 'Price Theory and Business Behaviour,' *Oxford Economic Papers*, No. 2 (1939), p. 30.

of sellers precedes the rise in price instead of following it. But the end result is the same—a multiplication of firms and a striking departure from the economic system which would result from each seller maximizing his profits along a Marshallian demand curve (which neglects repercussions), to say nothing of a system defined by pure competition.[9]

Most of the considerations just discussed which lead to excess capacity are unrelated to oligopoly and are mentioned only because they give results similar to those following from a particular solution of oligopoly, viz. that of 'mutual dependence recognized.' Although oligopoly theory has many solutions according to circumstances, it is not too much to say that this particular one has, in the minds of many, come to be thought of as *the* solution of the problem. It is necessary therefore to insist that it is not. It is quite possible—and quite rational—for oligopolists to compete vigorously against each other. Such competition may arise out of an attempt to secure a final victory in the struggle and eliminate all rivals—a perfectly rational objective—or it may arise simply out of a desire to get ahead of the other fellow and stay there. Furthermore, various elements of uncertainty as to how much effect a move will actually have upon a rival and whether or not he will react and how, may enter perfectly rationally into the calculations of anyone, as well as the perfectly rational objective of gaining customers who may remain with him even after a rival has matched his price cut. Finally, there is no reason to assume that human beings always act perfectly rationally; indeed, there is good reason not to assume it.

A great deal has been made in recent years of the considerable number of industries in which a large fraction of the total output is produced by three, four, or five large producers—a great deal too much in my opinion. The reason why so much has been

9. I am bound to say that it seems to me quite impossible to explain the economics of retailing in France, for example, with its endless small establishments, each doing such a restricted volume of business, except in terms of this particular feature of monopolistic competition theory. Another even more striking example is given in a recent study by Richard H. Holton of retailing in Puerto Rico, 'Marketing Structure and Economic Development,' *Quarterly Journal of Economics*, August 1953.

made of it is, I think, an identification of such a situation with behavior according to the 'mutual dependence recognized' rule. The answer is that this is only one possibility among many. Oligopoly is bad or not depending upon what kind of competition develops within its framework; and the theory of the subject yields no certain conclusion as to what will happen, given the bare minimum of information that the number of sellers is small.

Let me close this very general discussion of oligopoly problems with two brief observations. The first is that the subject needs to be rewritten in terms of that extremely useful concept which originated, I believe, with Mr. Kaldor, of cross-elasticity of demand, rather than in terms of the number of sellers in a market. In the typical chain relationship between sellers, which emerges so clearly from our earlier spatial example, there is in fact no market, commodity, or industry for which the number of sellers may be counted. A particular seller may be taken as a focal point and related to others near by; but when we move on to the next seller the grouping changes. In fact if we consider the extreme of an economy in which the phenomenon of 'isolation' does not exist, there can be as many groups of this sort as there are sellers. I do not know of any comprehensive development of the theory in these terms, but it seems to me to be indicated as a major consequence of recognizing that the product is heterogeneous.

The second observation has to do with the attitude that economists should take towards the discovery and recognition of oligopoly. It seems evident to me that oligopolistic elements are very general in the economic system and that economic study must be increasingly concerned with their influence upon prices and other economic categories. In so far as this factor interjects indeterminateness into the system it is certainly the job of the economist as a scientist to say so.

It may happen that situations are indeterminate because only a selection of the variables actually involved—the *economic* ones—has been included in formulating the problem. Thus the discovery that certain economic problems, narrowly conceived, are indeterminate may be a necessary preliminary to putting them into the wider context which will explain why in the real world they do in fact settle down into some form of stable relationship. After all, economics deals with only one aspect of social reality, and by trying to give complete explanations within itself may end up by giving false ones. However that may be, the only defensible scientific attitude seems to be to 'let the chips fall where they may,' to give full importance to the indeterminate as well as to the determinate, and carefully to avoid the temptation of formulating problems with the *objective* of assuring a determinate answer.[10]

I should like to make one more point as to the nature of monopoly power generally. It is common to associate monopoly power with a restriction or destruction of supply, or at least with a holding back of supply from the market. But this is misleading, for very few monopolists do this in the literal sense. Some commodities (wheat) may have their production restricted, and others (potatoes) may be destroyed after they are produced; but the typical monopolist, instead of reducing his supply and leaving it to the market to raise the price, raises his price and leaves it to the market to tell him how much he can sell. And having set his price (in accord with his monopoly power), he naturally tries to sell all he can—indeed, he usually advertises in order to sell more. A monopolist must be thought of as someone who simply *controls* the supply of something; in most cases he *operates* directly not on the supply, but on the price.

It remains to indicate how the theory of monopolistic competition permits us to pass over to the study of dynamics, and in particular to the problems of development and growth. On this matter the late Professor Schumpeter was the great authority. And in the theory of the subject which he developed it is significant that the entrepreneur who breaks away from the established order of things by introducing an 'innovation,' enjoys for a period of time a monopoly of it. From this temporary monopoly posi-

10. Professor Hicks holds the contrary view. Believing that 'a general abandonment of the assumption of perfect competition . . . must have very destructive consequences for economic theory,' he wishes to preserve the theory. (*Value and Capital,* pp. 83-5) At another period of history one might have argued similarly for continuing to believe that the world was flat.

tion he derives profits, and if he is clever enough, by the time others have caught up with him he will be out in front again with another innovation.

There are many major differences between Schumpeter's system and my own,[11] but with respect to the role of monopoly in the process of economic development there is agreement. How can one doubt that if a new product or variation of a product, or a new and more efficient technique of production, could be instantly imitated by others, the incentive to make it would for most people be lost? Since one could never gain even a temporary advantage there would be no use in trying, especially since he could be certain never to fall behind by merely copying at once anyone else who did try and who succeeded.

But it must now be recognized that dynamic monopoly of this kind builds a pretty hot fire under everyone—not only to get out in front with an improved product, but to keep from falling behind with an out-of-date one. It is a situation in which, as in the country of the Red Queen, 'it takes all the running you can do to keep in the same place.' Technical progress, of course, requires a favorable scientific environment, and a spirit of enterprise ready to create and exploit the potential opportunities for profit in new products and new ways of doing things. But in terms of the categories of competition and monopoly the essential requirement is a field as open as possible to the formation of *new* monopolies which will help to curb and destroy the old ones. Schumpeter has called this whole process 'creative destruction,' and it is an apt paradox.

Inevitably the prizes in this struggle fall unevenly, even to those who succeed. Some find just the product that the public wants and reap enormous gains before anyone catches up with them—if indeed anyone ever does. Others succeed more moderately, and large numbers contribute substantially to the output of the economic system although never 'enjoying' anything but losses. Even in the midst of the prosperous 'twenties, roughly half of the business corporations in the United States were operated either at a loss or at profits so negligible they would never

11. See Essay 10 below.

have attracted enterprise into the field in question, could the profits have been foreseen.

The conclusion from this unevenness is that there is no reason to expect a close connection between actual profits and entrepreneurial contribution in any particular enterprise. And judgment as to the 'reasonableness' of profits ought never to be made without looking *beyond the limits of the particular firm which earns them.*

Schumpeter has remarked that 'the bulk of what we call economic progress is incompatible with . . . perfect competition.' [12] But it must not be concluded that it is the product of monopoly without calling to mind again that a monopolist is subject to competition in varying degrees, and that it is not good for him, or for 'progress,' to have too little of it. A monopolist in a fairly well-protected position—as were the railroads before the development of motor and air transportation—is, as we know from much empirical evidence, only too likely to become fat and lazy. What is needed is both monopoly and competition, and particularly the leaven of competition from newcomers.

We turn now to a brief statement of the difference between monopolistic and imperfect competition.[13] It was, I think, highly unfortunate for both the *Theory of Monopolistic Competition* and the *Economics of Imperfect Competition* that, although actually written with roughly a six-year interval between them, they were published within the same calendar year of 1933; and, I might add, that they presented the superficial similarity that a small and rather unimportant part of each of them offered to a world of economists jaded by equilibria in terms of intersecting lines, what seemed to be a perfectly fascinating alternative, viz. the geometrical construction of tangency.[14] It was unfortunate in

12. *Capitalism, Socialism and Democracy*, p. 105.

13. I am confining myself here to the essential difference which appears to me to be the prime source of all others.

14. In fact, the role of the 'tangency solution' in the structure of the two theories is completely different. Also the 'solution' itself is different, since both the demand curves and the cost curves are differently defined.

that two quite distinct theories, with quite distinct origins [15] and objectives, have become so confused that they are now widely identified, with a corresponding failure on the part of most to understand either one.

In the year after our books appeared, Mrs. Robinson wrote an article [16] in which it seemed to me that she found fault with almost everything that I considered most important in my own theory, from the concept of purity to that of a differentiated product. *It ought to have been clear at once that we were thinking in quite different terms.* Yet the evidence that *Imperfect Competition* is *not* a blend of monopoly and competition revealed itself only slowly, and when I pointed out the differences between the two theories as I saw them in 1937,[17] Mr. Kaldor found nothing more than 'braces *v.* suspenders' and accused me

15. Mr. P. W. S. Andrews has recently restated the familiar and false interpretation against which I have already protested. 'When I refer to the modern theories of business behaviour,' he says, 'I am thinking especially of the doctrines which had their origin in the discussions in the *Economic Journal*, 1926-33, to which many economists contributed. These resulted [sic] in Professor Chamberlin's *Monopolistic Competition* and Mrs. Joan Robinson's *Economics of Imperfect Competition.*' ('Some Aspects of Competition in Retail Trade,' *Oxford Economic Papers* (New Series), June 1950, p. 138n.)

Actually my own work was first written in the years 1924-26, and filed as a doctor's thesis in Harvard University Library on 1 April 1927. It was subsequently revised and rewritten (see Preface), but its connection with the specific controversies of the late 'twenties and early 'thirties which form the background of Mrs. Robinson's book is literally *nil*. Not even in the revision was there any attempt made to integrate its content with post-1926 materials. The reader may observe for himself that the few footnote references designed in small part to 'bring it up to date' (cf., for instance, pp. 5, 14, 54, 73, 86, 126, and also the last four pages of Appendix A) do not grow out of the text, but are merely tacked on to it.

Holding as I do that the two theories are quite different, my interest is not in 'priorities,' but in trying again to put an end to the sloppy way in which the two are usually identified. Their supposed common origin has played a major part in this identification.

16. 'What Is Perfect Competition?' *Quarterly Journal of Economics*, November 1934.

17. 'Monopolistic or Imperfect Competition?' *Quarterly Journal of Economics*, August 1937; reprinted in the fifth and later editions of *Monopolistic Competition* as Chap. IX. The discussion with Mr. Kaldor is in the same *Journal* for May 1938.

of having fallen a victim to my own theory and of trying to 'differentiate my product too far.' However, his reply was eloquent in its support of my interpretation of Mrs. Robinson's theory, for he argued that the two theories were alike because there was no monopoly in either one! I can only ask anyone who thinks that monopoly is missing from *Monopolistic Competition* to go back and read again.[18]

This is indeed the fundamental difference between monopolistic and imperfect competition: that the former is a fusion of the hitherto separate theories of monopoly and competition, whereas the latter leaves the conventional dichotomy as sharp as ever.

The fact that *Imperfect Competition* contains no monopoly in the traditional sense of control over supply is fully documented in the latter half of my own Chapter ix. Mrs. Robinson is 'tempted' by the possibility of arranging 'actual cases in a series of which pure monopoly would be the limit at one end and pure competition at the other,' but finds that it cannot be done. Monopoly in the sense of control over supply therefore explicitly retains its association with an *industry*—and with a firm only if the firm coincides with the industry. This is as it always was. Consistent with this view, the various producers within an imperfectly competitive industry have no monopoly because the output of the industry is defined as homogeneous.[19] Mr. Kahn stated two years later that 'It is to be understood that the phrase *imperfection of competition* does not carry with it any of those implications with which by tradition the word *monopoly* is associated.' [20] And Mr. Kaldor still later said, in effect, that if I had ever seriously faced the question of defining pure monopoly, the difficulties of blending monopoly and competition would at once have been apparent, and I too should have seen that it could not be done.[21] But the question *is* faced and answered in Chapter iv. Mr. Kaldor had missed the definition given, and therefore, like so many others, had misread the meaning of the theory itself.

18. Suggestion: page 8 for the matter of numbers; Chap. iv for product differentiation.
19. *Imperfect Competition*, p. 17.
20. 'Some Notes on Ideal Output,' *Economic Journal*, March 1935, p. 20.
21. *Quarterly Journal of Economics*, May 1938, p. 526.

However one may judge the result, a way *was* found for doing it, and it is this blend of monopoly and competition (together with the more obvious blend on the scale of numbers) which is the essence of the theory.

A theory which aims to blend monopoly and competition could hardly neglect the scale of numbers and the intermediate area of oligopoly.[22] And having departed from the traditional assumption of a homogeneous commodity to insist upon the fact that each producer's product is different from those of others, it could hardly fail to include the possibilities of varying products (as well as prices) and of advertising and selling costs as types of competition growing out of heterogeneity. Such a theory presents an explanation of the economic system so different from that of the traditional dichotomy that one would expect it to have ramifications into the farthest corners of our thinking with respect both to general analysis and to questions of policy. And one would expect these ramifications to be different from those which have evolved from the theory of imperfect competition, where the dichotomy is consciously or unconsciously present.

In summary, let me call attention to the chief points of difference between this formulation of monopolistic competition theory and the one of 1933.

22. It must be clear from what has just been said that such a statement does not apply to Mrs. Robinson, who not only could but did neglect it, completely. And so Mr. K. W. Rothschild accuses us *jointly,* uniting the two theories into one and asserting that *the* theory 'badly neglects' oligopoly. ('Price Theory and Oligopoly,' *Economic Journal,* September 1947, pp. 301-2.) Yet not only was the subject given its present name in the *Theory of Monopolistic Competition* (see Essay 2), but it was clearly presented (Chap. 1) as co-ordinate with product differentiation—one of the *two* ways in which monopolistic and competitive elements may be blended; and it was given the most exhaustive analysis to which it had yet been subjected.

Let me add that I am unable to find any basis whatever in my treatment of oligopoly for Mr. Rothschild's strange statement that the idea of indeterminateness is 'abhorrent' to me, and further that I 'try hard to formulate my additional assumptions for the oligopolistic case in such a way as to obtain a determinate equilibrium price . . .' I am particularly distressed by such statements because I have for years held precisely the opposite view (cf. above, p. 61, the 'second observation').

In the original version the point was first made that monopoly and competition were blended in *two* ways: with respect to numbers and with respect to the differentiation of the product; and the proposal made to study each separately and then combine them. Oligopoly without product differentiation was then analyzed; after which came product differentiation without oligopoly, i.e. for both a single seller and for a very large number (the familiar 'large group') under the provisional assumption of uniformity of demand and cost conditions for all the firms in the group. In each case there was an analysis of the product as a variable. Oligopoly was then reintroduced, and thus combined with product differentiation. The full cost principle and other departures from profit maximization were added, and finally the uniformity assumption was dropped and the actual diversity of conditions incorporated into the theory. Selling costs, which had been excluded up to this point, were then added, and the whole analysis revised at each stage to include them.

The present formulation is much simpler. It begins with the individual seller and uses the spatial example to illustrate how the entire economic system may be viewed as an elaborate network of interrelated firms, each one being able to adjust from the beginning either its price, product, or selling outlay. The uniformity assumption is used only momentarily, and diversity appears at once in the form of concentrations of buyers. The individual firm is either isolated or related oligopolistically to others. The group has disappeared from the formulation here given,[23] and with it the concept of large numbers, since the individual seller in this latter instance is again correctly described as isolated, even in the special case of pure competition. The problem of entry disappears along with the group, and becomes absorbed

23. The 'group' was always meant to be a completely flexible concept—if it had meant an industry, the word industry would have been used—and there is clearly no reason why *any area whatever* within the whole economy may not be marked off, even quite arbitrarily, for separate study. But there is urgent need for examination of the variety of criteria by which areas intermediate between the firm and the whole economy may also be meaningfully defined. This more general statement of the theory without groups should be regarded as preliminary to a more critical study of the group problem.

into the larger problem of the distribution of resources throughout the entire economic system.

In the present formulation the importance of oligopolistic relations in the whole system emerges with greater force, as does that of the full cost principle and other departures from profit maximization, and the relation of the theory to problems of development and growth. I believe that this is only one of numerous ways in which the subject may be presented, but I hope it is one in which the theory emerges more clearly as a *general* one, designed to replace that of pure competition as a basis for analyzing the whole economy.

4

Measuring the Degree of Monopoly

and Competition [1]

1. DEFINITIONS

AN analysis of the problem of measuring monopoly and competition [2] should start from definitions, so that it may be clear from the first what it is whose measurement is being discussed. As a part of the intensive theoretical study of this field in recent years a number of new definitions of monopoly have appeared, and I should like to make clear from the beginning that I do not accept any of them. Dr. Triffin, after discussing some of these new definitions, comments that 'Professor Chamberlin seems to be the only one who has kept without a particle of change the old traditional definition of monopoly as control over supply.[3] This is what monopoly has always meant, and I see no reason to change it.

I do hold, however, that this traditional concept 'is meaningless without reference to the thing monopolized.[4] The traditional dichotomy between competition and monopoly is dissolved, not by a new definition of monopoly, but by applying the old and

---

1. Reprinted from *Monopoly and Competition and their Regulation. Papers and Proceedings of a Conference Held by the International Economic Association*, E. H. Chamberlin, ed., London, 1954.

2. See A. G. Papandreou, 'Market Structure and Monopoly Power,' *American Economic Review*, September 1949, for a fairly complete bibliography of the subject.

3. *Monopolistic Competition and General Equilibrium Theory*, p. 128.

4. *Monopolistic Competition*, p. 65.

familiar one with complete flexibility to cover any product whatever, no matter how broadly or narrowly defined. One can have a monopoly of Château d'Yquem, of all Sauternes, of all white wines from the Bordeaux region, or all Bordeaux wines, or of all white wines, of all wines, of all beverages, and so on indefinitely until we reach the limit of all economic goods. And whatever the area monopolized, the monopolist will always face competition in some degree from the wider area beyond its limits. Hence the paradoxical expression 'monopolistic competition.'

From this flexible *application* of the *established* definition of monopoly as control over supply, we arrive at the definition of pure monopoly. Since every monopolist is subject to competition in some degree from the area beyond that which he controls, pure monopoly from which all competition was eliminated would exist only if the area were co-extensive with the supply of all economic goods. Such a pure monopoly, of course, is hardly to be found in real life, although a completely isolated regime of State socialism would seem to satisfy its conditions. But it is essential as a theoretical limit, for it makes clear that all monopoly in real life, falling short of this extreme, is a phase of monopolistic competition, and not something outside of it. This point is evidently of prime importance in relation to the problem of measurement.

Just as pure monopoly must mean the absence of competition, so pure competition must mean the absence of any degree of monopoly control, i.e. the reduction of such control to a point where it is negligible and hence is in fact neglected by the individual seller. This involves (1) a large number of sellers for (2) a homogeneous product, defining the word product in a broad sense to include location in space and other circumstances surrounding the sale. Since, under these conditions, it would be possible for any seller by a very small reduction in price to increase his sales far beyond his possible production, the demand curve for his product is conceived as perfectly elastic within the relevant range. Prices will evidently be uniform for all sellers. But such uniformity is also frequent under monopolistic competition, and it is therefore not possible to identify pure competition, as is often done, with uniform prices and monopolistic competition with price differences.

2. Pure Competition as a Point of Departure for Measurement

If all rents are included within the cost curve of the firm, equilibrium for the firm under pure competition will always involve tangency of the demand curve and the cost curve at the minimum point for the latter, and hence the equality of price and marginal cost. But it does not follow that the equilibrium of a firm under monopolistic competition may be compared with such assumed conditions for *the same firm* in order to obtain a measure of the departure from pure competition. The reason is that *the definition of pure competition involves conditions beyond the individual firm.* Pure competition could be realized for the firm in question only if there were a very large number of *other* firms producing the identical product, and this is precisely what does not and cannot exist when as in real life the demand is for a diversified product. To imagine its existence is to indulge in flights of fancy which deprive the comparisons of any useful meaning. The difficulties are fundamental and must be explained further.

Since our firm is the *only one* producing the product in question, the requirement of large numbers might be met by conceiving the firm to be either (1) divided or (2) multiplied. If it were to be split into many smaller parts, the result would be higher unit costs by reason of the U-shaped cost curve, and we have an illustration of the paradoxical proposition which Schumpeter exploited so dramatically, that monopoly may be cheaper than competition. But such a situation is logically inconsistent with pure competition in spite of its large numbers because it is not in equilibrium. Unless, to be sure, the original firm in question owed its size predominantly to factors other than economies of scale, the 'atomized' firms, with perfectly elastic demands and falling unit costs, would soon eliminate each other, the movement continuing until the original single firm was re-established.

The alternative of multiplication involves imagining a multiplication of *demand* for this particular product sufficient to require a 'large number' of firms, *each* of optimum size. For example, if we suppose General Motors to be of about optimum size in the automobile industry, we must have a demand for the products *of this company*, say fifty times its present magnitude, with the forty-nine competing companies all manufacturing and selling Chevrolets, Buicks, etc., at the *identical places* where they are now manufactured and sold by General Motors. Putting aside the question of what to do with Ford, Chrysler, and other producers, the American public would have to have, instead of the conventional two-car garage, at least twenty-five-car garages and spend its entire income on automobiles, thereby making it impossible for any other product to be sold under purely competitive conditions at the same time. Why discuss such absurdities? it will be said, and I fully agree. The whole point to the illustration is to bring home that pure competition cannot be conceived in this way for purposes of measuring deviations from it.

A more sensible alternative to either dividing or multiplying the firm would seem to be to use the conventional 'industry' category which already includes a substantial number of firms, and assume away the actual diversity of products. This, as I understand it, is the meaning of Mrs. Robinson's imperfectly competitive industry with its explicitly homogeneous product and its consistent treatment of 'imperfections' within the industry as something to be removed so far as possible in the interest of increasing efficiency, of reducing 'exploitation,' etc. As most of you probably know, I have maintained elsewhere [5] that imperfect and monopolistic competition are two quite different theories, instead of being, as commonly thought, merely two different names for the same thing; and it is necessary to refer to their differences in relation to the problems of measurement. When Mr. Kaldor was in the process of discovering the differences in question in 1938 he made a number of significant remarks, two of which are particularly helpful in the present connection: (1) that he thought 'everybody was agreed by now' in accepting the measurement of the *degree* of imperfection of competition in terms

5. *Monopolistic Competition*, Chap. IX, especially the second half. See also Essay 5 below. [1957] See also pp. 26-30 above and Essay 16 below.

of the elasticity of individual firms' demand curves, and (2) that 'this measurement certainly cannot be used to denote the relative strength of the "monopoly" and "competitive" elements in a given situation, in the sense which Professor Chamberlin has in mind.' [6] The first remark bears out my contention that the theory of monopolistic competition has been widely misinterpreted, and the second, intended as a criticism of monopolistic competition, is seen to be instead a criticism of measurement. It agrees with, and fortifies, the position I have always taken, and the position developed in this paper, that the relative strength of monopoly and competition cannot be measured.

The fundamental difference between the two theories lies in the fact that *Imperfect Competition* contains no monopoly in the sense of control over supply, except in relation to a 'commodity,' defined as co-extensive with an *industry*. The individual seller *within* an imperfectly competitive industry has no monopoly whatever—indeed, since the industry is defined as producing a homogoneous commodity, his product must be indistinguishable from that of others, and there is, by definition, simply nothing the supply of which he might control. The idea of arranging 'actual cases in a series of which pure monopoly would be the limit at one end and pure competition at the other' was definitely abandoned by Mrs. Robinson in view of the supposed impossibility of defining a pure monopoly,[7] and this latter concept does not figure in her theory. If I ever had doubts as to this interpretation of Mrs. Robinson, they would have been allayed by Mr. Kaldor's saying at one stage that the theories of imperfect and of monopolistic competition were alike because *neither one* contains any monopoly, and, in effect, that if I had ever tried to define pure monopoly, I too would have seen, *as did Mrs. Robinson,* that it was impossible to blend the two theories.[8] I conclude that monopoly and competition are *not* blended in *Imperfect Competition;* and that the fact that they *are* blended in *Monopolistic Competition* was missed by Mr. Kaldor, who gave the theory a quite different interpretation, in part because he

6. *Quarterly Journal of Economics,* May 1938, pp. 519 and 526.
7. *Imperfect Competition,* pp. 4, 5.
8. *Op. cit.* p. 526.

had overlooked the definition of pure monopoly. And if anyone with the keen interest in the subject and boundless energies of Mr. Kaldor can make this mistake, perhaps it is too much to expect lesser mortals to do better.

A chief difficulty in assuming away the actual diversity of products is that there is no way of discovering the nature of the single product which the resulting purely competitive industry is to produce. For instance, if we are to imagine a purely competitive automobile industry, will its homogeneous product be Packards, Plymouths, or Peugeots? The question must be answered, for until it is, the cost curves for the firms in such an industry cannot be drawn. But even after it is answered, if Packards are chosen, what nonsense it is to compare the actual price of a Rolls-Royce or of a Renault under monopolistic competition with the ruling price in a purely competitive Packard industry! Incidentally, the cost curves would not even be those for Packards as at present manufactured, because of the external economies from standardization of parts and methods on an industry-wide basis. These are difficulties of *monopolistic* competition, where products are *recognized* to be heterogeneous. They do not appear under *imperfect* competition, where it is easy to measure the 'degree of imperfection' within an industry since the product is defined as homogeneous and therefore is presumably the same whether competition is perfect or imperfect.

There is a further and even more serious objection to assuming away the actual diversity of products within an 'industry' in order to obtain a purely competitive standard for measuring purposes. It is that such diversity is the natural consequence of the system of demands, in the same sense as is any variety whatever in the output of the economic system. I do not mean to assert that no qualifications are needed to the general proposition that demand guides production, but only that whatever qualifications *are* necessary with respect to 'rationality,' legal obstacles, or what not, are not peculiar to the intra-industry problem. A preference for the *New York Times* over the *Daily Record* is not to be dismissed as irrational or of no consequence merely because they are both a part of the newspaper industry. The general principle of free choice in the spending of one's income includes not only

freedom to vary the proportions between the larger categories of
food, shelter, etc., but freedom also to express a market demand
for Smith's sausages if one believes them superior to Jones's. Also
it must not be overlooked that tastes are only a part of what is at
issue. Diversity is demanded not only because people have different tastes but also because they have different incomes and because they have different locations in space. With regard to the
latter, a major element in the 'diversity' of product is the dispersion of shops and factories over space in response to the spatial
dispersion of buyers and hence of demand. To assume away actual diversity is to assume that all sellers are offering their products at the same spot, and unless buyers are also located at one
spot, the assumption does such violence to the system of demands
that one wonders how it could ever seriously be proposed.

The upshot of all these arguments is that, in so far as products
are actually heterogeneous by reason of buyers' demands being
dispersed over space and over a wide range of diverse tastes and
incomes, it is completely artificial to conceive of purely competitive industries at all, and hence quite impossible to compare an
actual situation, with its complex of monopoly and competitive
elements, with an assumed state in which the monopoly elements
were missing. In arguing that this is so, we have been led incidentally to indicate a fundamental position which I have developed much more at length elsewhere—that not only the real
world, but also the welfare ideal, is a complex of monopoly and
competition. It is only by considering both heterogeneity itself
and the demand for it within an industry as nonexistent or 'irrational' (which I suspect to be the real meaning of 'imperfect'
competition) that it becomes possible to consider perfect competition as the welfare ideal. Mr. Lerner's index is explicitly designed to measure departures from such a social optimum, and
follows in this respect imperfect, but not monopolistic, competition.

3. PURE MONOPOLY AND MONOPOLY AS POINTS OF DEPARTURE FOR MEASUREMENT

If it is not possible to take pure competition as a point of
departure for comparisons, what of pure monopoly at the other

extreme? It would seem, on the face of it, that since every firm is subject to competition from the rest of the economy, the larger it is, the smaller is the remaining area of competition; and a possible case appears for holding that a large firm is 'more monopolistic' than a small one simply because it embraces a larger segment of the whole economy. This approach to the problem raises quite a number of fundamental issues, especially when it is interpreted to include an agreement among producers (or a cartel) as one aspect of 'size,' consolidating as it does separate firms into one unit for purposes of price policy. In the simple case of a homogeneous product, it seems clear that the higher the percentage of the total output produced by one firm, or covered by an agreement, the greater the degree of monopoly control *of the product in question*. Here is a valid and important measure of monopoly control to which I see no objection whatever on technical grounds. It literally measures the degree of monopoly for the case of a particular product. From it we see at once that a firm may reach a certain size, or an agreement include a certain number of firms, consistent with *pure* competition, if the resulting control unit is still a small percentage of total output. Agreements are not *necessarily* monopolistic. But even with a high degree of monopoly or 'complete' monopoly of one product, the availability of substitute products is the other aspect of the problem. Complete control, even of some major category of product, may be of little consequence if the demand for it is highly elastic.

We are back to the general case of heterogeneous products, where *every* seller typically has a 'complete monopoly' of his own product, and where the important issues seem to turn on elasticity (and cross-elasticity). Here the problems of measuring monopoly in terms of size, or of percentages of some total, become much more complicated. Evidently a large firm may have a more elastic demand for its product than a small one, and a firm may expand in size, either by extending its control over a number of close substitutes, or by entering into a number of areas each of which is and remains highly competitive. It seems clear that size itself becomes a completely unreliable index of monopoly power in any sense.

As for percentages of a total, it is tempting to say that, since the term 'product' may be defined more or less broadly, it may be identified with 'industry' categories and monopoly measured, as was proposed a moment ago for really homogeneous products, on a percentage basis within such areas. The fundamental reason why this cannot be done is that it ignores all monopoly arising from the heterogeneity of the product within the area. Thus the cement industry in the United States with 162 mills operated by 75 companies (1938), the five largest of which produced under 40 per cent of the total, would appear by this measure to be almost purely competitive, whereas the element of spatial monopoly is actually so great as to make it one of the most striking cases of monopolistic competition. The field of retailing with its 1,-800,000 establishments in the United States (1948) is one endless example of the same phenomenon, with space in this instance only one of the many elements of heterogeneity. But it is sufficient to cite only the arbitrariness of the industry concept. Concentration ratios and similar measures are of little significance because they are predominantly the result of how broadly the categories are defined. Above all, the practice of classifying industries as *either* competitive *or* monopolistic on the basis of a percentage dividing line seems to me comparable to classifying all members of the human race as *either* geniuses *or* idiots.

4. CROSS-ELASTICITY AS A MEASURE

From this discussion, developed from the concept of pure monopoly as I insist it should be used, let us pass to another definition of pure monopoly which has, in fact, been widely used as a measure of monopoly power, in terms of the cross-elasticity of demand. A pure monopoly is defined by Triffin as a seller who is entirely unaffected by price changes of any other *individual* seller; technically, a seller whose cross-elasticity of demand with every other seller is zero, or approaches zero.[9] The coefficient of cross-elasticity, it will be recalled, is $\frac{p_j \delta q_i}{q_i \delta p_j}$, where i and j represent any two firms. It measures the effect upon the sales of firm i of a change in the price of firm j; and another coefficient with the

9. Op. cit. p. 103.

subscripts reversed would measure the effect upon the sales of firm *j* of a change in the price of firm *i*. I believe that this coefficient was first suggested by Mr. Kaldor, although its great vogue must be due for the most part to Mr. Triffin's extensive use of it in his classification of the problems of monopolistic competition, including the extreme of pure monopoly where its value is zero. It is this definition of pure monopoly which is now widespread in the textbook literature of the subject, where I do not recall ever having seen a reference, even critical, to my own.

Before discussing cross-elasticity as a measure of monopoly, I should like to protest further the definition of pure monopoly which is involved. The term pure monopoly (also pure competition) was first used to my knowledge in *The Theory of Monopolistic Competition,* where it was given the meaning described at the beginning of this paper as a part of the clarification of just what was meant by a theory embracing both competition and monopoly and lying between the limits of pure monopoly and pure competition. Any other meaning, therefore, is more than an alternative definition of a particular concept: by redefining one of the limits of the theory with which the term is inevitably associated, it distorts the whole meaning of the theory itself, and of the nature of the 'intermediate' area with which it is concerned. Triffin's pure monopolist is *not* free from competition. He is only 'isolated,' in the sense that the effect of his adjustments is so distributed among others that no *one* of them feels it appreciably; and he is similarly protected from any *one* of them. But both the position and the shape of the demand curve for his product are vitally affected by the competing substitutes for it, and it is essential to an understanding of the nature of monopolistic competition to realize that such isolated monopolists are a part of it, and not outside of it. Triffin quite rightly points out the relation between his definition of pure monopoly and the Marshallian theory of monopoly,[10] and it seems certain that its use has fortified the natural tendency to identify these two. It is easy merely to start calling a monopoly a pure monopoly, and this is now done very generally, thus falsifying what is the very essence of the theory.

10. Op. cit. p. 130.

Triffin states that his 'coefficient of interdependence measures the relative share of monopoly and competition in the situation of the sellers,' [11] since it ranges from infinity under pure competition to zero under pure monopoly. If this statement could be accepted as it stands, it would indeed entitle the coefficient to consideration as a universal index of the degree of competition. However, there are serious reservations. Before discussing them I should like to say that I think Triffin's analysis of these problems and in particular his elaborate use of the cross-elasticity coefficient in his classifications of market positions was a very substantial achievement. It has provoked and continues to provoke a great deal of fruitful discussion and has brought to the fore hitherto obscure aspects of the theory which are of the greatest importance.[12]

Triffin presents the three general categories of (1) pure monopoly (also called isolated selling), (2) heterogeneous competition, and (3) homogeneous competition, with coefficients of zero, a finite value, and infinity, respectively. This is supplemented by a 'circular test' for oligopoly in the last two categories. But the coefficient approaches zero, not only under isolated selling, but also under heterogeneous competition with 'large numbers,' this latter being interpreted as usual to mean that the price adjustment of any one seller has a negligible effect upon any other. And, as has been pointed out by several others, it also has a value of zero under *homogeneous* competition with large numbers, since it is a familiar aspect of pure competition that no one seller can have any substantial effect upon the sales of any other. The coefficient may be interpreted as having a value of infinity under pure competition only if the rising marginal cost curves of the individual sellers, which are essential to the existence of pure competition, are ignored, so that any individual seller could actually, by a slight diminution of price, swallow up the entire

11. Op. cit. p. 131.

12. [1957] The next two paragraphs are left 'for the record' as they appeared in the original article. See, however, some further comment in a Supplementary Note, p. 84, on several of the issues raised by the cross-elasticity coefficient and by Triffin's analysis in particular.

market, thus reducing the sales of all others to zero.[13] But if the output of any one seller is limited and if there are many of them, the coefficient is zero for a pure competitor as well as for a so-called 'pure monopolist.' Even if we ignore the rising cost curves, and interpret the coefficient as having a value of infinity for pure competition, its value skips discontinuously to zero with the slightest departure in terms of heterogeneity; it can only be made to proceed through a stage of finite values by operating on the scale of numbers. It is, in fact, a measure of monopoly and competition only in the sense of isolation from any other *individual;* and *as such* it is of prime importance. The following sellers are isolated in this sense: a monopolist with *no* near substitutes for his product, a monopolist with *many* near substitutes for his product,[14] and a pure competitor (with many *perfect* substitutes for his product). In all these cases the coefficient relating one individual seller to any other individual seller approaches zero. Whenever it is substantially greater than zero we have oligopoly.

The conclusion is that elasticity as well as cross-elasticity is needed to classify the problems of monopolistic competition. I propose the following classification in terms of these two concepts:

	ϵ (elasticity)	$\acute{\epsilon}$ (cross-elasticities)
Isolated selling		
(1) Heterogeneous product	finite	$\rightarrow$0
(2) Homogeneous product	∞	$\rightarrow$0
Nonisolated selling		
(3) Heterogeneous product	finite	>0
(4) Homogeneous product	∞	>0

This schema is only a beginning: it is limited to selling, and within this area it deals only with price-output relations, omit-

13. This is clearly the interpretation of Triffin.

14. [1957] Between these two extremes better substitutes and larger numbers work against each other, the former increasing, the latter decreasing, the value of the coefficient. (See Supplementary Note.) Thus the most frequent cases of isolation in the real world may well involve a moderate number of substitutes intermediate on the scale of remoteness.

ting the important problems of selling costs and of the many aspects of the product as a variable.

Four cases are distinguished, in order: (1) isolated monopoly, (2) pure competition, (3) oligopoly with product differentiation, and (4) oligopoly without product differentiation. Note that pure monopoly (in its original sense) does not appear in the table; and that the classification is independent of the concept of a group. This latter remains flexible, to be varied in accord with the needs of particular problems or studies.

It is necessary to specify that the demand curves in terms of which the elasticities and cross-elasticities are measured are defined as involving a price change by one firm, the prices of all others remaining fixed. The essence of the problem under non-isolated selling is, of course, that this may not correspond to market results, that a change in price by one seller may cause others to change theirs, and further, that if the first seller recognizes this he may not act in accord with such a demand curve. In fact it may be difficult to describe his actions in terms of a demand curve at all. In any event, the nature of a seller's action under oligopolistic conditions depends upon so many subsidiary factors and involves so many uncertainties that it could hardly be described by a single coefficient. The value of ϵ' under the conditions defined is an accurate measure of the degree to which an oligopolistic relationships *exists*—incidentally, far more accurate than is the 'number of sellers' in some specified area. Its purpose is to indicate the *presence* of this set of forces—not to predict the outcome of them.

As for the value of ϵ, the elasticity of demand, it is by long tradition one of the most important measures of the power of a particular monopolist over his price. It was objected to earlier in this paper, not in this role, but as a measure of the departure from pure competition, on the ground that this latter involves drastic assumptions extending far beyond the firm in question. (Incidentally, the Lerner measure is not, strictly speaking, the inverse of elasticity, as usually stated, but $\dfrac{P-C}{P}$, where $P =$ price and $C =$ marginal cost. The distinction is of some importance and is insisted upon by Mr. Lerner. He makes it in order to realize more exactly a measure of actual deviations from the alleged social optimum.) *Even for the firm,* ϵ measures only one aspect of monopoly. Neither elasticity nor the Lerner index measures anything beyond the effectiveness of existing substitutes; it gives no indication as to potential substitutes (the important problem of entry) or as to the presence or absence or 'degree' of oligopoly, and it passes over completely the important problems of competition and monopoly in the nonprice area: quality and other aspects of the 'product,' including location; and advertising and other forms of selling costs. (The Lerner index specifically subtracts out selling costs as a preliminary to measuring monopoly, although their very existence depends on the presence of monopoly!) *Beyond the firm* the relationships of these various aspects of competition and monopoly become even more complex. As a single example, competition on the basis of price may be very different, depending upon whether or not there is at the same time the possibility of competing also on the basis of quality. The possibility of a single index becomes still more remote.

5. Conclusion

Our general position is that the measurement of monopoly and competition is many-sided. Certain aspects of these two categories and of their relations to each other cannot be measured at all; and the indices of other aspects which can be measured merely reduce *parts* of a complicated problem to quantitative expression. The various indices which can be constructed are limited in their meaning and will always require further interpretation, particularly in relating them to each other. Here (as elsewhere) a comparison of economics with medical science may be helpful. Some aspects of health can be measured and others cannot. Among the former we have body temperature, blood pressure, metabolism, weight, etc. But these do not lend themselves to the construction of a *single* quantitative index of health. Similarly in economics it does not follow that because certain indices are quantitative themselves they can be averaged or in some way reduced to a single index, either of monopoly power (without reference to an 'ideal') or of deviations from a social optimum.

[1957] Supplementary Note on Cross-elasticity

In the argument of section 4 above, leading to the table on page 81, cross-elasticity of demand, although criticized as a general measure of monopoly, is retained as a criterion for isolation or nonisolation. This latter is in accord with Triffin's definition of isolation (though not of oligopoly, as explained below), and I believe also with general usage at the time the essay was written. But it appears now that cross-elasticity is inaccurate also as a criterion for isolation. Specifically, it involves an inaccurate translation into a mathematical symbol of my own earlier and different criterion which Triffin had taken as his point of departure in developing the 'coefficient of interdependence.' I must therefore revert to the earlier criterion.

The correct (and completely general) criterion for the isolation of a seller must be that *any* adjustment (of price, output, product or selling cost) which would be made by any other seller will have no more than a negligible impact upon him. The relevant 'impact' would normally be upon his profits, but (if we abstract from product variation and from selling outlays—and at this stage from factor prices and cost—as does Triffin) it would be via either output or price, or possibly both. Triffin first expresses the criterion in terms of the impact upon the revenue R_i of firm i, of an adjustment of the price p_j of firm j; but instead of saying that the impact, ΔR_i, must be negligible, he gives as the criterion that $\frac{\delta R_i}{\delta p_j}$ must be negligible.[15] This converts 'any adjustment of price' by firm j, which must mean some finite price adjustment with its consequent finite impact upon firm i, into a coefficient of relative rates of change, which is not the same thing at all. It is true that if the value of the indicated coefficient is 'of insignificant size,' ΔR_i must be negligible for any actual finite price adjustment, Δp_j, which would normally be made by firm j. Thus a negligible value for the coefficient is a sufficient condition

15. Op. cit. p. 100.

for a negligible ΔR_i. But it is not a necessary condition. For ΔR_i may be very small (say -1) and the coefficient still have a moderate or high value if Δp_j is still smaller (say $-.01$), as it may well be by virtue of an extremely high elasticity for the demand curve of firm j. An insignificant value for the coefficient is therefore not a necessary condition for isolation. The point is that it is ΔR_i, and not $\dfrac{\delta R_i}{\delta p_j}$, which must be zero or negligible.

For the very good reason of possible asymmetry between firms as to size, Triffin soon converts the coefficient into one 'of the elasticity type,' $\dfrac{p_j \delta R_i}{R_i \delta p_j}$ (p. 101). The correct requirement for isolation is now that $\dfrac{\Delta R_i}{R_i}$, and not $\dfrac{p_j \delta R_i}{R_i \delta p_j}$, be zero or negligible. For reasons similar to those just given, a negligible value for the coefficient is a sufficient, but not a necessary, condition for isolation.

In order (later) to extend the analysis to buying as well as selling, Triffin now substitutes quantity of sales, q, for revenue, R, and the coefficient becomes the familiar one, $\dfrac{p_j \delta q_i}{q_i \delta p_j}$ (pp. 102-3). If this change is accepted, the correct requirement for isolation is now that $\dfrac{\Delta q_i}{q_i}$, and not $\dfrac{p_j \delta q_i}{q_i \delta p_j}$, be zero or negligible. Again, a negligible value of the coefficient is a sufficient, but not a necessary, condition for isolation.

In any particular case, the magnitude of the impact on firm i will obviously depend on the magnitude of the change inaugurated by firm j. In testing for the isolation of firm i, this move by j must be conceived in relation to what it is in the interest and the power of j to make. This is a general proposition. As one application of it, the rising marginal cost curve of j will in the specific case of pure competition limit the increment of sales which j achieves by shading its price, and thus (because of the large number of sellers) leave $\dfrac{\Delta q_i}{q_i}$ very small, or negligible. This is the familiar proposition that no single seller can have any substantial effect upon another (absence of oligopoly) under pure competition; and there can be hardly a doubt that it has contributed, consciously or unconsciously, to the view held by many (including myself, above, p. 80) that cross-elasticity is zero under pure competition.

The same belief that the introduction of cost curves results in a very small cross-elasticity is found even in the case of some of those who, like R. L. Bishop, maintain that the correct value of the coefficient, conceived as a 'pure demand' relationship, is ∞, and therefore that it is a capital error to introduce cost at all.[16] In arguing against this position, I have maintained [17] that there is nothing wrong per se with a coefficient which embraces cost functions as a part of the system of relationships from which it is derived (cf. Triffin's 'general' coefficient on his page 115, and discussed below); but however one may settle this issue (and I shall not debate it further here), it appears to me now that it is irrelevant to the question of the value of the coefficient under pure competition. The reason must appear from the argument above—that the rising cost curve of j affects the absolute magnitude of its adjustment, rather than the value of the coefficient, which is a derivative. For example, it is consistent with a coefficient of ∞ that $\dfrac{\Delta q_i}{q_i}$ should be negligible because of the rising cost curve of firm j, which limits the magnitude of Δq_j (and hence of Δq_i) as firm j shades its price. The value of the coefficient under pure competition will be further discussed below, but our point here is that, whatever it may turn out to be, the correct requirement for isolation must remain simply that $\dfrac{\Delta q_i}{q_i}$ be very small for plausible variations in p_j.

From this discussion, and especially from the vexed case of pure competition discussed below, cross-elasticity emerges as a concept of only limited usefulness. *The distinctions of the table on page 81 between heterogeneity and homogeneity, isolation and nonisolation, remain, and they are as essential as ever.* But there seems to be no satisfactory symbol, or coefficient, which will serve as a criterion for isolation. This is unfortunate; but it may

16. 'Elasticities, Cross-Elasticities and Market Relationships,' *American Economic Review,* December 1952, p. 779.

17. Ibid. December 1953, p. 914.

be commented that, desirable as it would be to have a satisfactory symbol, this would not in itself make the criterion precise. The distinction would still have to turn on 'negligible' as against 'appreciable' values for it and could thus only be vague at best.

It will be noted that my own criterion for oligopoly is merely nonisolation, whereas Triffin, by contrast, introduces a circular test. This difference appears to be explained mainly by different conceptions of the nature of the oligopoly problem. My own stresses the ability of any *single seller* to influence appreciably the market situation of which he is a part.[18] It is not necessarily concerned with indeterminateness, nor with the specific possibility of sellers reacting upon each other. (For instance, the Cournot type of solution is to me a part of the oligopoly problem, although (1) it is determinate, and (2) it definitely ignores mutual dependence.[19] With its stress on the single seller, my own conception evidently includes situations where ability to influence the price or output of others may be enjoyed by only *one* of the several sellers. Indeed, in the usual case of asymmetry (symmetry is clearly a simplifying assumption) sellers may be expected to have different degrees of influence, and some of them perhaps none at all. It is quite possible for a large producer, *A*, to have an appreciable influence upon a small producer, *B*, at the same time that *B*'s influence on *A* is negligible. Such situations lie intermediate between single firm monopoly and pure competition: they are surely oligopoly problems, yet they would not satisfy a circular test between the two sellers, for the reason that the influence is in only one direction.

By contrast, Triffin, in introducing his circular test, stresses 'indeterminacy' and 'reactions,' referring to the 'mutual interaction that offers some leeway for the poker game element which characterizes the oligopolistic problem.'[20] A circular test is clearly necessary for these phenomena—one cannot play poker with himself. But such a test appears not to be necessary for oligopoly defined more generally, so as simply to embrace the

18. Cf. *Monopolistic Competition*, pp. 7, 30, 83, and *passim*.
19. Ibid. pp. 32ff.
20. Op. cit. p. 102; see also p. 104.

phenomena intermediate between the one and the many on the 'numbers scale.'

Triffin's circular test is actually given in several different and conflicting ways, so that its precise nature must remain in doubt. On page 104 the first coefficient is a 'price coefficient,' $\frac{p_j \delta q_i}{q_i \delta p_j}$, and the second appears as its reciprocal, $\frac{q_i \delta p_j}{p_j \delta q_i}$, a 'quantity coefficient.' But on page 138, the second coefficient is, like the first, a price coefficient, but with subscripts reversed, $\frac{p_i \delta q_j}{q_j \delta p_i}$, indicating the same type of influence, but in the opposite direction. On page 102 (where the problem is first discussed) it is said that under the symmetry assumption, since the influence of one seller on another is the same in both directions, a single (price) coefficient suffices. This would indicate that even without symmetry both are price coefficients; and Triffin's criterion for isolation is a price coefficient. (Actually, the terms price and quantity coefficient are not used by Triffin, and there is no discussion of differences in their meaning which would indicate a preference for one over the other.) For these and other reasons I thought for years that the reciprocal, or 'quantity coefficient' on page 104 was merely an error, but there seems to be no conclusive evidence either way.

However this question may be settled, there are further ambiguities, for the circular test as first presented and as so far discussed, based on the 'demand side alone,' is described (p. 104) as only an 'approximate' solution to be accepted 'provisionally,' and it is said that 'the distinction cannot be drawn in an exact and complete form without involving the cost aspect of the situation.' The sequel to this warning seems to be found on page 115, where it is sought to 'define the oligopolistic problem in its generality, instead of defining it with reference to demand alone or to cost alone,' and here new coefficients based on *profits* are presented. Profits are here differentiated with respect both to price and quantity, and the two possibilities are presented as *alternatives* for the first coefficient. The second coefficient is more complicated in form, with a choice of four alternative versions. In view of all these variations, can Triffin's circular test be given any definite interpretation at all? I believe that the stress should be merely on his evident desire to include influence in both directions, with a recognition that at the time he wrote he simply had not seen or faced many of the issues which have arisen since. And I repeat that, for reasons given above, a circular test, although significant for certain parts of the oligopoly problem, seems to me to conceive it too narrowly. The problem is in fact broader than mere indeterminacy and bluff, and when it is conceived more broadly the circular test, however defined, is superfluous.

A definite interpretation has, however, been given to it by R. L. Bishop,[21] who has ruled that Triffin's circular test for oligopoly is limited to the demand side and consists in a price, followed by a quantity, coefficient. Bishop attaches great significance to Triffin's alleged choice of such a combination of coefficients as the test for oligopoly, and without mentioning the conflicting evidence just cited. He also gives the two coefficients precise interpretations (1) as partial derivatives (2) of functions which he himself defines. But all these interpretations seem gratuitous at best. No equations are given by Triffin. Indeed, it may be seen from the account given earlier in this Note of the evolution of his 'coefficient of interdependence,' that it is 'constructed' rather than derived from equations. The term cross-elasticity is never used—only 'the coefficient'—and the symbol for partial differentiation, ∂, never appears—only the more general δ. Since Triffin is writing about general equilibrium theory, we must assume that he has in mind at least implicitly some general equations describing the economic system (although certainly not a 'group,' for it is the essence of his position that there are no groups). But there is no mention of partial differentiation and no certain indication of what variables, if any, are being held constant in deriving any of his coefficients. It must remain an open question whether many of the issues which have since been raised had really been faced by him at the time he wrote.

Finally, I should like to comment on the correct interpretation of the coefficient $\dfrac{p_j \delta q_i}{q_i \delta p_j}$ under pure competition. It has been

21. Op. cit.

argued above that the rising cost curve of the firm, although significant as an element in the test for isolation because it affects the absolute magnitudes involved, does not affect the value of the coefficient, which is a derivative. The value of this latter appears to be a rather complicated problem under the theory of limits, with different answers depending on how it is conceived mathematically. As indicated above, it is not free from ambiguity as to the nature of the functional relationships involved—whether, for instance, it is a total or a partial derivative, and if the latter, what is being held constant in the process of differentiation. These difficulties are present even under monopolistic competition, where each product has its price, and where it is meaningful to state the sales of one product as a function of its own price and a number of other prices. But if we now accept as an interpretation of the coefficient that it is a partial derivative obtained by differentiating such a function, q_i, partially with respect to another price, p_j, we have still to recognize that so long as one seller can undersell another even by a little, we are dealing mathematically with monopolistic, not pure, competition. In other words, pure competition is itself a limit; and since we seek the limiting value of the coefficient as we approach it, the question of *how* we approach it cannot be avoided. The problem may be put in this way: that if with (given) large numbers we let demand elasticities approach ∞, the coefficient approaches ∞; but if with (given) high elasticities we let the number of sellers approach ∞, the coefficient approaches 0. (Indeed, one can conceive of both numbers and elasticities increasing, the total situation thus approaching pure competition in *both* respects, in such a way that the coefficient would maintain any constant finite value indefinitely.) In any actual market where numbers and elasticities, although both high, are finite, and which therefore 'approximates' pure competition, the coefficient will be smaller the larger the numbers and larger the higher the elasticities. The ambiguity of the result seems inherent because of the requirement for pure competition, which includes *both* (1) product homogeneity and (2) large numbers.

Perhaps one should not say that cross-elasticity is 'indeterminate' under pure competition; it is simply capable of alternative definitions, and its value depends on how it is defined. Because of this complication it seems advisable to avoid the concept for pure competition. What is important here as elsewhere is isolation, and we know that the individual firm is isolated in the sense that no other firm can have any influence upon it.

5

Product Heterogeneity and Public

Policy (Welfare Economics) [1]

IT has been remarked by Mr. Triffin that 'for the historian of economic thought, the most revolutionary feature of monopolistic competition theories will probably be the unprecedented pace at which they conquered their audience.' [2] Interpreting this as he does, mainly in terms of the appearance in textbooks for the first time of chapters on oligopoly, product differentiation, and selling costs, he may be right. But I must again lament the widespread misunderstanding of the subject; so that what has 'conquered' appears often to be something quite foreign to the theory, at least as I understand it. Nowhere is this more true than in that part of the whole subject which is taken up in this paper: the reorientation of our ideas as to public policy in view of the fact of product heterogeneity.

Public policy must be presumed to seek in some sense the general welfare, and hence in the economic sphere it implies a welfare economics. The supremacy of pure competition with its corollary of prices equal to marginal costs as the economic welfare ideal is well known. Mr. A. P. Lerner's 'Rule' is a quick and familiar reference.[3] What is perhaps not so well appreciated is how

1. A paper given at the meetings of the American Economic Association at New York in December 1949. Reprinted from the *American Economic Review*, May 1950. The title has been clarified by the addition in parentheses.

2. *Monopolistic Competition and General Equilibrium Theory*, p. 17.

3. *The Economics of Control*, p. 64 and *passim*.

explicitly monopolistic competition has been interpreted as merely indicating the nature of the departures from the ideal which need to be corrected. Thus, although it may have reoriented in some degree our ideas as to how the economic system actually works, its impact upon our conception of the model towards which we would move appears to me to have been virtually nil. I say 'towards which' in recognition of the fact that pure competition is evidently a theoretical concept, and that the practical-minded economist is often ready enough to point out that 'no one has ever advocated that it be established.' What we want, to be sure, is some kind of 'workable' competition. But ordinary (purely) competitive theory remains the chief source of our criteria as to what should be done if possible, and of the direction in which we should move so far as we can. A striking instance is the subtitle of this part of the program of these meetings: 'Can the American economy be made more competitive?' The implication is evident that if it can be it should.

Now if pure competition is the ideal, the direction in which we should move is very clear. For it is easy enough to show that the actual economy is shot full of monopoly elements, and hence that any move to get rid of them or to diminish their importance is in the right direction. The main point I want to make is that the welfare ideal itself (as well as the description of reality) involves a blend of monopoly and competition and is therefore correctly described as one of monopolistic competition. If this is true, it is no longer self-evident which way we should move, for it is no longer self-evident on which side of the ideal lies the actuality for which a policy is sought. It is possible that the economy should be made 'more competitive'; but it is also quite possible that it should be made 'more monopolistic' instead. Or perhaps, if there are faults to be found with it, it should simply be changed, towards something else which again involves both monopoly and competition, with the frank admission that, since we cannot measure monopoly and competition quantitatively, there is no way of comparing the actual with the ideal on any yardstick involving these concepts.

Let us proceed at once to the proposition that monopoly is necessarily a part of the welfare norm. In abstract terms it seems to follow very directly from the recognition that human beings are individuals, diverse in their tastes and desires, and moreover widely dispersed spatially. In so far as demand has any force as a guide to production, one would expect entrepreneurs to appeal to them in diverse ways, and thus to render the output of the economy correspondingly heterogeneous, using this term in its broadest sense to embrace not only the qualitative aspects of the product itself, but also the conditions surrounding its sale, including spatial location.[4] And since what people want—an elaborate system of consumers' preferences—is the starting point in welfare economics, their wants for a heterogeneous product would seem to be as fundamental as anything could be. Heterogeneity as between producers is synonymous with the presence of monopoly; therefore monopoly is necessarily a part of the welfare ideal.

It must be emphasized that any and all monopoly is included within the general concept of heterogeneity or differentiation (although there is no implication of an identity between the actual and the ideal). A monopoly is simply a product under a single control and significantly different from others on the infinite chain of substitutes. This holds equally for a patent, a cement producer separated in space from others, a local gas utility, a toll bridge, or the A & P. And they are, of course, all without exception engaged in competition with others near by on the chain of substitutes and with others generally in the system. 'Industry' or 'commodity' boundaries are a snare and a delusion—in the highest degree arbitrarily drawn and, wherever drawn, establishing at once wholly false implications both as to competition of substitutes within their limits, which supposedly stops at their borders, and as to the possibility of ruling on the presence or absence of oligopolistic forces by the simple device of counting the number of producers included. As for the *conventional* categories of industries, it seems increasingly evident to me that they have their origin, not primarily in substitution at all, but in similarity of

4. Apart from the influence of demand, output will also be heterogeneous because of the diversity of nature on the side of production; as illustrated by human services, both directly and as reflected in the products they create; and by the fact that sellers are separated spatially.

raw materials or other inputs or of technical methods used. Glass, leather goods, drugs, and medicines are obvious examples. Apart from the wide diversity of products embraced by almost any so-called 'industry,' spatial separation of producers within it is an added prime obstacle to substitution in most cases. But the main point is that, even if lines were arbitrarily to be drawn, they would have literally nothing to do with the extent and character of the heterogeneity, either within such an industry or beyond it, which would be defensible from the point of view of welfare or of public policy.

All this is in striking contrast with prevailing notions of the significance of product heterogeneity for public policy. The reason is, I believe, mainly a difference in the implications of monopolistic competition on the one hand and of imperfect competition on the other; and the fact that the prevailing notions on public policy have been derived largely from an interpretation which follows the latter. It is worth noting that the terms product and market are used consistently in *Monopolistic Competition*, not in their usual broad sense, but with reference only to the individual firm. There are no 'commodities,' such as shoes, sheets, or shaving brushes, but only groupings of individual products. The term industry was carefully avoided, and does not appear at all (except where its limitations are being pointed out). By contrast, *Imperfect Competition* followed the tradition of competitive theory, not only in identifying a commodity (albeit elastically defined) with an industry, but in expressly assuming such a commodity to be homogeneous.[5] Such a theory involves no break whatever with the competitive tradition. The very terminology of 'imperfect competition' is heavy with implications that the objective is to move towards 'perfection.'

Even within the terminology of monopolistic competition, the same tendencies have appeared in the connotation which the term differentiation has taken on to many as of something superficial. (Hence the term heterogeneous in this paper.) It is often conceived as describing the reprehensible creation by businessmen of purely factitious differences between products which are by nature fundamentally uniform. In this vein, some have even

5. J. Robinson, *The Economics of Imperfect Competition*, p. 17.

gone so far as to attribute differentiation, and monopolistic competition generally, to 'imperfect knowledge,'[6] as though the individuality of particular products could be dismissed as an optical illusion based upon ignorance—a purely psychic phenomenon. There seems, on the contrary, to be as much reason for people to lack knowledge of the differences between products as for them to lack knowledge of their similarities; and there is a good prima facia case for believing that 'perfect knowledge' (while causing major shifts in individual preferences) would leave a system in which there were more and stronger preferences than ever. Certainly the consumer research organizations, which are engaged in perfecting the knowledge of their subscribers as to the goods they contemplate purchasing, are as much concerned with differences as with similarities.

Another device for leveling off the heterogeneous output of the economy into a series of purely competitive industries is the distinction between 'rational' and 'irrational' preferences, with its heavy implication that a substantial part of actual preferences are of the latter category. The distinction is not without its complications; but the test is supposedly simple: 'If a consumer were *forced* to have B's goods instead of A's goods, would he feel worse off after the change had taken place? If, in fact, he would consider himself to be worse off, the buyers' preference is rational; if not, it is irrational.'[7] The conclusion is, of course, that if irrational buyers' preference exists, 'then the community clearly gains by the concentration of the industry's output on a smaller number of firms.' It need only be commented that the argument, for whatever validity it may have, should not be limited in its application to an arbitrarily defined industry, but should be applied generally. On the one hand, it may be said that if Palmolive were abolished, people might be no 'worse off' after they had got used to using Lux and Lifebuoy instead. But on the other hand, it is equally true that if baseball were abolished and

---

6. F. H. Knight, *American Economic Review*, May 1946, p. 104; and G. J. Stigler, *Theory of Price* (1946), pp. 214-15, 329n, and *passim*.

7. Meade, *Economic Analysis and Policy*, p. 155. I believe the distinction was first made by R. F. Kahn in 'Some Notes on Ideal Output,' *Economic Journal*, March 1935, pp. 25-6. It is criticized by J. K. Galbraith, ibid. June 1938, p. 336.

bull fights substituted, people might be equally well or better satisfied after they were adjusted to the change, in which case their preferences for baseball should be classified as irrational. Similarly, many people have stopped smoking and, after they got used to it, were no more unhappy than before. There is a case, of course, for improving knowledge in all these matters, but no reason to think that improved knowledge would leave us with fewer or weaker preferences. In some cases it seems clear that increased standardization of certain products by public authority is indicated, as when oligopolistic forces are supporting an unduly large number of producers,[8] or when the gain in efficiency is judged by proper authorities to be more important than the losses in consumers' surplus through abandoning certain products. But the labeling of most preferences within an arbitrarily defined industry as irrational seems to me to indicate mainly a preference for the purely competitive ideal, and an attempt, perhaps largely unconscious, to salvage it. The alternative is not necessarily to assume that all preferences are rational, but only that they are on the same footing—in other words, to make no invidious distinctions between them as to rationality on the basis of the relative proximity of substitutes.

It might be added that no invidious distinctions are indicated either on the basis of whether or not the demands for particular products are influenced by selling expenditures. Here again, stress on irrational preferences makes an easy transition to the labeling of those established by advertising as irrational, and to the conventional sweeping condemnation of advertising as a 'competitive waste.'[9] Granted that the techniques of modern advertising are often a shocking affront to good taste, or objectionable on other grounds, it remains true, so far as I can see, that the question of whether advertising is wasteful or not, in the sense of being a misallocation of resources, simply cannot be answered by any criteria derived from market demand and cost curves— or from indifference curves either. Here is a major aspect of 'welfare' which appears to lie quite outside the conventional analysis of the subject. The general condemnation of advertising as a

8. *Monopolistic Competition,* pp. 100-109.
9. Meade, op. cit. pp. 165-6 (Meade and Hitch, pp. 176-7).

waste surely has its primary explanation in the irrelevancy that it could not exist under the perfectly competitive ideal.

The fact that equilibrium for the firm when products are heterogeneous normally takes place under conditions of falling average costs of production has generally been regarded as a departure from ideal conditions, these latter being associated with the minimum point on the curve; and various corrective measures have been proposed. However, if heterogeneity is part of the welfare ideal, there is no prima facie case for doing anything at all. It is true that the same total resources (either within some arbitrarily defined industry or within the whole economy) may be made to yield more units of product by being concentrated on fewer firms. The issue might be put as efficiency versus diversity—more of either one means less of the other. But unless it can be shown that the loss of satisfaction from a more standardized product (again, either within an 'industry' or for the economy as a whole) is less than the gain through producing more units, there is no 'waste' at all, even though every firm is producing to the left of its minimum point.

How are the two to be compared—a larger, less heterogeneous output as against a smaller, more heterogeneous one? The price system, especially in view of its all-pervasive oligopolistic forces and the omnipresence of selling costs whose welfare status is uncertain, appears to afford no test. If we may allow the individual producer his optimum selling expenditure, included as a lump sum in his fixed costs, and conceive a system in which every producer determines the equilibrium of his firm with reference to a demand curve which measures demand for his product at different prices while all other prices, products, and selling costs do not change, we have in the elasticity of demand one index of the strength of buyers' preferences for each product.[10] If adjustment of prices along demand curves of this type could be enforced, many firms whose profits (perhaps nominal) are protected by the

10. The curves of Mrs. Robinson's *Imperfect Competition* cannot be used for this purpose because they are defined as including oligopolistic reactions. Cf. *Imperfect Competition*, p. 21.

absence of vigorous price competition [11] would certainly be involved in losses and would be obliged to go out of business before a general equilibrium for the whole economy were realized. There would be less heterogeneity than we find at present, and it would seem that something like what I have described elsewhere as a 'sort of ideal' [12] would be established.

Another approach to the same problem is to test old products individually for survival and new products for admission to the economy by a consideration of the surpluses of satisfaction over cost which are sacrificed in one place and generated in another by the transfer of resources involved. Much of what has been written in this connection [13] seems to me to be vitiated by entanglement with the standard theory of 'exploitation' which has evolved out of 'imperfect' competition and which I have elsewhere [14] shown to be fallacious—a theory in which hired factors are held to be exploited by entrepreneurs. But the theoretical criterion involved can be adapted to an analysis from which this objectionable feature is absent. Of course the old bogey of interpersonal comparisons appears at once; also the familiar problem of subsidy to the expanded firms which, if they had no extra profits before, are now, at the lower prices necessary to sell the larger output, losing money. Unfortunately the matter is too complex to be developed in this short paper. Let us only observe that, for whatever it may be worth, the final welfare equilibrium which emerges from this analysis, as from the preceding one, would inevitably involve product heterogeneity; and that it would be characterized neither by the equation of price and marginal cost nor by production at minimum average cost for the firms involved. Indeed, by this procedure, the adjustment required from any starting point might as easily be to increase the supposedly

11. Cf. *Monopolistic Competition*, pp. 100-109.

12. Ibid. p. 94. With allowance made for the 'diversity of conditions surrounding each producer' (pp. 110-13) the ideal would evidently involve diverse outputs and prices for the individual producers in the system.

13. Cf. especially R. F. Kahn, op. cit. and J. E. Meade (also Meade and Hitch), op. cit. Part II, Ch. VI.

14. *Monopolistic Competition* (5th or later ed.), pp. 182-4, 215-18. [See also below, pp. 309ff.]

excess number of firms as to diminish it. As an indication of what is involved, one might under this principle even revive that good old newspaper, the *Boston Transcript*, under public subsidy, since many 'proper Bostonians' were strangely attached to it and no doubt lost heavily in consumers' surplus when it finally folded up.

Let us leave this question of how many products there should be, or of diversity, to say a word about the other major type of adjustment which has been analyzed in relation to product heterogeneity and welfare—that of the distribution of resources among a given number of products or among a given number of industries.

It has been proposed that resources be transferred from purely competitive industries, where price equals marginal cost, to 'imperfectly competitive industries,' where price is greater than marginal cost, and similarly from less imperfectly competitive to more imperfectly competitive industries, until the ratio of price to marginal cost is the same everywhere. Such a proposal may be dismissed at once on two grounds, either one of which alone is sufficient: (1) the boundaries of an industry being arbitrary, it is quite meaningless and (2) the demand and cost curves of different firms within any industry are highly diverse as to elasticity and shape. For these two reasons we must abandon altogether the idea of transferring resources in some vague way to an industry, and face the question of the firms to which they are to be attached.[15]

What, then, of equalizing the price-marginal cost ratio as between firms in the economy? Apart from other difficulties, I believe there is a fatal objection to such a conception; viz. the generally prevalent oligopolistic relationships between firms. The logic by which this proposition is usually developed envisages each firm as an isolated monopoly, isolated in the sense that its output and price may be adjusted without appreciable effect on any other single firm. But where oligopolistic influences are present, there are two points to be made. First, the demand curve for

15. Mr. Kahn's analysis explicitly assumes industries in which competition is 'uniformly imperfect' (op. cit. p. 21n.), and thus lays down principles for a wholly imaginary problem.

any one firm, which would indicate the effect on its price of adding resources to it, cannot be known without knowing which of the many possible patterns of behavior under oligopoly will govern the case at hand. In fact, since adding resources to any one firm would, by lowering its price, inevitably shift the demand curves of others economically near it (since every curve is drawn on the assumption of given prices for other firms), there seems to be no escape from abandoning the conception of transfers between firms considered to be independent, and reconceiving it in terms of groups of some kind. Second, the effect on welfare of adding resources to one firm, where oligopolistic interdependence is involved, is a function of whether or not, and in what quantity, resources are being added at the same time to others economically near. Even assuming that the price behavior could be directed according to some socially enforced rule, the major problem would still remain of finding the rule in welfare terms. I very much fear that, because of oligopolistic interrelationships between the welfare contributions of firms, we are reduced to asserting merely that resources should be transferred from one place to another in the system whenever the net effect will be to increase welfare. This is not very illuminating.

In conclusion, the consequences of product heterogeneity for welfare economics have been either ignored or seriously misunderstood. Monopoly elements are built into the economic system and the ideal necessarily involves them. Thus wherever there is a demand for diversity of product, pure competition turns out to be not the ideal but a departure from it. Marginal cost pricing no longer holds as a principle of welfare economics (not even for toll bridges); nor is the minimum point on the cost curve for the firm to be associated with the ideal. Selling costs may no longer be excluded from the problem or dismissed as an obvious waste; yet the impossibility of discovering from the standard welfare techniques what is the socially ideal expenditure on selling suggests that the techniques are unduly narrow. It has been impossible to discuss in this paper whole families of new problems which put in their appearance with a recognition of the fact that products themselves are variables and that there must be norms for them as well as for prices, costs, and outputs. What has been called the 'new welfare economics,' instead of being on a 'secure basis' as suggested by Professor Hicks,[16] has quite misconceived a whole set of major problems. It is badly in need of a general overhauling.

16. 'The Foundations of Welfare Economics,' *Economic Journal*, December 1939, p. 711.

Part

II

_____

NONPRICE COMPETITION

6

The Product as an Economic Variable [1,2]

1. INTRODUCTION

THE recognition that the fundamental structure of the economic world which the economist must explain is one of competition between monopolists, each with a product different in some degree from those of his rivals, may be regarded as having a twofold impact upon traditional economic theory. In the first place, it forces an integration into a single system of the two separate theories of monopoly and of competition, no longer to be looked upon as mutually exclusive alternatives, but as partial aspects of a much more complex structure. In the second place, it opens up broad new areas for investigation.

It is the first of those mentioned which has attracted almost exclusive attention, and the reason is not far to seek, for here at least we remain in the familiar territory of price-quantity relationships. The theory of pure competition, which has traditionally explained the economy, is a system of such relationships, as is the traditional theory of monopoly. It is clear by now that the integration of these two theories through the recognition of product heterogeneity and of oligopolistic forces creates a new way of

1. Reprinted from the *Quarterly Journal of Economics*, February 1953.
2. The substance of this article has been presented to successive generations of graduate students at Harvard since 1935, and a number of them have since carried the analysis much further than is done here. The present manuscript is a revision of one prepared and almost completed in 1936.
A note on bibliography appears at the end of the article.

looking at the economic system, raising a host of new problems and yielding new solutions for old ones. Yet it remains true that *mere* integration may still take place within a framework limited to the familiar variables of price and quantity.

But the recognition of heterogeneity in the output of the economic system further transforms and enlarges economic theory by opening it to new variables of major importance. The managements of individual firms will seek in their control of their market relationships not only to choose price most advantageously, but with it to combine (1) the best choice of the 'product' itself in its various qualitative aspects, and (2) the optimum expenditure for advertising and selling.

'Nonprice competition' is a term which has come to be rather widely accepted to describe the area covered by these new variables, the 'product' and selling costs. They are *new* in the sense that they are inconsistent with pure competition and therefore emerge only when the assumption of pure competition is dropped. They might, of course, be ruled out in a system of heterogeneous products by further assumptions carefully designed to exclude them, but such a procedure would be arbitrary indeed, and would require strong justification in view of their vital importance in the real economic world which the economist is charged with explaining. They have both from the beginning been part and parcel of the theory of monopolistic competition,[3] and any formu-

3. They are not a part of the theory of imperfect competition as developed by Mrs. Robinson. Alfred Sherrard, in his article 'Advertising, Product Variation, and the Limits of Economies' (*Journal of Political Economy*, April 1951), seems to recognize that they are not (p. 126n.1), yet gratuitously includes Mrs. Robinson (also Stackelberg) in his adverse criticisms of this type of theory. Surely this is a new level of absurdity in the history of this slipshod tradition which glosses over all differences between the two theories. Sherrard says that 'if Chamberlin's interpretation of Mrs. Robinson were accepted, her theory would have to be excluded from consideration in this article altogether, on the ground that "imperfect competition" does not encompass product variation.' But this is not my 'interpretation'—it is simply a fact. Mrs. Robinson herself would be the last to make any claim to have dealt with the subject, and in fact *necessarily* excludes it by defining the commodity co-extensive with her imperfectly competitive market as homogeneous (*Imperfect Competition*, p. 17) and consistently interpreting it in this way. Indeed there is no reason to suppose that she would be any more sympathetic towards the

lation of this theory which does not include them is no more than a piece of partial analysis—a facet of the whole theory.

The main concern of this paper is with the 'product' as a variable.[4] But since it is necessary to view the problem in its whole setting, let us first look briefly at the many-sided nature of competition in which four variables, instead of the familiar two of quantity and price, play a part.

If all four are truly variable, the functional relationships of any two of them, important as they may be, cannot be accepted as more than a partial explanation of the whole. It is not enough, for instance, to concern oneself with the proposition that the demand for a *given* product (under given selling outlays) varies with its price; one must also take into account that the demand at a *given* price (and under given selling outlays) varies with its 'quality.' One must take it into account because products [5] are not in fact given; they are continuously changed—improved, deteriorated, or just made different—as an essential part of the market process.

It may be said that the reactions of buyers to quality are so obvious that there is nothing to be said about them. Yet they

'product as a variable' than is Sherrard. She should therefore be spared his criticisms.

Sherrard cites Triffin in support of his rejection of my 'interpretation.' But Triffin's authority on this seemingly controversial matter is to the contrary. With reference to product variation and selling outlays Triffin states that in 'the expositions of Mrs. Robinson, von Stackelberg and Pareto . . . no attention is given to these problems.' Perhaps it is for this reason that he neglects them himself, and warns his readers that this neglect 'must be borne in mind when comparing *The Theory of Monopolistic Competition* with the expositions [in question].' (*Monopolistic Competition and General Equilibrium Theory*, p. 21n.6.) Unfortunately Mr. Sherrard failed to bear it in mind, and thereby contributed his bit to the prevailing obfuscation.

4. Product variation must not be confused with the familiar analysis of 'product differentiation' in which the products of different sellers, although different, are all *given,* so that the only variables studied are price and quantity.

5. 'Product' is used in the broad sense to include all aspects of the good or service exchanged, whether arising from materials or ingredients, mechanical construction, design, durability, taste, peculiarities of package or container, service, location of seller, or any other factor having significance for the buyer. Cf. *Monopolistic Competition*, pp. 56, 71, 78.

may be as complicated in their ramifications as are the equally 'obvious' reactions of buyers (and sellers) to prices, upon which the whole structure of economic theory has been built. Certainly they cannot be ignored in any realistic description of how the economic system works. In the same way the question of the behavior of *each* variable relative to the others inevitably poses itself. The quantity of a product which can be sold depends in part upon the price which is asked for it, in part upon its product attributes, and in part upon the amount spent to persuade people to buy it. And any one of the four may be regarded as dependent upon the other three in a similar manner.

Where the variables are two (price and quantity), there arises only the question of their relationships to each other. But when they are four, the number of possible paired relationships expands to six, as follows:

1. Price-quantity.
2. Product-quantity.
3. Advertising [6]-quantity.
4. Price-product.
5. Price-advertising.
6. Advertising-product.

Such a table must be regarded merely as a symbol, especially with reference to the product, which is seen at once to be a composite made up of a more or less indefinite number of aspects, such as location, size, design, workmanship, nutritive value, etc., depending on the nature of the product in question. But it is a very useful symbol. For instance, it indicates at once what an absurdly small part of a very broad problem is the first pair of variables—price-quantity relationships—to which economic theory has traditionally limited itself. And it provides sub-headings under which the general nature of the expansion in subject matter may be conveniently indicated. Passing over the first of these sub-headings as familiar, let us look briefly at each of the other five.

6. Advertising is used here for convenience as a more concise term to cover all forms of selling costs. The definition of these latter is discussed in *Monopolistic Competition*, Chap. VI.

Product-quantity relationships. It may be helpful at this point merely to suggest two of the many ways in which familiar concepts of price-quantity analysis may be taken as a starting point in analyzing the phenomena of this new area. First, elasticity of demand, in its general sense of the degree of responsiveness of demand to a change in price, is evidently applicable to the product as a variable, where the question becomes that of the responsiveness of demand to a change in the product. How much, for instance, will an improvement—better materials or a technical addition—(price remaining the same) increase the amount demanded; and how much will materials a little poorer or a few corners cut here and there diminish it? In addition to an analysis based on perfect knowledge, it is especially important here to admit also the highly realistic assumption of imperfect knowledge. If the product can be deteriorated in ways not easily detected, the demand may be quite inelastic with reference to such a change and the temptation will be strong to go ahead; but if the change is easily discovered, buyers will shift in greater numbers to something else. The special problem of 'product elasticity of demand' in the face of consumer ignorance is one of those brought into the open by the recognition of the product as a variable. It is relatively easy for the buyer to know the *price* of a product; but as to its *qualities* and their significance to him, perfect ignorance would often be a better assumption than perfect knowledge—and one leading to very different theoretical conclusions as to how products are 'determined,' as will be seen later on.

As a second example, 'cut-throat' price competition has its counterpart in product-quantity relations. In price analysis this term has referred to a severe struggle for business in which prices are cut to disastrous levels far below costs; in product analysis it would refer to a struggle in which products are improved with resulting higher costs until costs are above prices. Such a result may easily follow in any type of product competition where an improvement or an added service by one seller succeeds sufficiently well to oblige his rivals to 'follow suit,' and thus opens the way to a series of adjustments. A simple example may be found in the element of speed in transportation. Speed is a qualitative aspect of the product in this case, excluded from economic analysis unless the product is admitted as a variable; yet increased speed of transport has probably been as revolutionary in its effects upon the economic system as have lower costs. Our concern for the moment is with speed as a basis of competition, and in particular, of 'cut-throat' competition. There have been some famous 'speed wars' in the history of rail transport, with reference in particular to passenger transport. A reduction in the number of hours between, say, New York and Chicago, is a way of attracting customers, just as is a reduction in the price of a ticket. Increased speed increases costs (after an optimum has been reached) in terms of road ballast, fuel consumption, design of power units and trains, safety measures, lawsuits where safety measures fail, etc. Speed wars can be (and have been) as ruinous as rate wars. But apart from this particularly dramatic aspect of speed as an element of competition, it is evident that we have here a very simple, run-of-the-mill example of the product as a variable, one which is of major importance, perfectly measurable, and as capable of analysis in terms of cost and demand functions, profit maximization, etc., as is the conventional variable of price.[7]

Advertising-quantity relationships. With given prices and products, demand will vary with selling expenditures. The manner of its variation is highly complex and is only beginning to be studied and to be integrated into the main body of economic analysis. Selling costs must likewise be related to the general (production) cost analysis of economic theory. An attempt to develop a systematic analysis of these problems and to relate them to the other variables involved is contained in Chapter VII of *Monopolistic Competition.* It may be added here that the two problems just discussed with reference to product-quantity relationships as illustrative of the application of familiar concepts to these areas obviously have their counterparts in advertising-quantity relationships. The recognition of advertising as a means of creating and altering demands evidently introduces the distinction between demands as they are found by producers and

7. Many of the problems of this area have been examined by Herbert Ashton in an unpublished Ph.D. thesis, *Economic Analysis of the Element of Speed in Transportation,* Harvard University, 1936.

economically created demands. Economic theory has concerned itself only with the former.

Price-product relationships. Advertising outlay and quantity sold remaining the same, how will price vary with changes in the product? This type of relationship may be difficult to visualize in its isolated form because it would rarely happen in actuality that variations in price and in product would be unaccompanied by a change in advertising outlay and would take place in such a way as not to alter the amount sold. But the functional relationship exists as a part of the whole problem, and it is one of the most important. In general, it is elementary common sense that there will be a rough correlation between the quality of the product and its price, although the conventional analysis of price competition completely passes over such a correlation by confining its attention to price changes for *given* products. We have here a prime example of one of the pitfalls of partial analysis if it is not used with care. *Reasoning from a given product,* economists are much given to scolding businessmen because they are not sufficiently active in their (price) competition. The admission of the product as a variable not only adds to the picture an alternative area in which competition may in fact be quite active; it does much more than this: it supplies a powerful new force working *against* price competition. If products were actually 'given,' people would rush to buy from the seller whose price was cheapest because they would know they were getting the same thing for less money. Since products in the real world are not given, people will naturally recognize that the lower price may be accompanied by poorer quality and their response to it will be diminished; it may even be negative. Furthermore, intense price competition puts strong pressure on businessmen actually to lower the quality of their products, and the desire to maintain certain standards emerges as a natural and commonplace (partial) explanation of why businessmen do not like price competition. Neglect of price-product relationships gives a warped picture indeed of the actual competitive process.

Price-advertising and advertising-product relationships. Analytically, each of these may be separated from the complex whole in the same way that price-quantity relationships are ordinarily isolated—by holding constant the other two variables in the problem. In real life they do not stand out as clearly as the others for the reason that they do not so often vary in perfect isolation. Let us consider, for example, advertising and quality. There is no difficulty about conceiving of the price as held constant, for many products have fixed prices over long periods of time. But the quantity sold is so sensitive to changes both in selling expenditure and in quality that it is difficult to conceive in actuality of advertising and quality varying in such a way as to offset each other exactly, thereby leaving the quantity sold a constant amount. Nevertheless, we know that advertising is often used to maintain sales volume in the face of quality deterioration. And many firms choose to devote resources to improving their products as an alternative to advertising. It is also true that advertising and quality are often positively correlated, and it is a familiar maxim that 'it doesn't pay to advertise a poor product.' What is indicated by these apparently contradictory observations is not, as will at once be said, 'general indeterminateness,' but rather a state of general ignorance for lack of study. We know very little about the functional relationships involved for the simple reason that economic theory has been so conceived as to exclude them from its province. As soon as they are accepted as legitimate objects of analysis it seems not too much to hope that our knowledge of the forces involved and hence of the whole competitive process will improve. Clearly, equilibrium in any particular case must involve an optimum relationship between advertising and the product as well as between the other variables in question. Similarly, for a product of given quality, any particular output may be achieved by many possible different combinations of advertising outlay and price. The higher the price the greater must be the advertising outlay (and vice versa) in order to produce the demand necessary to take the given output from the market. Total profit will vary with different combinations and equilibrium must involve an optimum relationship between advertising and price as well as between the other variables. The isolation of price-advertising and advertising-product relationships suggests, among other things, studies as to the comparative qualities and prices of advertised as against nonadvertised goods on the market.

The discussion above has been framed in terms of pairs of variables as a familiar type of simplified partial analysis, but evidently three or more variables may be studied together by more complicated methods, and any *final* picture of the forces at work either for a firm, a group of firms, or the whole economy must embrace *all* the forces at work. The principles involved here are no different from those of economic analysis generally.

In looking into new problems opened up by the recognition of the product and of advertising (in addition to price and quantity) as economic variables, a word may be said about variations over time. Time series of prices and of quantities produced or consumed (either for individual commodities or in the form of indexes) are, of course, among the most familiar of economic data. Familiar, too, are the difficulties encountered both in the construction and interpretation of such series because of the qualitative changes over time in the products which compose them. It is not necessary, then, to argue for the existence of such changes. What is necessary is to recognize them as variations of vital importance in themselves, rather than as disturbing elements in the problem of price and quantity indexes. We know next to nothing about the history, even the recent history, of the qualitative improvement or deterioration of products, either individually, by classes, or in general. There is a limitless field for investigation here. Of course, to a considerable extent, descriptions of product changes would have to be in nonquantitative terms, but the extent to which quality may be reduced to quantitative terms is apt to be underestimated.[8] The nutritive qualities of foodstuffs, tensile strength and thread count of materials, durability and performance of mechanical devices, are simple examples of tests highly relevant to the capacities of goods to satisfy wants. Even such elusive aspects of quality as taste, appearance, etc., have been successfully reduced to quantitative terms in some of the products (as butter) for which standards and grades have already been promulgated by the Federal gov-

8. It was definitely underestimated in *Monopolistic Competition*, p. 79.

ernment. Quality series could be related to the business cycle (To what extent are products deteriorated in time of depression?); and data bearing on quality could be related to the growth of competition or monopoly, to the scale of production, to the growth of production for the market as opposed to production for direct use, and to many other familiar economic categories in a way which would tremendously increase our knowledge of the working of the economic system.

2. THE MEANING OF PRODUCT DETERMINATION

Let us turn now to one part of the whole process considered up to this point—that part having to do specifically with the product as a variable. In view of the generally sanctioned procedure of studying price-quantity relationships for *given* products it is of the utmost importance at the outset to realize that there is literally no such thing as a given product. Products are actually the most volatile things in the economic system—much more so than prices. To begin with, almost every 'product' has a variable element at least in the circumstances surrounding its sale: convenience of location, peculiarities of shop and environment, personalities, service, methods of doing business, etc. These factors are, of course, of varying importance in the individual case.

As for products in the narrower sense, evidently consumers' goods may be of different materials, design, or standards of workmanship, whether we are speaking of furniture, clothing, or household equipment. The preparation of food for sale, whether by canning, baking, or other type of manufacture for consumption at home, or by cooking and serving in a restaurant, affords infinite possibilities of variation with respect to the selection of ingredients, their quality, and the manner in which they are combined and prepared. The perfect and infinite variability of such 'products' as services—public utility, professional, and personal—is evident. In the case of barber shops, beauty parlors, laundries, cleaning establishments, etc., the quality of what is sold is a major element in the consumer's decision to buy from one seller rather than another—his choice is made as much on the basis of product as of price, and probably much more so.

Moving back in the productive process from consumers' goods

to capital goods, it is evident without further elaboration that similar considerations apply, and that *all* products beyond the raw material stage are highly variable, for the most part on a continuous scale.

Where, then, do we find fixed products? It would seem that when we get back to raw materials, we might find something given by nature—perhaps some metals in their pure form. But agricultural products can be varied a great deal—the quality of meat is obviously varied by feeding, by breeding, and so on; grains, fruits, and vegetables are changed a great deal by human control of seed, methods of culture, etc.; and all these things are done constantly in order to improve profits by the people who are producing them. A student once suggested that the given product we were looking for was an egg. This might have been a good illustration before the scientific age. But eggs are actually among the most variable of products and nowadays are *made* to vary in size, color, chemistry of contents, hardness of shell, freshness, etc., to say nothing of such new-fangled inventions as that described in the following item: 'Government experts claim to have developed an egg with a non-porous shell that will remain edible about twice as long as the average egg.' [9]

If products are in fact so elusive, how can we as economists justify freezing them at some arbitrary point, and consider that we have done our job when we have explained prices and outputs *for the particular resulting entities?* There can be no true equilibrium until products themselves as well as prices and outputs have been determined; and they are in fact determined along with these latter by the interaction of entrepreneurs' decisions in the face of market forces, often with the familiar objective of maximizing profits. The study of these 'nonprice' aspects of the economic system should add substantially to our knowledge of how it operates, as compared with the limited partial picture we get when we assume that everything is given except price and quantity.

It may be said by some that traditional economic theory already contains a theory of products, holding as it does, at least

9. From *Looking Ahead Toward the Better World of Tomorrow,* a monthly bulletin published by the State Street Trust Co., Boston.

implicitly, that entrepreneurs will engage in the production of those goods for which, in the light of demand and cost conditions, there are the greatest possibilities of profit. But the proposition that products are determined by the maximum profit decisions of entrepreneurs reveals itself as no more than a plausible initial assumption. It is inadequate to explain products for the same reason that the bare proposition that prices will be such as to maximize profits does not constitute a theory of value. The system of products may actually be much more intricate and complicated in its functional relationships than is the system of prices.

To appreciate fully what is meant by the problem of 'product determination' it will be helpful to elaborate the idea of a wide range of product 'possibilities,' only a few of which are realized in actuality. We are accustomed to thinking of wants as expressing themselves in the market in terms of demand curves or schedules for the particular goods there offered. Yet it must be evident at once that these are only a fragment of the whole system of wants. Just as the demands for any particular good at prices other than the one actually ruling make up a part of the system, so it is with the demands for products other than those actually produced. After all, the only wants which *actually* express themselves, even for the given products, are those at the prices which actually come into existence. If the demands for these same products at other prices constitute a part of the system, so equally do the demands for other products at the same prices (and therefore at other prices as well). The wants in which we are interested, then, are those for all possible products at all possible prices. Only with this conception clearly before us do the same potentialities for product variation appear as are always recognized for prices in the familiar demand curve.[10]

The diversity of these wants is disguised by the degree of uni-

10. There is no reason to dismiss such a notion on the ground that it involves an infinity of possibilities which are absurdly remote and which the entrepreneur would never consider. The same is true of prices. Realistically, the entrepreneur will naturally not waste his time in considering remote product possibilities any more than he will waste it in considering whether or not to set a price of $1000 on a lead pencil.

formity present in the goods brought forth in the market.[11] The explanation of such uniformity lies, of course, in economies of scale, economies which vary widely in importance as between products. If all products were made to order, production would clearly be very much less efficient and fewer wants would be satisfied. But they would be satisfied with greater precision.

This failure of actual products to satisfy wants exactly may be visualized by imagining all buyers to be distributed uniformly along a line in space and considering the product of all to be homogeneous except for the single element of convenience. The variety of product desired by each would be produced only if there were a shop at every point on the line, and this would be the case (barring obstacles to entry) if there were no economies of scale. Where such economies exist, a maximum of *efficiency* for each firm would be realized only if there were such a limited number of them that each was producing at the minimum point on its cost curve. But since willingness to pay something for convenience means that the demand curve for the product of each firm is tipped from the horizontal, the number of firms would in our example adjust itself by familiar principles so that their demand and cost curves would be tangent; their size would be smaller and there would be more of them than under conditions of maximum efficiency.[12] The exact number of shops in any particular case would evidently be larger the greater the importance which buyers attached to convenience, and smaller the greater the importance of the economies of scale. Even if we suppose the equilibrium number of shops in this final adjustment to be located at equal intervals along the line so as to give a maximum of convenience, the only buyers who are getting *exactly* what they want are those few located at the identical points with the shops. The others purchase at the nearest shop because it affords the next best substitute.

In this example the diversity of wants was infinitely graded on

11. By uniformity is meant not merely that sometimes existing as between producers, but, what is much more important, uniformity in the product of any one producer as compared with the diversity of wants on the part of those who purchase from him.

12. Cf. *Monopolistic Competition*, p. 84.

a scale of distance. When we pass to other phases of the product, and recognize that no two individuals are either identical in tastes or identically situated relative to their environment, we might by analogy regard buyers as distributed along symbolical lines in multidimensional space with respect to other aspects of the product. Certain it is that they are not concentrated at precise points corresponding to the particular products actually produced. The demands for products 'in between' those actually upon the market are analogous to those for locations in between those actually established on the line of distance.[13] The economic problem of products, like that of prices, is simply to discover and elaborate the principles that determine which of the many potential products (prices) become, or tend to become, actual.

3. THREE MAIN DETERMINANTS OF PRODUCTS

It is possible in the remainder of this article, to present only a few suggestions for a theory of products, and to develop some of them in a limited way.[14] Let us distinguish three main determinants of products under the general headings of (1) custom, (2) standards, and (3) profit maximization.

The first will be passed over quickly. Many products and some aspects of almost all products are determined by custom—and let us add, inertia; sometimes for long periods, more often for short periods.[15] Here a comparison with prices is highly suggestive.

13. Because we usually become habituated to what we can get and accept it without too much grumbling, the extent to which products fail to satisfy our wants is underestimated. Yet it is a familiar experience not to find exactly what one wants upon the market. Many 'in-between' products might be as profitable to produce as others actually on the market if the surrounding products were different.

14. Product decisions are evidently made with reference to the whole range of time periods; and there is no reason to think that the element of time is of any less importance here than in price theory. But it will not be developed in what follows, except incidentally. It may be remarked in passing that a product, say an automobile, by reason of its many aspects, may, at any one time (unlike a price) be a *composite* of decisions made with reference to different time periods.

15. It is of interest to recall that John Stuart Mill clearly (and correctly) distinguished custom from 'competition' in value theory. It is a force separate and distinct from the laws of supply and demand and of cost, and he gave it

Economists, believing on the whole in the 'law of supply and demand,' and recognizing, as they must, that supply and demand conditions change more or less constantly, have been much concerned with explaining the phenomenon of rigid, or 'sticky,' prices—prices which remain unchanged over any substantial period of time. At the same time, since the possible variation in products has been covered up by the device of *assuming* them constant, the stickiness of these latter over time has been taken as a matter of course. Once the product has been recognized as a variable, a parallel treatment of prices and products is suggested. Sticky products, equally with prices, require explaining. If rigid prices over a period of time raise suspicions of an antisocial price agreement, then rigid products suggest the possibility of an equally antisocial product agreement. Similarly, if it is a matter of no concern that certain aspects of products become 'frozen' over periods of time by reason of custom or inertia, the same forces may explain why prices too do not move for substantial periods. It is suggested that active price competition with given products may in general be not more nor less 'competitive' than active product competition with given prices. When competition takes place over an area which includes both prices and products, rigidity in any portion of this area, whether caused by a monopolistic agreement, by custom, or by inertia, is at least not inconsistent with flexibility in other portions of it and even with intense competition. Finally, it would seem that new light on all the problems of this area is to be had by recognizing the fundamental variability of both products and prices and hence the possible parallels in the explanations of their failures to vary.

We may discuss at this point two other explanations of short-run product rigidity logically independent of custom, yet involving it finally in the form of generally accepted, industry-wide procedures. The first is the influence of technical change on the frequency with which types or models of certain products are altered; the second is the style factor.

It happens that both of these may be illustrated by the automobile industry. In the United States automobile models are

great importance, both in the long and in the short run. (*Principles of Political Economy,* Ashley Edition, Book ii, Chap. 4 and *passim.*)

changed yearly. Why once a year instead of once a month, or once every five years? What determines the period during which this particular product becomes fixed? There would perhaps be disagreement as to whether the period of one year in the automobile industry is in fact predominantly the result of technological or of style considerations. But let us for the moment turn attention merely to the former. Research is constantly going on, of course, and possible improvements over the model which is in production accumulate. If, for the sake of incorporating such improvements, producers were to set up new models, say every week, they would never produce very many of any particular one; and so, in order to realize the economies which come with large aggregate production of a particular type on a production line basis, they have to freeze the product for a substantial period. If the period is too long, the gains from cheap production are more than offset by the deficiencies of the product relative to the developing state of technical knowledge.[16] From this point of view the annual change of models is simply the compromise which has been worked out between the conflicting objectives of low cost and improved quality.

There are similar problems in connection with style. Here the issue is not technical but aesthetic 'improvement,' in the sense that human beings tire of a particular design, whether of automobiles or of clothing, and are refreshed by a change, the new product being in this sense an 'improvement' (again for a time). This fundamental desire for variety is of course greatly accentuated in its influence by the social interdependence of want satisfactions, illustrated by the satisfaction derived (or the dissatisfaction avoided) from being 'in style' once the cycle has been established. Be this as it may, the style cycle for many products, of which women's clothing is perhaps the best example, repre-

16. The related problem of just when to freeze the production of a particular model of airplane or tank for military purposes is one which similarly involves the foregoing of subsequent improvements in order to gain quantity output. Its solution is, of course, quite different because of the totally different objective of optimum defense, which introduces important new variables such as the relative strength of the enemy, the time when he is most likely to attack, and the inevitable oligopolistic element of his probable reaction to any decision taken.

sents again a compromise between the conflicting objectives of
frequent change ('improvement') and of low cost, the latter resulting not only from the popularization and quantity output
of a particular design or general type of product, but also from
a period of use on the part of the purchaser sufficiently long to
reduce to a reasonable level the cost to him per unit of time.
The style cycle is full of special problems and is certainly one
of the most interesting and important aspects of the product
as an economic variable.[17]

The second determinant of products may be called 'standards,'
and they are of various kinds. Speaking generally, a certain conception of what a product ought to be often exists, and although
it may be freely variable in a 'technical' sense, there is disapproval
of variations which involve a departure from, and in particular
a deterioration of, the standard set. Perhaps the simplest example
of such a standard is one established and maintained by organized society through the machinery of the state. Thus legal en-
actments in the form of building codes determine in great detail
the types of houses that may be constructed, laws and commission regulations set standards of service for transport and public
utilities, public authority regulates sizes and shapes of food con-
tainers and in diverse respects the qualitative aspects of food and
drug products themselves, etc., etc. For the most part (but not
entirely) the imposition of such legal standards seems to be explained by the alternative dramatic deterioration of products in
a system in which they are determined by profit maximization.
The circumstances under which such deterioration is 'normal'
are discussed further on.

Standards are also established and maintained by various
classes and sub-groups within society, as well as by firms and
individuals. Thus there are professional standards, and the conception of the professions as an area of activity in which objectives
other than profit maximization supposedly prevail is familiar.
With reference to the product this means, to take medicine as
an example, that a doctor is restrained by the weight of generally

17. The problem of 'variety over time' bears an obvious analogy to that discussed above of variety in general, and illustrated by a spatial example.

accepted professional practice from depreciating the quality of his medical services, even where such depreciation, combined with the proper price policy, might increase his income. Indeed, the taboo on commercialism in the form both of advertising and of price competition is a part of a system designed to protect a standard-determined service from being put on the scale of profit maximization.

Closely related to standards in the professions are artistic, ethical, and moral standards, and standards of purity, of quality, or of workmanship. An artist or writer may be faithful to his best creative ideals—a standard—or he may deliberately alter his product in favor of what will sell more readily. In like manner the character of sports will be vitally affected by whether the persons taking part in them are competing for the sake of the sport itself or to make money, and so we have the distinction (increasingly difficult to maintain) between amateur and professional sports. Even where all participants are amateur, profit maximization by other control units may enter in, as illustrated by the recent crisis in college football in which leading American universities suddenly became aware that their eagerness to exploit the market possibilities of great football spectacles had altered the 'product' in numerous undesirable respects.[18]

The services of the politician may be dedicated uncompromisingly to the public interest, or they may depart from this standard in all degrees by reason of inducements pressed upon him by those who seek to influence his views or to obtain political favors: in our terminology the product (his services) is in the latter case no longer determined by a standard of integrity but has been altered in favor of income maximization.[19] Similarly,

18. Typically, however, the 'maximum profits' from football, since they were used to offest the losses in other sports, were consistent with no profits (or a deficit) for the athletic program as a whole.

19. There has been much discussion of this particular problem in the United States recently. In the revelations of gifts to public servants by interested parties, an accused income tax official startled the community by his defense of accepting a ham on the ground that it weighed only twelve pounds. A politician is in fact up against a perplexing problem in protecting his 'product.' Since gifts are constantly pressed upon him which range from a casual cigarette or a luncheon to expensive entertainment and articles of great value, the

maple syrup, the product of the maple tree, may be produced and marketed as such or it may be allowed to depart from this standard by diluting it in various degrees with cheaper cane syrup. This latter may seem a less serious 'loss of integrity,' than in the case of the politician, and one which would be fairly well taken care of by informing the purchasers of what had been done, but analytically the contrast between a product determined by a standard on the one hand or by profit maximization on the other is the same in the two cases.

Individual businessmen, of course, constantly set standards for their products or services, and, as has been noted, their aversion to price competition is in some part explained by the downward pressure it puts upon quality. Typically, a trade-marked product is carefully defined and its quality scrupulously maintained so that buyers will get exactly what they have come to expect. However, although the product definition *may* involve a standard independent of profit maximization (consistent, incidentally, with the determination of *price* by this latter principle), more often it will merely represent the 'freezing,' of a product determined by the maximization principle.

As an example of 'standards of workmanship' I might mention a recent article by a French chef explaining how he made several of his most famous dishes, in which he began with the comment that if you permitted yourself to think about money you were 'ruined from the start.' Here the standard appears to be the 'maximum excellence of the product,' a maximum about which we read nothing in economic literature although it would seem to be a category which should figure prominently in welfare economics. A standard of workmanship implies a feeling strongly held that a product 'ought' by its very nature to be made in a certain way. The artisan who feels thus and who revolts at the idea of cutting corners in order to make his product more cheaply still exists but he is increasingly difficult to find.

important practical question is raised of where to draw the line in order not to be a prig and yet to maintain a satisfactory standard of ethics. Senator Paul H. Douglas has discussed the practical and ethical aspects of the question and mentioned his own rule-of-thumb limit, designed to avoid 'major involvements,' as $2.50. (*Ethics in Government*, Harvard University Press, 1952, pp. 45-9.)

This all-too-brief discussion of standards with its few scattered illustrations may at least serve the purpose of emphasizing that products, which are by their nature highly variable, are often determined by important forces other than the maximizing of profits.[20] It seems clear that, at least in this area, profit maximization is not nearly as universal as it is commonly assumed to be in price-quantity analysis. And, by analogy, one may be led to wonder whether it is actually as important as has been thought in this latter area as well, or if other determinants should not receive more attention.

The third of our main determinants of products is profit maximization. Here we are on familiar ground so far as the objective goes, but not with respect either to the variables manipulated or to the variety of functional relationships which describe the paths along which they may move. Only a few of many types of problems may be mentioned here. First of all, the whole subject of product agreements must be passed over, although, as with price theory, collusive action opens up a broad area for study.

Let us begin by returning to the subject of spatial location. Space is in fact one of the leading aspects of product differentiation and of product variation. It is obviously mensurable, and many of the leading problems of monopolistic competition may helpfully be conceived, by analogy, as spatial problems.[21] Although location in the economic system is normally a matter of two dimensions, we may, without loss of generality for our present purpose, limit our brief comments to the simplified one-dimen-

20. The economist may of course restrict himself to describing; but if he permits himself to pass judgments he will probably recognize that, in some fields at least, preserving standards seems preferable to maximizing profits. Education (in which he himself is usually engaged) is perhaps a clear example. The disturbing question is raised of the criteria by which such areas are to be distinguished from those in which standards are thought to be of no importance.

21. Although space is given substantial importance in *Monopolistic Competition,* it appears (with small exceptions) simply as one of the many types of product differentiation. In Essay 3 above it is used as a device to develop by analogy the whole conception of a monopolistically competitive economic system.

sional version already mentioned—that of the distribution of sellers along a line. It is a familiar problem with a substantial and growing literature, to which the reader is referred for a more extended discussion.

We assume at first that buyers are uniformly distributed along the line, which may be thought of as a street. Prices are given and uniform for all sellers, and products are homogeneous except for location, so that there is no basis of competition other than convenience, each buyer trading with the seller who locates nearest to him. The actual number of sellers on any such line would of course be worked out as always by the interplay of the desire for 'diversity' (in this case, more convenience) on the one hand, and economies of scale on the other, as expressed by the demand and cost curves involved.[22] But this problem may be abstracted from in discussing the location of any particular number of sellers.

The major problem is whether the sellers will concentrate at a point on the line or whether they will be dispersed over its length, as are the buyers. If we assume, with Hotelling,[23] that the distribution of sales as between sellers is a function of location, but that *aggregate* sales on the line are a constant, a single seller would locate anywhere at all. But two sellers would be concentrated at the center [24] instead of dispersed at the quartile points, where convenience would be maximized. This is because either one would, by the general principle that the market of each extends halfway to his nearest rival in any direction, increase his sales by moving towards the other; and if, when they met, they were not already at the center, the one nearer to an end of the line, and hence with the smaller market of the two, would gain by moving around to the other side of his rival. Such movements would continue until they were side by side in the middle of the line where, their markets being equal, neither one could improve his position by a further adjustment. A substantial development of the problem has taken place for this special case

22. Cf. above, p. 117.

23. 'Stability in Competition,' *Economic Journal*, March 1929.

24. Hotelling argues merely that two or a larger number of sellers will 'cluster unduly.' Since he never *isolates* the spatial factor as we have done, he reaches no conclusion as to *where* the cluster will take place.

of duopoly, including the obvious possibility of oligopolistic reactions, both as to location and as to price.[25] But let us pass on
to larger numbers where the issue of concentration versus dispersion appears in more general form. Assuming two sellers already grouped together, Hotelling argued that a third would also
maximize his market by closing in on them as explained above,
and that a fourth and a fifth and so on would likewise pile up
at the same spot, the general conclusion being excessive concentration. The reasoning was extended by analogy to cider, political parties, and even to religions: products in general are 'too
homogeneous.'

The falsity of this result for more than two sellers was argued
in my own Appendix C,[26] where the general principle of dispersion along the line was established for three or more sellers, it
being held that groups of two were possible, but not groups of
three (or more). Groups of three are impossible because the 'one
who is caught between the other two will move to the outer edge
of the group, and a series of such moves, always by the one left
in the center, will disperse the group.' Groups of two, however,
are possible because any seller located *between two others* will
make the same total sales wherever he locates within the limits
of their positions, and hence *may* locate next to one of them.
In general, n sellers must be dispersed so that 'the space between
the last sellers at either end and the ends of the line can never
exceed $1/n$ . . . and that the space between any two sellers can
never exceed $2/n$ (taking the length of the line as unity), this
limit being reached only in the extreme case where the sellers
are grouped by twos.' The dispersion would, of course, go even
further if groups of two did not come into being.

Lerner and Singer, in addition to presenting an elaborate analysis of the duopoly case, also discuss the general problem for larger
numbers, and, although *expressing* strong dissent from my own
conclusions, seem with two exceptions to agree with them.[27]

25. I mention specifically only two of the numerous articles: A. P. Lerner
and H. W. Singer, 'Some Notes on Duopoly and Spatial Competition,' *Journal
of Political Economy*, April 1937, and Arthur Smithies, 'Optimum Location in
Spatial Competition,' *Journal of Political Economy*, June 1941.

26. *Monopolistic Competition*, Appendix C, 'Pure Spatial Competition.'

27. Op. cit. pp. 176-82. See especially diagram on page 177.

The first exception is the case of three (and only three) sellers where an intriguing alternative possibility is suggested of the three milling about indefinitely at the center of the line or possibly waltzing up and down it in an 'unstable cycle.' The second exception is the discovery that, although 'groups' of sellers may in general consist of either one or two, the *end* groups must necessarily consist of two sellers.[28] The necessity arises from the fact that a lone seller at either end would always gain by closing in on his neighbor until he was as near him as possible, just as in the case of two sellers described above. This is a correction of greater importance than seemed to be realized, for it now appears that when there are only two sellers on the line, they will crowd together at a point not because they are duopolists, but because they are a special case of the 'end problem.' That this is so can be seen at once by getting rid of the ends.

The ends may be got rid of by the expedient of bending them around and joining them, in other words by assuming a 'circular street.' This is of course only a symbol, but as a symbol it is probably more meaningful than a line with ends, since the idea of a 'chain of substitutes' without sharp breaks and which therefore 'defies subdivision' [29] has become a commonplace. On a circular street the first seller would locate at any place on the circle, as would the second, since in any event total sales would be split between them by the familiar principle that each sells halfway to the other. Thus with two sellers equilibrium no longer *requires* their concentration, since if they were dispersed there would be no gain for either one by moving towards the other. But there would also be no loss, and in general, with two or more sellers, we still have the *possibility*, as on the straight line, of sellers grouping accidentally by twos (but not by threes) for the reason explained earlier that any seller may wander about between his two neighbors, even coming up very close to one of them, without effect upon the size of his market.

However, this latter type of indeterminacy disappears at one stroke when the unrealistic assumption is dropped that *aggregate*

28. Ibid. p. 181.
29. *Monopolistic Competition*, p. 103.

demand on the line is the same regardless of the number and location of the sellers. In general people do take space into account in some degree in deciding whether to buy at all, so that if the product is too far away and it is too much trouble to obtain it they will do without it. For this reason a single seller will sell more if he locates at the center of the line than if he locates anywhere else. 'Convenience' is maximized at that point (more generally, the discrepancy between products and wants is minimized), and just as demand is greater at a lower price, so it is greater if convenience is increased. Similarly, two sellers located one each at the quartile points on the line will sell more than two located side by side at the mid-point.[30] And similarly a seller will always increase his sales by choosing the mid-point between his neighbors in either direction. The way is opened to further instructive analysis in the case of duopoly (also oligopoly) on a line with ends, as Lerner and Singer and particularly Smithies have shown; but if we rid ourselves of the 'end problem' by some device such as the circular street, it is clear that two or any larger number of sellers will always adjust themselves to a pattern involving equal spacing. There remains one small element of indeterminacy—there is no answer to the question of *where* sellers will locate; all we know is that they will be equally far apart. If there are four, for instance, they may be at 12, 3, 6, and 9 o'clock on the circle, or they may be at 1, 4, 7, and 10. This conclusion in its general application appears to present a major difficulty for welfare economics. In the special case of one seller, he may again locate anywhere.

All the discussion so far has assumed buyers to be distributed *evenly* along the line, and has established the general principle (contrary to Hotelling) of an adjustment of sellers roughly conforming to buyers' locations. The problem takes on new and im-

30. Thus, although two sellers on a line with ends will, if 'competing' in the sense of ignoring their mutual dependence, move towards the center, the solution of 'mutual dependence recognized' will lead them to move to the quartile points, where their joint sales are a maximum. A product (location) agreement would also put them at the quartile points. Agreement in this case is socially preferable to 'competition'—a result most distressing to any competitive theorist.

portant developments when it is recognized that buyers are in fact unevenly distributed and often highly concentrated at certain points. The locations of sellers and the sizes of firms will of course adapt themselves to such concentrations, and there will be some rather complicated interactions and cumulative effects which are passed over here.[31] But it is clear that the piling up of sellers and the growth in their scale of output at any point or in any area will usually be explained by the fact that buyers are concentrated there instead of being dispersed as we have been assuming up to now. Such 'concentrations of population' are obvious for the spatial problem in the literal sense, and a moment's reflection will show that they exist very generally too in 'economic space' and yield important general conclusions for the way in which products are determined. Concentrations of buyers around a successful type of economics textbook, of beach costume, or of toothpaste (chlorophyll!) bring sellers rushing to the area and result in an outpouring of products which are 'close together' in certain leading characteristics, although divergent in others.

Consider for example the scale of taste in general terms. By the reasoning already developed, one would expect products to be distributed over a wide range of human tastes; but we must also expect them to be concentrated wherever tastes are concentrated, and especially heavily where there is the greatest concentration of all—the mass market. So it is for example with the entertainment field generally, where it is significant that even in the case of classic literary productions, where one might hope that the product would be determined once for all by a standard of fidelity, reproduction for the moving pictures under principles of profit maximization will usually lead to substantial alterations being made in the interest of widening the market. For similar reasons the most sensational and/or catastrophic news of the day is heavily exploited by most newspapers in the belief, apparently borne out by the facts, that mass tastes are concentrated at this level. In a highly penetrating discussion of these and related matters, H. A. Overstreet has commented that 'where money-

31. Some of these are discussed in *Monopolistic Competition*, Appendix C.

making is the paramount interest, a constant search will be made to discover what most people *as they are* can be relied upon to like most of the time,' with little or no interest in 'what a few discriminating people like,' 'what many people might eventually like' or 'what most people like once in a while.' [32] Evidently maximum profits do not lie in these areas where the population is thinly distributed. Fundamentally the reason for this must go back to economies of scale. In fields of activity where small-scale production is not too heavily penalized so that there can be a large number of sellers over the field as a whole, it is likely that the thinly populated areas will not be left out entirely. But it is, after all, familiar and rather obvious that the economies of mass production require the existence (or the development) of mass tastes, and put heavy pressure on all others for survival.[33]

Another example is furnished by the scale of incomes, with its heavy concentration at the lower end. Since there is a concentration of population at levels of moderate or low incomes, profit maximization requires, by principles already developed, that the great mass of products be determined *qualitatively* with reference to what people of such incomes can afford to pay. Indeed, to take the extreme, one of the simple and obvious results of a complete leveling down of incomes would seem to be the complete disappearance from the market of goods of the highest quality and most skilled workmanship—goods which are expensive to make and which only those of high incomes can afford to buy. But even long before this extreme has been reached, the economies of scale play heavily in favor of the mass market and against those products higher up the scale of quality which could be bought only by those in the thinly populated income areas.

A corollary to these effects of income distribution on the deter-

32. *The Mature Mind* (New York: W. W. Norton & Co., 1949), p. 206. Italics in original.

33. An interesting study of the adaptation of products to preferences in the field of radio broadcasting has been made by Peter O. Steiner in his article, 'Program Patterns and Preferences and the Workability of Competition in Radio Broadcasting,' *Quarterly Journal of Economics*, May 1952. A field which seems to the author to cry out for analysis from this point of view is that of book publishing; also that of magazine publishing.

mination of products is the pressure on quality exerted by the outpouring of new products. The appearance on the market of every
new product creates pressure in some degree on the markets for
others, and when products are variable and determined by profit
maximization some of this pressure is bound to be exerted on
quality in order to maintain prices which people can afford to pay.
Thus in a world whose technology is constantly creating new
products, it should not be surprising to find that a part of the
whole process is the deterioration of other products in order to
make room for the new ones at the mass market level where the
population is concentrated.

Who is there who has not heard many times the observation
that 'they don't make them that way any more'? Any reader could
supply his own illustrations; but let me mention several from
recent personal experience. A plumber (who ought to know about
such matters) inspected a water boiler in my cellar and informed
me that if it had been made more recently it would already be
worn out, but being an 'old-timer' it still had many years of life
in it. Again, an honest but apparently unenterprising radio dealer
has repeatedly advised me against discarding a small radio purchased twenty years ago, for the reason that it 'has better stuff in
it' than those currently on the market at double the price. And a
jeweler recently informed me on his own initiative that the really
beautifully made watch is virtually extinct because, as he put it,
nowadays all watches are 'made to sell at a price.' One feels foolish
substantiating by illustration what is a commonplace to most people, but my impression is that in this matter, whereas most people
are quite aware of what goes on, economists on the whole are de-
luded. Perhaps they have been blinded as the joint result of (1)
a system of thought which takes products as data and hence does
not even raise the question of how they are determined, and (2)
an unconsciously held conviction that, since we live in an age
of 'progress,' whenever products do change they must change
for the better. One might add (3) a technique of welfare analysis
which (at least for the unwary, and how few are not!) seems to
grind out the answer that so long as free choice is preserved we
are bound to get the best of all possible worlds. Let it be noted
that I am not denying that technology often gives us new and

better products, but only insisting that its equally notable achievement in giving us poorer ones whenever these will maximize profits must not be overlooked.

Let us leave the family of problems flowing from the spatial analogy and look briefly at profit maximization in two other settings. The first of these has to do with durability. Durability is an aspect of products which is exceedingly variable, and incidentally quite measurable, like space, speed of transportation, and others we have discussed. Since it is variable, the producer has to face the question of how durable to make his product. Evidently if he makes it too durable, as soon as people have bought one unit they will not need another for a substantial period during which there will be no repeat demand for his product.[34] He has an interest then in making it less durable so that people will come back that much sooner to buy another unit. On the other hand, just as he must not set his price too high, so he must not offer a product which wears out too fast in comparison with others on the market. The problem is to find that length of life for his product which will maximize his profit.

I have been told by people who ought to know, that it is possible to make at reasonable cost a razor blade which would last a lifetime. I will not vouch for the fact—let us take it merely as a hypothetical illustration. What is clear is that if razor blades of this kind were made, as soon as everybody had one there would be no more sold. Probably most products not consumed in a single use could be made more durable than they are at somewhat higher cost. On the other hand, in some cases—as when there is a style factor—buyers do not want durability beyond a certain point. The question is raised: what governs the durability of different types of products, and under different conditions of competition and monopoly; and how does the optimum defined by profit maximization compare with standards defined by a public interest or welfare criterion?

Finally, let us raise explicitly the question of imperfect knowl-

34. Thus an executive of the men's apparel industry recently observed that 'the business suffers from a lack of obsolescence.' The subject of durability is evidently (or should be) closely linked to Keynesian economics, since aggregate demand may fall off and unemployment result if products last too long.

edge, and begin with an example. In 1934 a letter was received by the Consumers' Advisory Board of the NRA from a manufacturer of mayonnaise in Texas which read substantially as follows: 'I started making mayonnaise several years ago. I was making it out of the best ingredients and selling it at a fair profit. Everything went all right for a while until a competitor came in and started making mayonnaise with about 10 per cent gum arabic in it and lowering the price. I had to lower the price along with him in order to stay in business, and so I had to put in 10 per cent gum arabic too because I couldn't produce 100 per cent good mayonnaise at this lower price. What did my competitor do but increase the gum arabic to 20 per cent and lower the price again. Of course I had to do the same thing in order not to lose my customers. This has been going on until I am now putting in 55 per cent gum arabic with 45 per cent mayonnaise. Can't you do something so that I can go back again to making a good product?' As it happened, the Consumers' Advisory Board could do nothing (about this or anything else); but what interests us here is the principle of product determination involved.

The phenomenon of product deterioration has already received substantial discussion and explanation, but without any particular reference to the consumer's imperfect knowledge of products. An added element of major importance now appears in the recognition of the fact that this knowledge is extremely limited. With respect to food products, consumers are not chemists as a rule, and therefore cannot test them to find out about their ingredients. What is perhaps more to the point is that even if they had the necessary technical knowledge and equipment, and the necessary passion for testing things, they would be unable individually to find out about even a small fraction of the myriad varieties of products and services made available by modern industry for them to purchase. They have of course some limited defenses, as in the case of food the faculty of taste, but these are feeble indeed when pitted against the achievements of modern science.[35] In particular it often happens that alterations in products may be effected so gradually that small changes cannot be

35. It is this situation of course which provides a market for the services of the consumers' counsel and testing agencies.

detected at all. In any such situation the logic of profit maximization leads to definite and clear-cut results. Any producer, by deteriorating his product slightly, can reduce his cost and increase his profits, either by selling at the same price as before, which would give him a greater profit per unit, or by combining the deterioration with a lower price, which is what happens more usually, and thereby increasing profits by taking business away from his rivals. In a succession of such moves there appears to be no limit until the technological possibilities of deterioration have been exhausted—in the case at hand, if the producer had put any more gum arabic into the mayonnaise, it would probably have disintegrated.

The general principle may be formulated as follows: assuming profit maximization and complete lack of knowledge with respect to certain aspects of products, these aspects will undergo such qualitative change as will reduce cost, until a limit set by *technological* considerations is reached. In actuality, since knowledge is hardly ever either perfect or completely lacking, deterioration will be carried further in some cases than in others, and intermediate equilibria may be defined in any particular case by demand considerations reflecting buyers' expected responses to further deterioration, as governed by their knowledge or suspicions as to what is happening and in particular by the question of whether the situation is general or whether substitute products *of assured quality* are available. The general tendency described might be termed Gresham's Law of products: bad products drive good products off the market.

Let us look at one more example. Alsberg, in his pioneering and authoritative study in this field,[36] has described the process by which sole leather came over the years to be 'weighted' more and more by leaving in excessive amounts of tanning extract, or by impregnating the leather with glucose or epsom salts; those who introduced these practices being able in the early stage 'to sell tanning extract, glucose or epsom salts, as the case might be, at the price of sole leather . . . The limit for water-soluble sub-

36. C. R. Alsberg, 'Economic Aspects of Adulteration and Imitation,' *Quarterly Journal of Economics,* November 1931. The discussion of sole leather is on pages 8-11.

stances,' he says, 'has climbed continuously upward' until 'in the federal specifications for sole leather . . . [it] is now [1931] being raised to 33 per cent to conform with "good commercial practice." The figure cannot well go much higher, because the tanner cannot get much more into the leather without risk of resulting trouble from spewing of the load.' Again, the limit is technological.

To what extent in real life are products determined in this way? Certainly the average citizen (whose lack of knowledge is what accounts for the phenomenon!) is in no position to answer, and in the absence of an unmitigated faith in the virtues of 'free enterprise' no reason presents itself for supposing that the two examples mentioned are in any way exceptional. On the contrary, since the results in both cases followed from the two main conditions of (a) profit maximization and (b) imperfect knowledge, and since these conditions are widespread, a presumption would seem to be established that they are typical. It should not be forgotten that what is involved is not merely major and spectacular changes, but also countless lesser ones, sometimes of subsidiary importance for particular products, sometimes compounded into a significant aggregate, and often overshadowed by an 'improvement' of some sort to which the buyer's attention is directed by skillful advertising.

The principle must of course be understood as one operating in the absence of measures designed to offset it; and substantial evidence as to its validity and importance is to be had by observing the extent to which it has in fact led to countervailing action on the part of government to protect consumers from its consequences. The regulation of service and safety in the public utility and transport industries is a familiar example. Standards of safety, for instance, are set and enforced by governments because it is recognized that if they were not, private companies would, in order to maximize their profits, avoid the outlays necessary for this purpose. Similarly, standards of container fill for food products are established because when they were not, some producers had a tendency to maximize profits by converting a given amount of food into more cans of food through putting less food into each can. Similarly, informative labeling as to ingredients is required for some food and drug products as a means of preventing or discouraging certain types of adulteration, and as an aid to the consumer in detecting and judging the acceptability of others in the light of lower price and other considerations. All that was said earlier [37] about the determination of products by government standards should be recalled at this point. The principle of product deterioration explains such measures of social control in just the same way that the principle of monopoly profits explains the regulation of monopoly.

There are of course factors other than those of government control which operate against product deterioration, and which similarly attest to its importance in the sense that they have arisen or continue as countervailing forces. They include in general all the alternatives to profit maximization, especially standards in all the senses of this word discussed above,[38] of which those established by governments are only one. They include the attempts of producers to avoid price competition in so far as these represent attempts to avoid pressure on products. They include such monopoly elements as trade marks, names, etc., in their role of guarantors of quality. And they include all informational activity designed to improve the state of knowledge of consumers. The net result is difficult to evaluate, but in any event the importance of the principle in question is not to be judged by the amount of product deterioration that remains after a few of the worst instances of it have been counteracted by regulation, any more than the importance of the principle of monopoly price is to be judged by the residuum after some degree of monopoly control. There seems on the whole to be no reason to doubt that the tendencies described are an important part of the larger subject of product determination.

By way of general summary, it seems difficult to understand how the economist can pretend to explain (or to prescribe for) the economic system and leave products out of the picture. Why not leave prices out? And why is one more important than the other? It is perhaps unnecessary to argue the point, since nonprice

37. Above, p. 121.
38. Pp. 121-4.

competition seems already to have achieved some substantial recognition in the literature.[39] But many are still afraid of it, in particular the traditionalists who do not like to rock the boat. From their point of view I think they are right. One thing seems certain—nonprice competition will not stay quietly in a separate compartment, leaving the rest of economic theory to go its way unaffected and undisturbed by its recognition. For it pervades, and pervades vitally, the whole competitive process.[40]

39. Nonprice competition has its counterpart in other areas, as for instance in the field of incomes, where, in particular, 'nonwage' elements in the labor bargain are always important and often more important than the wage itself, both from a private and a public point of view. Yet they have been completely passed over in wage theory until quite recently, when they have begun to receive some small attention.

40. *Bibliographical Note* [1957]. The original article contained references by number to items in the general bibliography at the end of the sixth edition of *Monopolistic Competition* (1948) which deal with the product as a variable, including spatial competition; and a few items since 1948 were also mentioned. Since that time, however, in the seventh edition, the bibliography has been extended to 1956, and by consequence more than doubled, so that it now contains almost 1500 items. The number of these which deal with the product as a variable is now several hundred, and it would be quite impracticable to list them here.

7

Some Aspects of Nonprice Competition [1]

I COME before this group of marketing experts, certainly not as a fellow expert but as a general economic theorist. I suppose I am here in part for having put forward a system of monopolistically competitive theory which breaks sharply with the traditional theory of pure competition in many ways—among them that it embraces nonprice competition whereas traditional theory left it severely out in the cold.

I may begin by reporting briefly on what success has been met in persuading general, as distinct from business, economists to open the theoretical doors and let nonprice competition in. The answer is easy: very little. It has perhaps had its best success in the textbooks, where it is not at all unusual in recent years to find a chapter on advertising, or perhaps more generally on nonprice competition, together with others on product differentiation, oligopoly, and so forth. But any number of general and recent treatises in economic theory could be named in which it is not even mentioned.

A few years ago I spoke with a well-known French theorist on the theoretical problems in this area. He was so enthusiastic that when two years later he sent me a copy of the treatise in theory which he had just completed and I found it to be a system of pure competition without even a word on these problems, I

1. A paper given before a marketing symposium at the University of Illinois, November 1953. Reprinted from *The Role and Nature of Competition in our Marketing Economy*, Harvey W. Huegy, ed., University of Illinois Bulletin, Vol. 51, No. 76, June 1954.

wrote to ask him why. 'Ah!' he replied, 'you misunderstand. This is my book on *theory*. Monopolistic competition will be discussed in Volume II, which will deal with *reality*.' Unfortunately this identification of *theory* with *purely competitive* theory is so common that it may almost be described as typical. I have long ago given up trying to convert my old teacher, Frank Knight, from any other view than this. Keynes has well stated in the last sentence of his Preface to the *General Theory* the essential difficulty in 'assaulting' 'habitual modes of thought.' It lies, he says, 'not in the new ideas, but in escaping from old ones, which ramify, for those brought up as most of us have been, into every corner of our minds.' Sometimes the difficulty lies, as with J. R. Hicks, in a kind of reverence for things past. '. . . it has to be recognized,' he says, 'that a general abandonment of the assumption of perfect competition . . . must have very destructive consequences for economic theory.' After more argument in this vein, he concludes: 'Let us, then, return to the case of perfect competition.' [2]

There is also a definable 'school' of opposition to the theory, with a set of preposterous misinterpretations so standardized that there could be no questioning the fact of their common intellectual origin.[3]

.   .   .   .

In spite of the protests and the discouragingly slow recognition by those plying the theorist's trade, progress is being made. In addition to journal articles appearing constantly there has recently appeared a whole book on the subject of *Product Equilibrium under Monopolistic Competition* by Hans Brems. The most encouraging statement of the changing situation which I have found is by the late Professor Joseph Schumpeter, especially significant because it is by a leading theorist, who made a more genuine effort than anyone else I know of in his generation to understand what it was all about. He says, 'The first thing to go is the traditional conception of the *modus operandi* of competition. Economists are at long last emerging from the stage in which price competition was all they saw. As soon as quality competition and sales effort are admitted into the sacred precincts of theory, the price variable

2. *Value and Capital*, pp. 83-5.
3. [1957] See below, Essay 15, p. 296, on 'The Chicago School.'

is ousted from its dominant position.' [4] Let us hope that in this
definitely optimistic statement he was not unduly influenced by
the Harvard environment in which he wrote.

I may perhaps summarize this part of my paper by referring
those economic theorists who cling desperately to perfect competition, to an admonition by that great American League pitcher,
Satchel Paige, of indeterminate birthday. In a recent and much-
quoted article he gave six rules of conduct, one of which was:
'Don't look back. Something might be gaining on you.' I do
believe that, even though slowly, it is gaining.

However, the legacy of pure competition is a heavy one. Let us
look at several aspects of it.

Pure competition involves homogeneous products; and so it is
only natural for those trained in and committed to traditional
economic theory to regard products as *fundamentally* homogeneous, and actual heterogeneity as a sort of aberration. In my own
use of the term product differentiation, nothing whatever of this
sort is implied or stated, but the phrase seems to have an unfortunate connotation. Thus, Knight identifies product differentiation with 'such "adventitious" features in the product as
name, design, ornament, packaging, "services," suggestion or
sheer "puffing," etc.,' and for some strange reason seems to link
them all with 'imperfectly economic behavior.' [5] He also—believe
it or not—attributes monopoly to 'buyer ignorance'—anything to
get rid of it. Stigler refers to firms differentiating 'virtually identical commodities,' [6] and again says that 'the product of the individual firm may be differentiated (in consumers' eyes) from products of other firms which are technologically very similar or even
identical' [7] and attributes the phenomenon clearly to 'consumer
ignorance' without which, he seems to tell us, products would in
fact be homogeneous. Similarly, Lerner says that 'the same or
practically similar goods are sold to different people at different
prices under different labels so that . . . the optimum allocation

4. *Capitalism, Socialism and Democracy*, p. 84.
5. 'Immutable Law in Economics: Its Reality and Limitations,' *American
Economic Review*, May 1946, pp. 103-4.
6. *Theory of Price* (1946), p. 215.
7. Ibid. p. 218.

of goods is not reached,' [8] and Sherrard speaks of '*deliberate* product differentiation.' [9] There is, of course, a minimum of truth in this point of view, so that those who find product differentiation intruding into their 'habitual mode of thought' readily interpret it as something factitious and even as an example of downright evil deception on the part of businessmen.

But businessmen also, deliberately or not, make products which are actually different seem deceptively similar, so why not treat the idea of deception for whatever it may be worth as a separate problem, and ask the question of whether, apart from this, products are *fundamentally* heterogeneous or homogeneous? The answer seems clear: they are fundamentally heterogeneous for two basic reasons: (1) nature, which has made every individual different as to personality and ability; which separates enterprises and products in space and in time; and which turns out agricultural and other products so diverse that they become homogeneous for practical purposes only by the man-made device of grading; (2) adaptation by producers to the diverse tastes and desires of human beings in their role as buyers. Who can deny that the fundamental fact is heterogeneity, and that the artificial creation is homogeneity for purposes such as facilitating trade in the large organized markets, reducing costs through mass production methods, and so on? Why not establish a 'mode of thought' in economics which, instead of asking 'to what extent are products *really* differentiated?' will recognize this elementary characteristic of the economic system, and ask instead 'to what extent are they *really* homogeneous?'

This legacy of pure competition is nowhere more in evidence than in Mrs. Robinson's *Economics of Imperfect Competition*, where the commodity in her imperfectly competitive market is expressly defined [10] *and consistently treated* as homogeneous. Those who so readily look upon Mrs. Robinson's theory and my own as one 'standardized' commodity overlook (among a multitude of striking differences) the fact that her first reaction to the

8. *Economics of Control*, p. 43.

9. 'Advertising, Product Variation and the Limits of Economics,' *Journal of Political Economy*, April 1951, p. 142.

10. P. 17.

term product differentiation was to *object* to associating it with imperfect competition and to insist that it is neither necessary nor sufficient to market imperfection in her meaning of the term.[11] Only reflect that she might have said, 'I agree. Although to be sure I defined my "commodity" as homogeneous, to call it "differentiated" expresses exactly what I had in mind.' But she did not.

Mrs. Robinson gets a result superficially similar in some respects to one segment of the theory of monopolistic competition by stressing the idea of 'preferences' (within the area of her homogeneous commodity). This concept soon led to a distinction first presented, I believe, by Mr. Kahn,[12] between 'irrational' and 'rational' preferences. I am led to wonder if this distinction may not have been the fruit of discussion in Cambridge (England) of the clash between our two views. The terms are almost self-explanatory, but they were given precise definitions in terms of welfare economics. The question is: 'If a consumer were forced to have B's goods instead of A's goods, would he feel worse off after the change had taken place? If, in fact, he would consider himself to be worse off, the buyers' preference is rational; if not, it is irrational.' [13] When I lectured at Oxford in 1951 I was asked the question in discussion afterwards if the difference between Mrs. Robinson's theory and my own could not be put as follows: that for Mrs. Robinson the preferences within her imperfect market were irrational, whereas for me those between differentiated products were rational. I think that, apart from the answer to this question, it is highly significant that it should be *asked* in England. I had not been discussing this issue at all; yet coming out of a clear sky it succeeds in describing Mrs. Robinson to a T. As for the answer, I should rather say that my own theory is neutral with respect to the welfare distinction involved; but the evidence abounds that Mrs. Robinson actually thinks of the preferences within her imperfectly competitive market as of little, if any, consequence. After all, this is implied in the very language of 'imper-

11. 'What Is Perfect Competition?' *Quarterly Journal of Economics,* November 1934, p. 112.

12. 'Some Notes on Ideal Output,' *Economic Journal,* March 1935, pp. 25-6.

13. J. E. Meade, *Economic Analysis and Policy,* p. 155. (Meade and Hitch, p. 165.)

fect' competition, which suggests that the imperfections are to be perfected or removed if possible; or if this is impossible, at least to be ignored in any serious matter of social policy.

A variation on this thesis that variety is of little or no importance is the idea which recurs again and again that there is 'excessive' differentiation. This may well be so, although it is hard to define the standard by which to judge it. It seems to me that since differentiation apparently starts out with two strikes against it—and this is the legacy of pure competition—any degree whatever is going to seem excessive. I was told a few years ago by an English economist visiting in this country what I had not known before: that the works of Mrs. Robinson and myself had been extensively used in left-wing circles in England as the basis for fundamental criticisms of the capitalist system in terms of waste (also exploitation and other matters which do not concern us here); they are supposed to show that under capitalism there are 'too many' firms and that production is therefore inefficient as compared with a planned economy. True for Mrs. Robinson's theory, but certainly not for mine.

A good summary of what I may call the prevailing view among technical economists in England is found in Meade,[14] where, although the distinction between rational and irrational preferences is made and used, there is an unmistakable general flavor of 'too many firms' and hence of waste. It is instructive in this connection to quote from J. R. Hicks's well-known article on 'The Foundations of Welfare Economics.' [15] He too makes some allowance for variety, but he makes the significant statement that 'The rule usually given [sic]' is one where, because 'the products of the different firms are very close substitutes, or merely distinguished by "irrational preferences," ' the consumers' surplus (crucial to the argument for variety) can be neglected; and that with this (and other) simplifications, 'the number of firms in an imperfectly competitive industry is always excessive.' Regardless of his own more cautious (and inconclusive) position, it remains true that this is the rule 'usually given,' which I regard very simply as a vestige of pure competition as the 'habitual mode of thought.' It certainly

14. Op. cit. Part II, Chap. VI. (Also Meade and Hitch.)
15. *Economic Journal*, December 1939, pp. 710-11.

cannot be shown by the techniques of welfare economics (or by any others I know of) that in an area where buyers want variety the social optimum requires producing at the minimum points on all the cost curves involved. The fact that under pure competition equilibrium is correctly identified with maximum efficiency in this sense is irrelevant. Given a general desire for variety expressed in a definite system of demand curves, the maximum of efficiency *consistent with these curves* will always be different from that of pure competition where presumably no such desire for variety exists.

Another part of the legacy of pure competition is the standard treatment of advertising. It too has had two strikes against it from the beginning, for the simple reason that it is not compatible with either pure or perfect competition. Hence it is often dismissed as sheer 'waste,' this disposition being strongly fortified by the fact that superficially it appears to be a type of 'predatory' activity: the gains of one are the losses of someone else, and if all advertise, a plausible case can be made for general cancellation. Occasionally, however, the exception has been made for 'new products' where it seems only common sense to recognize that people have to be told about them. What is overlooked is that as soon as products are recognized to be heterogeneous and product variation is brought into the picture, any qualitative change (including changes in service and so forth) means a 'new product'; and since products are in fact constantly changing in this sense, it may now be said with complete generality that people must be told about the changes. In fact, of course, this application of the argument will not be admitted when products are regarded as 'fundamentally homogeneous.'

Marshall long ago distinguished between 'constructive' and 'combative' advertisement, and the common trend recently has been to make some grudging concession to the view that not all advertising is bad. Nowadays the distinction is usually made on the basis of whether or not the advertising is 'informative,' thus contributing to a closer approach to one of the requirements of perfect competition, viz. perfect knowledge.

But note the tendency to belittle this aspect of it. Meade says, 'In the real world a *large part* of the expenditure on advertisement is undertaken . . . without in fact giving consumers any greater knowledge . . .' and that 'all such expenditure . . . is a waste, due to monopolistic conditions in the sale of commodities.' [16] He gives only qualified approval to the presumably smaller part which increases knowledge. A. P. Lerner says that 'some advertising . . . [provides] useful information to consumers, but most of it has the effect of stressing partly or wholly imaginary differences between goods . . .' [17] K. W. Rothschild, in a paper on 'The Wastes of Competition,' [18] refers to Marshall's distinction, and rules that 'the bulk of present-day advertising is of the "combative" type,' and so on. (It is interesting to note that Marshall himself expressed no such judgment.) Rothschild also makes the significant statement that informational advertising is 'compatible with pure competition where knowledge is not perfect,' and in effect *defines* the combative type as that which 'is connected with a differentiated product, with a partial monopoly.' I say that the statement is 'significant' because it again identifies the supposedly good with pure competition and the supposedly bad with a differentiated product. And I may comment in passing that advertising, whether constructive or combative, is logically incompatible with pure competition, even with imperfect knowledge.

The very assumption that improved knowledge would mean more perfect competition is a giveaway. Listen to Meade: 'If a trustworthy and authoritative body were enabled to spend on consumers' research one tenth of the sums now spent on wasteful competitive advertisement, a large amount of buyers' preference would disappear.' [19] Here again is the tacit assumption that products are really more homogeneous than people think, whereas a better case can surely be made for the reverse proposition that they are really more different. More perfect knowledge would certainly create a revolution in people's preferences, but these latter might be stronger than ever as a result. Political campaign

16. Op. cit. p. 166, my italics. (Meade and Hitch, p. 177.)
17. Op. cit. p. 43.
18. *Monopoly and Competition and Their Regulation*, E. H. Chamberlin, ed., p. 305.
19. Op. cit. p. 171. (Meade and Hitch, p. 183.)

speeches, we like to think, give us a better knowledge of the candidates running for an election, but even if the speeches were purely informational and truthful, they would hardly reduce the candidates involved to homogeneity in the sense of being perfect substitutes for each other.

I think the stress on information has been greatly overdone. Those who stress it evidently have in mind *technical* information about the product and its uses, and presented with zero emotional appeal. This kind of information is of course useful and desirable, but it is not the only kind people want. They are perhaps more interested in knowing that a famous movie star smokes a certain brand of cigarette than in knowing what the cigarette is made of; and both are information. They care more to know that a certain kind of perfume carries a name of such propitious omen as 'My Sin' than to know anything else about it, even its price. We are evidently bordering on the 'emotional,' and it may be observed that sex and the bathing beauty now advertise almost everything from beer to motor oil. People must want this kind of advertising; if they did not, it would soon be known, and something else would replace it.

It seems to be assumed by those economists who identify the welfare maximum with socialism that in a socialist regime all the supposedly wasteful advertising that they object to would be eliminated, so that there would be nothing left but informational advertising in the best sense. But present government practice does not bear this out. When the United States Navy wants recruits, it does not give the truth, the whole truth, and nothing but the truth about life in the Navy; it says 'Join the Navy and see the world.' Another example: A few years ago I ran across in a magazine the caption, 'Bob Hope and Bing Crosby agree,' with a picture of these two gentlemen looking very happy and shaking hands. I was intrigued to discover that what they were agreed upon was that it was advisable to buy government bonds. Now the fact that Hope and Crosby agree upon something is no doubt information, but its relevance to bond buying may at least be questioned. Perhaps it only goes to show that the Treasury knows its business after all. I conclude that the line between information and emotional appeal is not easy to draw, and also that human beings actually enjoy appeals to their emotions as well as to their limited rational powers. In short, the information approach to the problem of judging particular advertisements seems to me quite unsatisfatcory.

Let me close with a suggestion for what I should regard as a more defensible approach to the problem of testing the social utility of advertising. Advertisements (whether informational or not) may be regarded as products like any others, and the question raised of whether people want them badly enough to pay for them. This possibility of regarding advertisements as products is clarified by reflecting that people do in fact buy items which are no different from much that is supplied free as advertising. In the category of information, they buy catalogues, directories, guide books, road maps, cook books, and so forth, and certainly they buy the daily newspaper as much for the advertising it contains as for the news and comics. To put the matter in reverse, if the Sears, Roebuck catalogue were sold instead of being distributed as advertising, it would probably be a best seller. Outside the category of informational advertising, radio and television programs are a leading example, and they illustrate the matter at issue especially well because they are actually sold as products in England, whereas they are distributed free as advertising in the United States. The test to which I refer is simply whether the advertising could be sold separate from the product at a price sufficient to cover its cost. Certainly a great deal of advertising would, and a great deal would not, pass this test.

From this approach it emerges clearly that information is not the only type of advertising that people might be willing to buy. It emerges also that they would not necessarily buy advertising *merely* because it was informational. Thus to look upon advertising as itself a product which might be separated from the product advertised has the merit of bringing squarely to the fore the question of whether or not people want it enough to pay the cost of the social resources that are used up in providing it.

It will be said that people *do* pay for the advertising they get: the price of the product must be high enough to cover all costs including selling costs, or the producer must go out of business. But this is wrong because the people who pay for the advertising are not necessarily the ones who get it. Many who buy the product and, therefore, have no escape from also helping to pay for the radio program, do not listen to the program; and many who listen to the program do not buy the product. In other words, the *market* provides a test only if the advertising is actually offered and sold *separately* from the product itself. If it *could* be sold separately, however, it would be socially defensible by our criterion, which consists merely in subjecting it (hypothetically) to the same market test as other products.

It should be noted that I have said merely that the test proposed is 'more defensible' than that of whether or not advertising is informative. It will still have all the well-known inadequacies of the market test generally in welfare economics, and a full discussion of these would be quite impossible on the present occasion. The test proposed does, I think, contribute something to illuminating the problem, and it has the particular merit that it is *not* derived from the fallacious ideal of perfect competition.

8

Advertising Costs and Equilibrium [1]

1. A CORRECTION

IN reviewing recently some of the literature of selling costs, I have discovered that Mr. Henry Smith's article with the title above in Volume II, Number 1 (October 1934) of this *Review:* (1) is based upon an erroneous interpretation of one of the diagrams in my own *Theory of Monopolistic Competition,* and (2) in turn, wrongly defines the position of equilibrium in question. In spite of the lapse of time, I believe the error should be pointed out for the benefit of those interested in and working on the subject of selling costs. In addition to the specific points at issue, a discussion of Mr. Smith's analysis may derive added interest from the fact that he has employed a technique, implicit in Mrs. Robinson's brief reference to advertising costs, [2] of subtracting them from price, thus obtaining what he calls a 'net receipts' curve, in contrast to what would appear to be the more normal one of including them with the other costs in the cost curve.

1. Reprinted from the *Review of Economic Studies,* Vol. XII (2), 1944-45, p. 116 ('A Correction'); and Vol. XVII (3), 1949-50, p. 226 ('A Rejoinder'). For a full account of the matters discussed the reader should refer also to Mr. Smith's original article, which appeared ibid. Vol. II (1), 1934, and to his 'Reply,' ibid. Vol. XV (1), 1947-48, p. 40. I believe, however, that enough is given here by way of summary of Mr. Smith's arguments to make these two fragments intelligible and useful as they stand to anyone who is willing to work through the intricate analysis involved. I make no apology for this latter—it seems to be in the nature of the problem. For further comment see below, p. 152n.6.

2. *The Economics of Imperfect Competition,* p. 21.

(1) First, as to the misinterpretation. Mr. Smith says (p. 63) that the diagram on page 148 of *The Theory of Monopolistic Competition* (which depicts in one graph the optimum adjustment both of selling cost and of price for the individual firm) shows a 'conditional equilibrium only' in which there is 'only established a fortuitous relation between advertising expenditure and the new demand curve,' whereas, by contrast, the conditions of full equilibrium are to be derived from the diagram he presents.[3] My own diagram does, however. show full equilibrium, not a conditional one. There are no 'unexplored possibilities' which might increase profits, as Mr. Smith seems to think; they are all explored in the text (p. 147) from which the diagram explicitly emerges: 'A graphic summary of the characteristics *of this optimum adjustment,* except for the variations in "product," is possible, and is presented in Figure 24.'[4] What the figure shows, more specifically, is (1) variations in price, selling outlay being held constant *at its optimum value,* and (2) variations in selling outlay, price being held constant *at its optimum value.* Evidently such a diagram could be drawn only after full equilibrium were known, and Mr. Smith is correct in pointing out that equilibrium cannot be *derived from it.* The process of derivation is, however, fully described in the text with the help of cross sections of the surfaces involved, and what Mr. Smith really proposes (in effect) is to illustrate a portion of this argument graphically. We pass, then, to the positive part of his analysis.

3. Oddly enough, having made this claim, he does not in fact show full equilibrium in his own diagram, which is suggestive only and not carried to completion.

4. P. 148. (Italics added.) The reference to variations in product should be explained. Such variations are discussed in the text, but not shown in the figure, which is assumed to be drawn for the optimum product. Mr. Smith does not discuss this added variable at all and therefore falls short of his objective ('the conditions of full equilibrium') on this count, quite apart from the objections raised below to his solution within the range of variables considered.

It may be remarked further that, although my own figure represents the 'tangency' solution, it is made clear (p. 148) that this is an arbitrary choice. Tangency is not, for me, as it is for Mr. Smith (p. 63), a condition of equilibrium.

(2) Mr. Smith's diagram [5] is reproduced herewith as Figure 1, and his own explanation of it may be quoted:

Let *DD* be the demand curve, *CC* be the cost curve, of a firm which without any advertisement is in equilibrium. . . Draw the line *PQ* from the point *P* so that the vertical distance between any point on *PP* (the price line) represents the average cost per unit of selling the

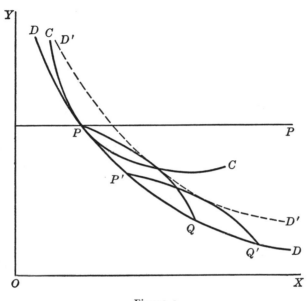

Figure 1

quantity indicated at the price *P*. *PQ* is thus the net average receipts curve, after deducting the cost of advertising, at the price *P*. Thus, at the price *P*, the firm can now make a profit: this profit shall be at its maximum, for that price, at the point at which it is possible to describe the largest rectangle from *OY* with the top of the right-hand upright at a point on *PQ* and its bottom at a point on *CC*.

It is then explained that the result so far is a 'conditional' equilibrium only, so that full equilibrium has still to be discovered. For this purpose an 'envelope' curve is introduced:

5. He specifically credits 'its present shape' to Mr. A. P. Lerner.

$D'D'$ is the envelope of curves similar to PQ drawn from each point on DD, and is the average net receipts curve, representing the maximum net receipts which it is possible for the firm to obtain by the means of advertising. Thus the conditions of full equilibrium must of necessity lie in the relation of the cost curve to $D'D'$.

In the case represented in our diagram it is obvious that the summed cost curve for the price P (*not* shown) would cut PP at a point immediately above the intersection of CC and PQ, and that the maximum average profit position, for that price, would be at a point to the left of the intersection of the summed cost curve with PP. [The intersection of CC and PQ is evidently unrelated to the point of tangency of PQ with $D'D'$, and their coincidence in the figure is accidental.]

The absolute maximum profit position is that at which it is possible to describe the largest rectangle from OY with the top of its right-hand upright at a point on *any* of the PQ curves and with the bottom at a point on CC. As $D'D'$ is the envelope of all PQ curves, this is also the largest rectangle with its right-hand upright limited by $D'D'$ and CC.

The envelope curve $D'D'$ appears to be quite without significance, however, and the conditions of full equilibrium are not related to it.[6] In the preceding quoted paragraph the first sentence is correct; the second is incorrect and does not follow from the first. This is the error which it is the main purpose of this note to point out.

The envelope curve in Mr. Smith's analysis is defined as 'the average net receipts curve, representing the maximum net receipts which it is possible for the firm to obtain by the means of advertising'; but it is, in fact, only the north and east limit of the PQ family of curves, unrelated to maximum average net receipts. The phrase 'maximum average net receipts' is not a happy one, but it must refer to total output, not to a single unit. (Maximum average net receipts *per unit* for the price line PP would evidently

6. [1957] This statement is incorrect, and the error is acknowledged in the 'Rejoinder' below, p. 157. In fact, the solution of Mr. Smith and my own 'correction' are shown in the 'Rejoinder' to be *co-ordinate* and hence of 'equal' significance. Each of us was wrong in thinking that he and *not the other* was right. The discussion thus yielded a correct *total* solution—and, perhaps more important, a warning against either (1) misinterpreting the parts or (2) substituting one of them for the whole.

be at P where selling costs are zero.) Interpreting the phrase to mean the average net receipts for which total net receipts are a maximum, it would be indicated for the price line PP by the maximum rectangle bounded by the x and y axes and touching PQ—at the point, of course, where the elasticity of PQ is unity. This point is unrelated to the envelope curve, which may, therefore, be discarded at once from our analysis.

But the point of 'maximum average net receipts' is, in turn, also subject to discard as irrelevant. We seek the point of maximum *profits*, and this is unrelated to the maximum of an aggregate which includes both profits and production costs (as it would be also, one might add, to the maximum of an aggregate of profits plus selling costs). The maximum profit rectangle for each price would, as Mr. Smith states, have the top of its right-hand upright located on the appropriate PQ curve, but, in general, neither on the envelope curve $D'D'$ nor on a locus curve of maximum average net receipts for all prices. In the figure as drawn, for the price line PP, the point would appear to be located about midway between P and the intersection of the curves PQ and CC. What is required is a curve of the locus of these tops of the right-hand uprights of the series of optimum profit rectangles.

The exact shape of such a curve is difficult to generalize about, but one thing is certain—that it would *not* be as now developed from Mr. Smith's diagram. Of the entire family of PQ curves, the two which have been drawn in the figure, PQ and $P'Q'$, are of roughly the same length and curvature—and the envelope $D'D'$ is parallel to DD; from which one must presume that the family of PQ curves is taken to be of about the same length and curvature throughout, being simply moved up and down along the demand curve DD. Accepting for the moment this interpretation, let us complete the figure by drawing in the locus curve described above. It would appear to be an arc concave to P, tangent to $D'D'$, and beginning and ending on CC at the two points of tangency of CC with one of the family of PQ curves. One of these points of tangency can be seen by moving $P'Q'$ slightly to the left along DD in the figure; the other would lie correspondingly on the portion of CC between P and the *upper* intersection of CC with $D'D'$.[7] The 'absolute maximum' of profit would then be given by the largest rectangle from OY with its right-hand upright limited at the top by this arc and at the bottom by CC. It would be unrelated to the point of tangency of this arc with $D'D'$, as also to the point of tangency of CC with DD.

But all this is quite misleading and even definitely erroneous, for the different PQ curves are not of the same length and curvature.[8] They are, as Mr. Smith recognizes, merely my own 'combined cost curves' upside down, and these vary in length, curvature, and position over a wide range depending upon circumstances. In general (but not always), starting from some point above which they would not extend to the right of DD at all, they would expand both in length and amplitude with each fall in price. For any particular set of assumptions as to prices, products, and selling outlays of near-by competitors, a locus curve of the type described could be drawn, but conclusions dependent upon its shape or location with reference to a demand curve which assumes no advertising at all could not be generalized.[9] It would remain true in any case, however, that, *given the locus curve*, the optimum solution would be defined by the largest rectangle from OY with its right-hand upright limited at the top by this locus curve and at the bottom by CC.

It should be pointed out that the procedure followed by Mr. Smith of finding the optimum profit, and hence selling outlay

7. If the minimizing of losses as well as the maximizing of profits were included, the curve would extend beyond these points.

8. As one example of where this analysis leads, it would appear that, as the diagram has now been developed, the optimum adjustment involves a price substantially higher than the one indicated by the price line PP (defined as the equilibrium price without advertising); from which one should conclude that advertising inevitably raises the price. This is not so, however (Cf. *Monopolistic Competition*, Chap. VII, especially pp. 166-7. The statement of the argument on these two pages has been recast, beginning with the second printing of the third edition).

9. In the tangency (no profit) solution which Mr. Smith identifies in the text with equilibrium but does not illustrate, the diagram would have to be redrawn. DD (representing demand without advertising) would lie to the left of CC at all points and the locus curve (now representing minimum losses) would be tangent to CC at the equilibrium output.

for a series of prices, has an element of arbitrariness in the sense that it is only one of several possibilities. For instance, one might equally well reverse the process, finding the optimum profit and hence price for a series of selling outlays.[10] Furthermore, full equilibrium involves generally the maximization of profits through adjustments in the product itself, so that still further loci of relative optima could be represented graphically for those aspects of the product whose variation was mensurable. Recognition of this added element in the problem seems to make it quite impossible to display the derivation of *full* equilibrium in a single two-dimensional diagram.

It should also be pointed out that a graphic presentation consisting of the original demand curve, production cost curve, and the locus curve as defined, although serving to illuminate certain aspects of the problem, would fail, unless supplemented, to provide information of prime importance. When the maximum profit area had been discovered from the figure, equilibrium output, production cost, and profit could be read off at once. But not the equilibrium price; nor the selling outlay. The price would appear only when the appropriate *PQ* curve had been added and its (upper) intersection with *DD* discovered. And equilibrium selling outlay would be revealed only after the price had been discovered, a horizontal price line drawn, and a perpendicular dropped from it to the equilibrium point on the *PQ* curve. These last two steps represent the addition to the locus diagram of a portion of the information provided by my own Figure 24, page 148; and of course a variety of amalgamations between the two types could be worked out. To put the matter in another way, it is evidently possible either to supplement the locus type of diagram which Mr. Smith means to propose, with cross sections showing how individual variables behave, the others remaining constant; or conversely, to project upon curves of the latter type (as my own Figure 24) curves of the loci of relative maxima.

One final comment on the technique of subtracting selling cost from price as a preliminary to profit maximization. Certainly it does not lead to happy results graphically, nor does it appear

10. Cf. *Monopolistic Competition*, p. 147.

to be a natural procedure in any event. It would be natural only
if it were intended to eliminate these costs from subsequent analysis,[11] which is evidently not the case with Mr. Smith, he being
among the few to have recognized their importance and to have
contributed to the literature on the subject. The only apparent
gain from the procedure in the present instance seems to be that
the production cost curve is made to serve as one (the lower) of
the two locus curves for the right-hand side of the profit rectangle,
thus requiring the addition of only one other; whereas two such
curves (top and bottom) would be necessary in my own type of
figure. To offset this we have the awkward result that a part of
the total costs is left floating in mid-air, as it were, with profit
wedged between it and the remainder. Total costs are thus made
difficult to discover; indeed, Mr. Smith, having drawn his diagram
in this way, at once finds it useful to describe and use a 'summed
cost curve' (my own 'combined cost curve') without, however,
adding it to his figure.

The explanation of thus separating the two parts of costs by
profits may possibly lie in the belief expressed in his final paragraph that his methods seem to be preferable in that they are
'compatible with the use of marginal as well as average curves,'
clearly implying that my own are not. I am at a loss to know,
however, what he finds in my own analysis which is incompatible
with marginal curves. They appear from time to time (e.g. in
diagrams on pages 75 and 142) and could be added to the figure
on page 148 without the slightest difficulty.

Mr. Smith took as the point of departure for his note a reflection from Mrs. Robinson which raises wider issues of the utmost
import, and the opportunity is afforded again to call them to the
attention of the professional economist. 'The fact that in the real
world the demand curve and the cost curve of individual firms

11. This appears clearly to have been the purpose of Mrs. Robinson (loc. cit.)
who says, 'Complications are introduced into the problem of the individual
demand curve by the existence of advertising, but these have been ignored. It
may be assumed that expenditure on advertising necessary to increase the sales
of a firm, can be treated as equivalent from the point of view of the entrepreneur, to a reduction in price having the same effect upon sales.'

are not independent presents a very formidable problem to economic analysis.' Indeed, it seems obvious that hardly a firm in the real world is without selling costs of some kind, and hence that there is hardly a firm whose demand curve is not functionally dependent upon its cost curve. How, then, can one explain the fact that in the world of economic theorizing there exists hardly a firm for which the two curves are not treated as functionally independent? How, above all, can this procedure be explained on the part of those who otherwise have seemed to accept a revision of economic theory in the direction of monopolistic competition; and finally, even among so many of those who have contributed to the development of substantial portions of this field? The problem *is* formidable, without any question, but this is surely not the reason. A good part of the explanation lies in the fundamental character of the change, and the overwhelming psychological barriers to casting off established modes of thought which are so much a part of our theoretical tradition. The remainder lies, I believe, in conscious avoidance: the interdependence in question is not admitted because it badly messes up what is otherwise a more tractable theoretical model. It would be easy to cite instances—not one or two, but many. Should not the question be squarely faced of whether we are willing really to admit that theorizing in economics is not an end in itself, but has for its purpose the explanation of the 'real world'?

2. A Rejoinder

The recent reply [12] of Mr. Henry Smith to my criticism [13] of his earlier analysis [14] of advertising costs leaves the whole discussion at a point where it is about to bear fruit, and therefore indicates a brief continuation. . . . In his 'Reply,' Mr. Smith generously concedes a number of points, but maintains what appears to be an essential one, viz. that the point of maximum profit lies on $D'D'$, whereas I had asserted that it did not. In this he is correct, and I hasten to contribute a *mea culpa* which will broaden further

12. *Review of Economic Studies*, 1947-48, Vol. xv (1), p. 40.
13. Ibid. 1944-5, Vol. xii (2), p. 116. [Above, p. 149.]
14. Ibid. 1934, Vol. ii (1), p. 62.

the area of agreement. But the fundamental ambiguity which gave rise to the error remains in Mr. Smith's earlier analysis, and the whole truth of the matter appears not yet to have been given.

It is still true that Mr. Smith wrongly identifies the envelope curve with the one which I contended should replace it, viz. with a curve of optimum advertising expenditure (and hence maximum profit) at each price. The method of finding the point of maximum profit by the use of this latter curve is described in my 'Correction.' What is evident now is that the solution lies on *both* of these two curves at their point of tangency, and could thus be discovered graphically by the use of *either* one of them. There emerges the importance of distinguishing between the two curves and of understanding the meaning and limitations of each. Mr. Smith wrongly failed to make the distinction, identifying his single curve with both; whereas, having made the distinction, I wrongly concluded that one of the curves was 'without significance.'

In straightening matters out, let us first complete the picture by pointing out that there are three curves of relative maxima, not two. Assuming a given product [15] with a given curve of production cost, we seek the point of maximum profit with reference to the three variables of price, advertising expenditure, and output. The solution is, of course, graphically a point; we get curves of relative maxima only by considering the best adjustment of two of the variables for a succession of assumed values of the third.[16] The three possibilities are: (1) a curve of the locus of

15. The fact that full equilibrium involves the *additional* important variable of the product itself has already been commented upon.

16. I believe Mr. Smith, in his first article, misunderstood my original analysis (*Monopolistic Competition,* Chap. VII) in part because I did not employ such locus curves. My Figure 22 shows variations of selling costs and output (demand) under a *single* assumed price, explaining in words, not graphically, the repetition of the process at each price; similarly, Figure 23 shows variations of price and output (demand) for a *single* assumed total of selling costs; and Figure 24 shows both types of variations in the same diagram, assuming the price and selling cost in each case to be the optimum ones. The third type of variation—that of price and selling cost for an assumed output (which, when repeated for all outputs and plotted as the locus of price minus selling costs for each, would give Mr. Smith's envelope curve)—I confess never even occurred to me, probably because of its extreme remoteness from economic

optimum combinations of advertising expenditure and resulting output (sales) at each price; (2) a curve of the locus of optimum combinations of advertising expenditure and price for each output; and (3) a curve of the locus of optimum combinations of price and output (sales) for each total advertising expenditure.[17]

We are concerned with the first two of these curves, and since each of them depicts optimum advertising expenditure in some sense, it is easy to see how they could become confused. A further source of confusion is that, in the technique before us, the procedure of defining a succession of PQ curves each for a different *price* seems to indicate as its objective the first locus curve, at the same time that (under the subtraction process) it generates an envelope which turns out to be the second.

In his original *Review* article, Mr. Smith describes the envelope curve as 'representing the maximum net receipts which it is possible for the firm to obtain by the means of advertising,' which is ambiguous, to say the least. In his 'Reply,' he refers to his note in the *Quarterly Journal of Economics* for May 1935, as presenting the relevant 'full diagram,' and it is in this latter place that he describes the curve repeatedly as showing the optimum advertising expenditure at each price, which identifies it with curve number 1, and is wrong.[18] It seems evident that neither of us had seen clearly that there were *two* curves of 'optimum advertising expenditure.'

Let us now make explicit in terms of the diagram the distinctions involved. PQ is drawn with reference to the price P. At this price, total profits for various outputs will be indicated by

reality. *Geometrically* on a par with the others of course, when interpreted *economically* it would picture the output, not as a market result of decisions with respect to price and advertising, but as a decision in itself, to be maintained at different prices by nicely calculated compensating adjustments of advertising expenditure.

17. The exact definition of these functions would vary according to the terms in which their relationship was described: for instance, whether selling costs are subtracted from price, as with Mr. Smith, or added to production costs, as in my own treatment.

18. Pp. 544, line 4; 545, line 13; and 547, line 9. At the same time, he says in a footnote (p. 544), that it is 'identical with the net revenue curve employed by A. P. Lerner, "The Concept of Monopoly Power," *Review of Economic Studies*, June 1934,' which is quite explicitly curve number 2, and correct.

rectangles whose right-hand uprights are bounded by PQ at the top and CC at the bottom. The maximum profit rectangle would appear to be located at an output about midway between P and the intersection of the curves PQ and CC; and the optimum (total) advertising expenditure *for this price* is given (per unit) by the vertical distance from PQ to PP *at this output*. The point on PQ which defines this optimum is evidently unrelated to $D'D'$. But moving along PQ to its point of tangency with $D'D'$ we arrive at another optimum advertising expenditure, viz. that for the corresponding *output*. If a perpendicular is dropped from this point of tangency to OX, it is evident that PQ is the highest of those of the family of such curves (compare $P'Q'$) which are cut by this perpendicular, and therefore gives the highest 'net revenue' (price less advertising expenditure) for this output. *At this output* total profits for various prices will be indicated by rectangles whose right-hand uprights all lie on the perpendicular just drawn and are all bounded at the bottom by the same point, viz. the intersection of the CC curve with the perpendicular.[19] The top boundary of the upright at each price will lie on the particular member of the family of PQ type curves defined by that price, so that the maximum profit possibility is given by the envelope $D'D'$. Optimum (total) advertising expenditure *for this output* is given (per unit) by the vertical distance *at this output* from PQ to a price line PP. Thus it is seen that on *each PQ* type of curve there are *two* points of 'optimum advertising expenditure': one relative to the price which defines the curve, the other relative to the particular output for which this curve is higher than all others.[20] There is a locus curve for each of the two types of relative maximum, and either one will, together with the cost of production curve, define the position of maximum profit for the three variables.

19. In the Figure this point appears to coincide with the point of tangency of PQ and $D'D'$, but this is accidental.

20. Under certain conditions, for instance, of discontinuity, the second optimum would not exist at all because the PQ curve would lie below the envelope at all points. An example is afforded in Mr. Smith's diagram on page 546 of the *Quarterly Journal* article (reproduced below), where this is true for all PQ curves departing from the original demand curve between points P and P'.

We must now note that the further development of this technique in the *Quarterly Journal* article already cited is open to serious criticism arising out of the distinctions just made. The development is as follows: from each point on the envelope curve the appropriate (tangent) *PQ* curve is constructed and the price before selling costs were deducted is discovered at its intersection with the original demand curve. This price is now plotted directly above the original point, so that the difference between them measures the selling cost for the output in question. We now have the proposition that 'the locus of all such points is . . . the "demand" curve for the product when all the resources of publicity are fully exploited by the producer.' [21] But if the word demand is to be used at all in connection with such a construction, it is not *the* demand curve, but one out of two such curves. It shows the price for each output when advertising expenditure is best adjusted for that output; another curve similarly constructed from the other maximum on each of the family of *PQ* curves will show the output for each price when advertising expenditure is best adjusted for that price. On the ground that entrepreneurs are much more likely in real life to choose a price than an output, the second has more to commend it. But geometrically they seem to be on a par. In my own judgment, it is a mistake to call either one a 'demand' curve (even in quotation marks), since the familiar requirement of 'given conditions' is not met: in both cases the price-output relationship pictured holds only under an assumption as to advertising expenditures which constantly changes with movement along the curve; and the curve showing relative optima at different *prices* has the added peculiarity of being defined in part by production costs.

The importance of these objections could not be better illustrated than in Mr. Smith's note here under discussion. It is necessary to refer back to an earlier article by Mr. A. J. Nichol,[22] who had argued for the importance of cases where the demand curve confronting a firm might, even under product differentiation, be perfectly elastic over a certain range. In such cases it was held

21. Op. cit. p. 545.

22. 'The Influence of Marginal Buyers on Monopolistic Competition,' *Quarterly Journal of Economics*, November 1934, p. 121.

that the production cost curve might be tangent to the demand
curve within this range, so that the price would be the same
under monopolistic as under pure competition. The purpose of
Mr. Smith's note was to illustrate a special case 'which allows of
the application of Mr. Nichol's analysis,' and he finds it in a
situation where the so-called 'demand' curve described in the
last paragraph is horizontal within a certain range. The diagram

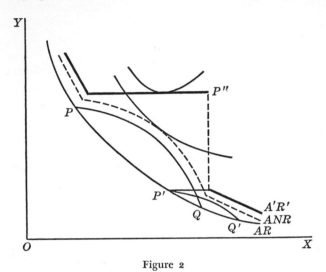

Figure 2

is reproduced as Figure 2. $A'R'$ is the 'demand' curve in question,
its horizontal segment being explained by the fact that advertising at the price P will render the effect of advertising very much
less productive at any other price. The following observations
are now indicated: (1) Such a curve gives optimum advertising
expenditure for each *output,* but not for each *price.* The latter
would be defined within the 'discontinuous' range by drawing
in the appropriate PQ curves for all prices between P and P',
and proceeding in the manner already indicated. It would have
no horizontal segment, but a single discontinuous value at the
price P, corresponding to the optimum output and advertising
expenditure for the PQ curve as it appears in the diagram. But
let us, merely for the sake of argument, accept the curve as drawn,

in order to examine into some further difficulties of its interpretation. (2) The tangency of the cost curve to the horizontal portion of the 'demand' curve, which looks like pure competition graphically, is achieved only by the arbitrary initial assumption of a production cost curve tangent to PQ. For a production cost curve located in any other way, this purely graphic resemblance to pure competition would appear only if monopoly profits were added into the cost curve—a strange procedure for a situation which is supposed to illustrate 'the same equilibrium price as under perfect competition.' [23] (3) The U-shaped cost curve whose minimum point rests on the horizontal segment of the 'demand' curve is not the production cost curve, as it would have to be if Mr. Nichol's arguments were to be applicable, but a combined production and selling cost curve. Its minimum point is unrelated to purely competitive conditions because it includes selling costs, which are incompatible with pure competition. (4) The horizontal segment of the so-called 'demand' curve to which the cost curve is tangent bears no resemblance (except geometrically) to the perfectly elastic demand curve of pure competition, nor to such segments in Mr. Nichol's curves. It is not only defined by selling costs, which are incompatible with pure competition, but it is defined by a different amount of selling costs at every point! It does not indicate, as under pure competition, the absence within its limits of any obstacle to increased sales at the going price; on the contrary, the obstacles are such that every added unit of output sold requires advertising expenditure at an ever-increasing rate.

In my earlier note of 'Correction,' I protested against the technique of subtracting selling cost from price on several grounds, one of which was that it had the effect of eliminating these costs from subsequent analysis, and was therefore a natural procedure only if, as with Mrs. Robinson, this were the intended result. Now Mr. Smith certainly does not want to eliminate them—in fact we seem to be in complete accord as to the importance of giving them full prominence. And because he does not, it is particularly significant to observe that the false conclusion to which he is led—of a result conforming to 'perfect competition' in ac-

23. Nichol, op. cit. p. 135.

cord with Mr. Nichol's arguments—involves interpreting the case as if the selling costs were not there. It is hard to believe that the technique of incorporating 'optimum advertising' into the so-called 'demand' curve did not, quite unconsciously, contribute its part to the result.

It was Mr. A. P. Lerner, I believe, who devised the 'average net revenue' (price minus advertising) curve which Mr. Smith developed further; and it is significant that with him its function was explicitly to remove 'marketing costs' from the picture so as to apply his measure of monopoly power to the remainder. 'In such cases [marketing costs],' he says, 'what becomes of the elasticity of demand? . . . how are we to find the falling demand curve which will entitle us to put these cases into this category and enable us to deal with them in the same way? . . . The marketing costs involved in selling a given quantity of product must be subtracted from the gross receipts, just as if they were all direct or indirect reductions in price . . . the Average Net Receipts curve . . . is the "demand curve" which we need.' [24]

Mr. Lerner states explicitly, to be sure, that 'The social loss, if any, due to the expenditure of resources on advertising, is *not* taken into account in the measurement of monopoly,' but '. . . constitutes a quite separate problem.' Yet how strange it is deliberately to remove one of the prime manifestations of monopoly, and hence one of the prime causes of the divergences supposedly to be measured, as a preliminary to performing the measurement! One can only conclude that Mr. Lerner does not associate selling costs with monopoly—indeed, he states explicitly that 'If the average net receipts curve is horizontal where the marginal net costs curve cuts it, there is no monopoly. The existence of marketing costs is quite another matter.' [25]

All this is, of course, in accord with Mrs. Robinson's analysis of 'imperfect' competition, where selling costs are rejected because they (supposedly) interfere with the marginal revenue technique which is to be developed, and where, as I have shown elsewhere in detail,[26] the problem is not conceived as one of blending

24. Op. cit. pp. 172-3.
25. Op. cit. p. 173.
26. *Monopolistic Competition*, 5th or later ed., pp. 204-12.

monopoly and competition. By contrast, selling costs are an integral part of the subject of *monopolistic* competition. In my own Chapter v, so often carelessly identified with the theory itself, they are omitted only through being explicitly impounded for the time being in *ceteris paribus*.[27] It should be clear to any careful reader that the full statement of the theory is achieved, not in Chapter v, but in Chapter vii, where selling costs finally take their place in the whole structure.

I am obliged to reaffirm my conviction that the device of subtracting selling costs from the price so as to obtain a curve of 'net average receipts' is willy-nilly a device for getting rid of them. Such a result may be sought as a conscious objective (as in the case of Mrs. Robinson, Mr. Lerner, and numerous others), or it may come about unconsciously (as illustrated by Mr. Smith's analysis of discontinuous curves) in the form of a misinterpretation of the analysis subsequent to the subtraction. In the present state of neglect under which selling cost finds itself in the corpus of economic theory, it would seem that addition, not subtraction, is in order.[28]

27. Ibid. any ed., pp. 71-2. This tendency to look upon selling costs as something 'added on,' but not really a part of the theory, has perhaps been encouraged by the complete neglect of this part of the theory in R. Triffin's exhaustive comparison between my own theory and those of Mrs. Robinson, von Stackelberg, and Pareto (see his *Monopolistic Competition and General Equilibrium Theory*, p. 21n.).

28. In the same issue with Mr. Smith's 'Reply,' Mr. T. H. Silcock has an article entitled 'Professor Chamberlin and Mr. Smith on Advertising.' He presents the following 'justification for Mr. Smith's analysis': '(1) the need to distinguish production costs and selling costs as two entirely distinct species from the economist's point of view; (2) the desirability of showing these two types of cost and their relation to demand, in visual form, for purposes of exposition; (3) the possibility of using the technique to investigate the effects of selling costs on the size of firms in imperfect competition.' He then states that 'Professor Chamberlin does not appear to recognize (1); (2) he presumably regards as a vain aspiration; (3) is, I believe, discussed in this article for the first time.' It is difficult to comment with restraint.

On (1) Mr. Silcock is referred to Chapter vi, and on (2) and (3) to Chapter vii, of *Monopolistic Competition*. He has evidently undertaken to discuss my views on selling costs and to inform the readers of the *Review* about them without having taken the trouble to find out what they are.

Part III

COST ANALYSIS

9

Proportionality, Divisibility,

and Economies of Scale [1]

THE long-run average cost curve of the firm must be interpreted as the *joint* result of the proportions of factors employed and of their aggregate amount. It will be held below that the common practice of treating proportions and size as separate problems has caused the current theory of the subject to go seriously astray, mainly through its becoming almost entirely a theory of proportions.

As a part of this development the erroneous thesis has come to be widely held that under the 'perfect divisibility' of theory, as applied to the factors of production, there would be no economies or diseconomies of scale. From this absence of economies and diseconomies there follows directly (under the assumption of pure competition) an economy without firms. The reason is that, efficiency being the same at all outputs, the size of the firm is indeterminate, hence the number of firms also; so that the very concept of a firm has ceased to have any meaning. As a further consequence the state of competition cannot be defined, since the number of sellers is not discoverable.

There has been concern in many quarters over this alleged propensity of the firm to disappear theoretically, and many

1. Reprinted with minor changes from the *Quarterly Journal of Economics*, February 1948. This Essay also appears in the sixth (1948) and later editions of *The Theory of Monopolistic Competition* as Appendix B.

strange and even wonderful lines of analysis owe their inspiration to it. It will be argued that these developments were not necessary—the firm exists, in theory as well as in fact. This simple proposition, if established, should lead beyond itself to a reconsideration of those lines of thought which have derived both (*a*) directly from the 'imperfect divisibility' thesis of economies, and (*b*) from the unnecessary attempts to escape from its consequences. The analysis will be carried out initially in terms of unit cost curves, and reformulated later in terms of the indifference curve technique, where the two methods will be related to each other.

1. 'PLANT' AND ENVELOPE CURVES

The variety of U-shaped cost curves for the individual firm which assumes a fixed 'plant' has become a textbook common-

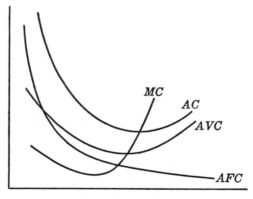

Figure 1

place. It is reproduced for reference in Figure 1, where cost per unit of product is measured on the vertical axis, and output on the horizontal one. The prices of the factors are taken as given for the firm in question, that is, as not influenced by its own adjustments to different outputs.[2] The curves of average fixed

2. Thus the influence upon the cost curves of monopsony in the purchase of factors is not within the scope of this analysis. It should also be clear that we are dealing with production costs only. The behavior of selling costs—those

cost, average variable cost, average (total unit) cost, and marginal cost are indicated by appropriate letters.

Remembering that a similar set of curves may be drawn for each and every fixed aggregate of factors,[3] hereafter called a 'plant,' let us carry forward only the AC curve, henceforth labeled PAC for 'plant average cost.'

In order to describe completely the cost conditions under which any particular good may be produced, it seems evident that thousands of such PAC curves would be required. Let us begin by showing only five of them in Figure 2, assuming for the moment that these five constitute all possibilities. The optimum manner of producing all outputs is then given by the heavy line in three 'scallops,' made up of portions of PAC_1, PAC_3, and PAC_5. It is simply the lowest point on *any* curve for each output, discovered by measuring upward from each point on the x axis until a plant curve is encountered. This scalloped curve of optimum average costs, being more general than any of the plant curves, we shall now designate as the curve of average costs, or AC.[4]

devoted to creating or increasing the demand for a product, as distinct from creating the product itself—is a different matter. But the selling cost curve may be added directly to the production cost curve. (See *Monopolistic Competition*, Chaps. vi, vii.)

3. The possibilities include not only plants of different size (aggregate investment) but also of different qualitative or technological character (for each investment total). They also include different possible assumptions as to how the total resources used are apportioned as between the fixed and variable categories. *All* factors being variable in the long run, what is taken to be fixed and what variable in any particular case is in a sense arbitrary, depending upon the nature of the problem and of the decisions to be taken by the entrepreneur. Thus in an analysis in which capital outlays were variable and labor fixed, labor would become the 'plant.'

4. The possibility of choosing the best plant for each output (evidently to be associated only with the 'long run'), rules out portions of curves PAC_1, PAC_3, and PAC_5, and all of curves PAC_2 and PAC_4. These latter curves, although not forming a part of AC, are not without significance. In the first place, it would not be possible from the outset to omit such curves on the plea that they lie entirely above AC, for we do not yet know where AC is. To draw them in, therefore, as has been done, clarifies the manner in which the AC curve was discovered. In the second place, in so far as the plant cannot be varied in the 'short run,' not only may the lighter portions of curves PAC_1, PAC_3, and PAC_5 be significant for short-run problems, but also curves such

   The next step must be to consider the more general case where
the plant possibilities are more numerous; and the limiting case
where they are so numerous and so 'close together' as to make
it legitimate to treat them as continuously variable. In Figure

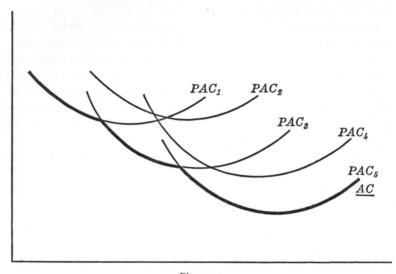

Figure 2

3, we have a number of plant curves drawn close together, and
an AC curve of tiny scallops composed of small segments of the
plant curves. Segments of the plant marginal cost curves for each
plant corresponding to the range of outputs within which it con-

as PAC_2 and PAC_4. This is true because the long run situation to which it is
assumed adjustment cannot be made in the short run involves not merely
variations in output along given plant cost curves which contribute to the AC
curve, but also changes in amounts of factors and in techniques, which redefine
all plant curves and hence the AC curve itself. If AC in our diagram is taken
to be the *present* long-run average cost curve, then curves such as PAC_2 and
PAC_4 may represent plants built under earlier long-run optimum conditions.
It would seem that any short-run period would include such plants, and that
short-run economic analysis should not confine itself, as it usually does (at
least by implication), to those curves of fixed equipment which touch the
'envelope' or long-run curve.

tributes to the AC curve are also drawn, constituting a discontinuous marginal cost curve, MC, to the general average cost curve.[5] The numbers along the base line indicate the range within which the indicated plant average and marginal cost curves contribute to the AC and MC curves.

In Figure 4 the number of plant possibilities has been multi-

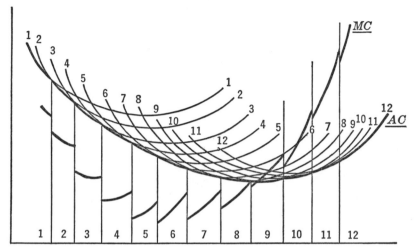

Figure 3

plied to the point where they may be considered as continuous, so that AC and also MC have become smooth curves. Three of the theoretically infinite number of plant curves are drawn in: PAC_1, PAC_2, and PAC_3, for the plants best adapted respectively to producing the outputs OA, OB, and OC. (Let the curves CP_1, CP_2, and CP_3 be ignored for the present.) Under the assumption of continuity, even a very small movement along the AC curve

5. In case the marginal revenue curve for the firm cuts more than one segment of this discontinuous marginal cost curve, equilibrium will be defined by the intersection which yields the highest of the several relative profit maxima; and there would be 'multiple equilibrium' only if two or more of the maxima were identical. Mr. Higgins has analyzed this problem differently ('Indeterminacy in Non-Perfect Competition,' *American Economic Review*, September 1939, pp. 471-3).

involves a change in the plant as well as in the variable factors used with it—in other words, *all* factors, as well as their proportions to each other, are continuously variable. This is the familiar 'envelope' cost curve.[6]

Whether the AC curve is continuous or not will be a question of fact in any particular economic situation; but always it will

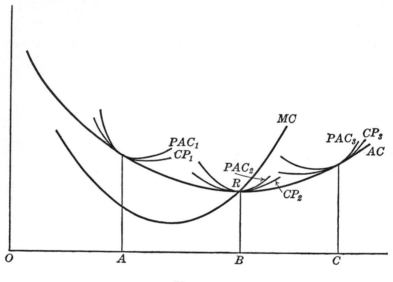

Figure 4

be true that this curve should be looked upon, not as a separate construction, drawn in a particular way with reference to the

6. We have here an advance indication of the nature of the fallacy that economies of scale disappear with perfect divisibility of the factors. (Assuming the variable factor to be finely divisible), 'perfect divisibility' is achieved when the 'plant' possibilities are continuous, and is therefore defined by the limiting position of the AC curve as the number of 'plants' approaches infinity. Economies of scale would be eliminated by perfect divisibility only if the envelope curve were a horizontal line, i.e. if all the plant curves had the same minimum value. The issue then turns on the location of the plant curves. There seems to be general agreement that they are located as drawn, although, of course, this may not be taken for granted without begging the question. It will be discussed further on.

plant curves, but as made up of segments of the plant curves themselves. It is composed of plant curves: it *is* the plant curves. The problem therefore is *not,* having drawn all relevant plant curves, to draw in the envelope curve, either through their minimum points (wrong, of course) or tangent to them, or in some other way. It is merely to draw in all the plant curves. The envelope curve is there already, and the question of how to draw it does not arise.

The urge to give significance to the minimum points on the plant curves is perennial,[7] yet they are clearly of no (long-run) significance whatever. Unless the plant curves are spaced very far apart, their minimum points will not even lie on the AC curve; and even in the unusual case of a great gap between some particular plant and the next possible larger one, such that the minimum point on the first PAC curve lay within the segment it contributed to the AC curve, this minimum would be no more significant than any other point. It is evident that in this matter there has been, and continues to be, a serious confusion between two different optima which are quite unrelated: the optimum way of producing a given output and the optimum way of utilizing a given plant.

2. DIVISIBILITY AND ECONOMIES OF SCALE

With this preparation we may now turn to our central problem, which is the U-shape of the AC curve and its explanation. Let us consider the falling and rising phases of the curve in turn.

The plant curves which compose the average cost curve have, for a time, successively lower minima, and hence define a downward course for the latter until its minimum is reached, primarily for two reasons: (1) increased specialization, made possible in general by the fact that the aggregate of resources is larger, and (2) qualitatively different and technologically more efficient

7. Beginning with the now classic argument between Professor Viner and his admirably obstinate Chinese draftsman (*Zeitschrift für Nationalökonomie,* Band III, Heft 1, p. 36n.). Not only does the envelope curve there drawn pass through the minimum points of the plant curves, but it is suggested that it may be significant only at these points!

units or factors,[8] particularly machinery, made possible by a wise
selection from among the greater range of technical possibilities
opened up by the greater resources.[9] These two explanations over-
lap substantially (machinery, for instance, being often the expression of further 'specialization' in the capital factor); and numerous other reasons, probably of lesser importance, could certainly be added. On the positive side we shall be content here,
however, with the summary statement above, since our main
purpose is the negative one of refuting the 'imperfect divisibility'
explanation, which has so largely pushed into the background
the one just given.

The explanation of economies of scale as a matter of imperfect
divisibility of factors derives from an approach to the problem
which, by contrast with that just summarized, stresses proportionality. There is a certain optimum proportion of factors; and,
because factors may be had only in discrete units, some of them
quite large or 'lumpy,' this optimum proportion is attainable
with precision only when the aggregate of factors is large. Thus
the relative inefficiency of small-scale production is explained
merely as a matter of failure to achieve the optimum proportions.
With perfect divisibility, it is argued, they could be realized by
subdivision for *any* aggregate, no matter how small, and economies of scale would be nonexistent. *Ergo,* economies are explained
by imperfect divisibility.

The fundamental fault with this argument is that it omits the
effect of divisibility upon efficiency. But before going into this
matter, the extent to which the explanation has been turned into

8. Incidentally, the product itself ordinarily undergoes qualitative change,
often quite drastic, as a function of the scale of production, thus calling into
question the whole concept of economies of scale, since what is produced more
economically, say under mass production methods, is not at all the same thing
as what is produced by the simpler methods of small-scale industry. This is
a phase of the general problem of 'product variation,' to which little enough
attention has been paid in economics. Unfortunately, it cannot be developed
here, where the usual assumption of a given product for each firm is made.

9. The downward course of the curve follows, as stated, from successively
lower plant curves; movement along the curve, however, involves *both* more
efficient plants *and* their more efficient utilization, until at the minimum point
we have (*a*) the most efficient plant (*b*) most efficiently utilized.

a tautology, by including in the *definition* of divisibility the requirement that efficiency be unaffected, should be made clear. Professor Stigler reflects this recent trend when he states explicitly: 'It is tautological that economies of scale rest on indivisibilities, for an indivisible productive service is *defined* as one which is not equally efficient in all sizes (measured in terms of output).' [10]

Much more common is a treatment in which the tautology, though not explicitly acknowledged, is nevertheless equally present. Thus Mr. Kaldor states that 'it appears *methodologically convenient* to treat all cases of large-scale economies under the heading "indivisibility";' and in order to bring a refractory case under the rule, immediately explains that it may be 'not so much the "original factors," but the specialized functions of those factors, which are indivisible.' [11] Divisibility is thus *defined* to include the availability for small scales of those 'specialized functions' which depend in fact upon large-scale operations, 'specialization' being of the essence of economies of scale. To affirm now that where everything is 'perfectly divisible' economies of scale are completely absent is merely to repeat oneself.

Similarly, Mr. Lerner's exhaustive analysis of divisibilities in relation to the welfare problem leans heavily on the proposition that under perfect divisibility of 'factors, products, and methods of production,' economies of scale are absent, and far-reaching conclusions are drawn from the alleged resulting conditions of constant cost. Here the explicit inclusion of 'methods of produc-

10. *The Theory of Price* (1946), p. 202n. (Italics supplied.) It should be added that with Stigler the tautology is incidental rather than fundamental. At an earlier point (p. 133) it is not mentioned; and he lists both (*a*) indivisibilities and (*b*) the 'human factor,' this latter being illustrated by specialization and by the problems of management. But the 'human factor' is at once transmuted back into indivisibilities. The arguments are dubious (and only too familiar). For example, management, although described as more than doubled [sic] while labor is doubled, is nevertheless called 'indivisible,' apparently for the reason that it is 'used more intensively.' (If 'more than doubled,' it would be used *less* intensively.) It is finally held, however, that the envelope curve 'usually' descends to a minimum and rises again, for reasons which include those given in this essay.

11. 'The Equilibrium of the Firm,' *Economic Journal*, March 1934, p. 65n. (Italics supplied.)

tion' automatically takes care of the efficiency problem, since the 'divisibility' of this item 'permits any particular method of production, involving certain proportions between factors and products, to be repeated in exactly the same way on a larger or on a smaller scale.' [12] The phrase 'in exactly the same way' clearly means with exactly the same efficiency (otherwise economies of scale would remain, even with the perfect divisibility of 'method'). What is being *assumed* is that the superior methods made possible by a larger aggregate of resources, such as assembly lines, are equally available with smaller aggregates—in other words, divisibility of method is simply a euphemism for absence of economies.

Professor Knight has given the earliest statement of the divisibility argument of which I am aware, perhaps the one from which, in view of his great influence, the more explicitly tautological formulations of recent years have evolved. He argued that *'If* the amounts of *all* elements in a combination were freely variable without limit and the product also continuously divisible, it is evident that one size of combination would be precisely similar in its workings to any other similarly composed.' [13] Such a proposition is 'evident' only if the effect upon efficiency of dividing factors is ignored; in other words, if the issue of economies of scale is assumed away.

Let us pass from the question of tautologies to still another false approach to the problem: a common line of reasoning which holds that there is something in the 'mathematics' of divisibility which washes out the economies. I have encountered this again and again in discussing the matter with students and with colleagues—indeed, it would seem to be not unreasonable to ascribe the ascendency of the divisibility thesis in recent years in some measure to the ascendency of mathematics, not merely as a tool, but often as a substitute for economics. In the present instance it is a bad substitute—and it is not even mathematics. To assume

12. *Economics of Control,* p. 143. On the absence of economies of scale under 'perfect divisibility,' see pages 165-7 and *passim*. On the principle that a change in scale will not change the marginal productivity of any of the factors, see pages 144, 154, and *passim*.

13. *Risk, Uncertainty and Profit,* p. 98. Italics in original.

that factors are 'perfectly divisible' carries with it no implication whatever as to how their efficiency will be affected in the process. In other words, mathematics as such contributes literally nothing to the question at issue.

The *actual* economic function is discontinuous in any event, and from the point of view of mathematics, to assume 'perfect' divisibility is merely to substitute a smooth function for it. Unless the substituted function follows closely the one which expresses the economic realities, the results derived from its use will be worthless. A mathematician called in for consultation as to how to draw the continuous cost function for the firm under an assumption of perfect divisibility would be obliged to ask the economist what divisibility meant concretely in the problem at hand, and how it would affect efficiency. Only when the economist had told him could he proceed; the question is one of economics, not mathematics.[14]

What, if anything, does divisibility do to efficiency?—that is the question; and the answer depends in part on what we mean concretely by 'dividing up' a factor.[15] A further question must be

14. Mr. Kaldor must again be cited in this connection. 'We see therefore,' he says, 'that the mathematical economists in taking "perfect competition" as their starting point, weren't such fools after all. For they assumed perfect divisibility of everything; and where everything is perfectly divisible, and consequently economies of scale completely absent, "perfect competition" [instead of monopolistic competition] must necessarily establish itself solely as a result of the "free play of economic forces." ' ('Market Imperfection and Excess Capacity,' *Economica*, February 1935, p. 42. The absence of economies of scale is crucial to his argument, which, however, involves other matters as well. Cf. *Monopolistic Competition*, pp. 198-9.) Here not only are economies of scale cast out, but monopoly as well; and 'mathematics' appears as a sort of mad queen striding about the economic croquet grounds and shouting 'Off with their heads!' Perhaps it should be recalled that when Alice's patience with such procedures had worn thin she retorted, 'Stuff and nonsense! . . . Who cares for you?' (and promptly woke up).

Unfortunately, this identification of mathematical economics with perfect competition is not limited to Mr. Kaldor. Closely related is the idea that 'economic theory' is the theory of perfect competition, monopolistic competition having to do, by contrast, with 'reality.'

15. The analysis of divisibility has gained in clarity through the helpful criticisms of my colleague, Dr. A. E. Monroe.

answered: what is to be done with the case where a factor *cannot* be divided, and hence where the question of its efficiency in fractional units does not arise?

Let us begin with the case where divisibility is in some sense possible, and suppose that under the most efficient conditions of production for the firm (the minimum point on its envelope cost curve) there were 100 laborers employed, assuming further, in order to simplify the problem, that no other factors of production are involved. There is no difficulty whatever in dividing the total labor force into any fraction which has a whole number for the numerator and 100 for the denominator, by merely taking the proper number of units. Until a single unit is reached, this is what division means concretely, and we know very well its effect upon efficiency: the fewer the laborers the less specialized they will be and hence the less efficient, for reasons explained in detail by Adam Smith—briefly, that they would achieve less 'dexterity' and that they would lose more time 'in passing from one species of work to another.' Plotting the unit costs of the outputs in question, we obtain a discontinuous series of 100 dots, each one a point on the falling phase of the average cost curve. *Full divisibility* of the labor force of 100, whatever it may mean for the intermediate points, must *include* the fractions 1/100, 2/100 . . . 100/100, and there is no avoiding the conclusion that these points must lie on the curve. This being so, it would appear that what happens between them is really of minor importance, for as long as it is established that the curve of perfect divisibility must pass through these points, it is, for practical purposes, defined: it is perfectly clear, for instance, that it cannot be the horizontal line which negates economies of scale.

But let us look into the further divisibilities involved in *fractional* units of a factor. There are a number of ways in which units of different economic entities may be 'divided.' The commodity beefsteak is infinitely divisible by the use of a meat cleaver; a steam boiler may be 'divided' in manufacture by making it smaller (or larger), and again the gradations are infinite. The reflection that neither of these processes is available for the labor factor is not made in order to be facetious, but to make clear that the interpretation to be given to divisibility is not derived from the mathematical blue, but from the economic realities of the problem at hand.

It would appear that one meaningful and realistic way to divide a unit of labor is on a time basis.

Let us suppose that an output is desired intermediate between that provided by 50 laborers and by 51 laborers. If laborers may be hired on a part-time basis, either directly, or indirectly by contracting out certain types of work, the matter becomes simply one of inquiring into the efficiency of production under such arrangements and filling in the gaps. The most favorable circumstances would seem to be where a worker could be hired part time with an effect upon efficiency such that cost per unit of product at the intermediate point would conform to the trend, that is, lie on the smooth curve drawn through our original 100 points. This would involve the application, to ranges between any two of these points, of the same type of analysis as that just developed for the range from 0 to 100 laborers. Thus, if we assume a fractional unit of labor to be five minutes, there will be roughly 100 of them to the day, and 10 such five-minute units of labor will be generally less efficient than 100, for the same reason that 10 days labor will be less efficient than 100 days. This conclusion makes efficiency depend upon the *amount* of a factor, the size of the unit being completely arbitrary. It is certainly the simplest and would seem to be the most defensible *general* assumption as to the effect of divisibility upon efficiency in the problem at hand.

It should be noted that, as a consequence of this interpretation, the efficiency of a fractional unit depends upon the total amount of labor to which it is *added*. It is different at every point on the curve, and corresponds approximately to the efficiency which obtains at the point where the division takes place, not at that which obtains at some other distant point, such as the minimum one on the cost curve. For example, because 50 whole laborers might be thought of as arithmetically equal to 100 half-laborers, one may not conclude that their efficiency will be that of 100 whole laborers at the minimum point because the number of 'units' is the same. Their number being *actually* 50, each will have to master more operations than if there were 100 and shift more frequently from one to the other, and so on. For these and similar reasons they will be less efficient.

Nor is there an escape from this conclusion by the alternative of actually hiring 100 laborers for half time. In this case there will be inefficiencies because of the hiring, training, and maintaining of twice as many workers as necessary, of the changeovers from one worker to another, and so forth, so that the results would in fact be worse, not better, than with 50 whole laborers. One need only contrast the extreme of one person working eight hours a day with 96 persons succeeding each other in five-minute shifts, to see that subdivision, although it may reproduce for smaller outputs the same number of 'units' as under the optimum output, will not reproduce the same conditions of efficiency.

From this example of units which are too small, we are led to a consideration of the very real complications which are introduced by the size of the unit. To produce any particular output most efficiently it is clearly not a matter of indifference whether there be a single laborer working 100 days, 100 laborers working one day, or 10,000 laborers working for 4.8 minutes. The envelope curve requires by definition that for each output the units of the factors be always chosen so as to achieve maximum efficiency. (They will evidently be of diverse sizes in such a broad category as 'labor.') But if the size of the unit matters, we have still another problem of divisibility: a fractional unit may involve a loss in efficiency merely because it is fractional—because, for instance, the time lost in starting and stopping work is the same for a part-time as for a full-time worker. In this case, wherever a fractional unit appears in our hitherto smooth curve, there will be a slight break to a higher point and within the range of the divided unit a more rapid descent to the smooth curve at the point where a whole unit is again reached. Such considerations may be important where the divided units are large relative to the total, but the inefficiencies of such fractional units would always be averaged over *all* units, and would usually become inconsequential for anything but the smallest outputs. Herein lies the justification in most cases for ignoring them, and considering that the efficiency of part-time workers conforms to the trend, that is, that unit cost is a *continuous* function of output. (Wherever the inefficiencies were consequential, an alternative would be to fit a smooth curve to the actual data.)

In addition to the time basis just discussed, another meaningful and realistic way to achieve continuous divisibility of a factor is to change it qualitatively. Instead of part-time laborers, more (or less) efficient laborers, or perhaps just *different* ones, are now the answer. The fact that human beings are strikingly diverse in their capabilities and economic attributes is a commonplace, and there would surely be no dissent from the proposition that the general factor 'labor' is continuously divisible in the sense here discussed; it only remains to call to mind the effect of such divisibility on economies. Here, too, I believe there would be general agreement that such qualitative considerations yield in themselves an important new source of economies of scale. The reason is that the employment of more highly specialized and superior abilities is often conditioned upon larger outputs, since the units in which such abilities are embodied are too large to be fully utilized for small ones. Hence the 'division' of an aggregate of labor corresponding to minimum cost conditions (as in our earlier case of 100 laborers) will diminish efficiency by narrowing the choice of the types of units used. Such units may, of course, be divisible on a time basis, in which case our earlier analysis will apply as an alternative to substituting less efficient units, and the better possibility will be chosen.

An analysis parallel to that for human beings may be made for machines (also for land), and need only be indicated briefly. Just as it does with the number of laborers, specialization increases with the number of machines, both in the manner of use of identical units and in the construction and design of different ones. 'Fractional' units on a time basis are again possible in some degree through rental, sharing, or contractual arrangements, although these considerations are probably not of great importance in the ordinary operations of manufacturing. Where they are present the analysis already given for labor seems applicable without important modifications.

It would appear that by far the most meaningful and important interpretation of divisibility in the case of machinery and capital equipment is in terms of qualitative change. While human beings are diverse by nature and training, capital instruments are so by manufacture. Variations in design are infinite, and all machines are also continuously divisible in a new dimension of physical size, with important consequences, of course, for efficiency. It would appear that continuous divisibility in the capital factor would be completely general, were it not for economies in the production of capital instruments themselves, through concentration on a limited number of models, thus creating the possibility of 'gaps' between the different types of units available to the firm. Wherever such gaps occur (unless a fractional unit is to be had on some other basis, such as time), particular units will be used with varying degrees of intensity over a certain range by changing the quantities of other factors employed with them, and the result will be a scalloped curve as in Figure 3. In large organizational complexes, however, such gaps are almost certain to come at different points for different types of equipment, thus shortening the scallops and perhaps re-establishing complete divisibility of capital outlay at all points.

So much for the question of continuity; what now of the shape of the curve—the effect of divisibility upon economies in this case of qualitative change? Here again, as for labor, I believe there would be general agreement that larger outputs widen the choice of units, constantly opening up new and more efficient technological possibilities which would be too costly for smaller outputs, because too badly underutilized. Hence, to look at the matter the other way around, the division of an aggregate of capital, as of labor, corresponding to minimum cost conditions, will diminish efficiency by narrowing the choice of units used.

Let us turn now to the case where a unit, or a factor, is not divisible at all. Thus it may be said that, although the general factor 'capital' is divisible, the particular machines in which it is embodied are not, and that this is the source, or at least a source, of economies of scale. But there appears to be no truth in this proposition. Evidently, if a machine may not be divided, the 'amount' of it must be held constant so long as it is used at all, and the amounts of other factors used with it will be varied, yielding a U-shaped plant curve with economies in its descending phase. However, in the case of continuous qualitative variation, movement along the envelope curve involves constant passage from one such curve to another, and the descending phase of the envelope curve is the result, not of the *shapes* of the plant curves composing it, but of their *position* relative to each other. This is clear at once when it is recalled that if the U-shaped plant curves all had the same minimum value, the envelope curve would be a horizontal line.

In the alternative case where substantial 'gaps' exist between the units of a factor, or between 'plants,' the contribution of particular plant curves to the long-run average cost curve will be finite, and perhaps substantial. It may then be said, of course, that each 'scallop' is governed by the laws of the fixed factor analysis, as symbolized in Figure 1. But, as in the case of continuity, the particular *portion* of any plant curve which contributes to the long-run average cost curve is governed by the position of the plant curves relative to each other, not by their shape. Thus again, if all plant curves had the same minimum value, the AC curve would be made up of segments around these minimum values; there would be as many rising as falling portions, and a smooth curve fitted to it would be horizontal. Even in the case of 'gaps' we may conclude, therefore, that the trend of the curve is governed by the nature of the movement from plant to plant, rather than by the movement within any particular plant curve. At the same time, there is no objection, of course, to saying that the behavior of the curve within any particular (perhaps substantial) segment is governed by the fixed factor analysis.

There *is* objection, however, in any case, to saying that the economies in the falling phase of a plant curve are explained by the *indivisibility* of the fixed plant, interpreting this to mean that if the plant were divisible there would be no economies. Such a proposition is part and parcel of the tautological conception of the problem, which derives in turn from the premise that if the same (allegedly 'best') proportions are reproduced for all outputs, there will be no economies (or diseconomies) of scale. The prevalence of this conception of divisibility as including 'without loss of efficiency' is evidently the measure of how sweeping has been the victory of proportions over size in the explanation of economies; whereas at best, divisibility here, if meaningful at all, would make possible the reproduction for smaller outputs of the conditions at the minimum point on the plant curve *only with respect to proportions.* All the forces discussed above which affect efficiency and which are a function of *size* would remain. The real objection, however, to explaining the shape of a plant curve in terms of 'indivisibility' is that it has no meaning. If a factor is indivisible, that is the end of the matter: there is no way of finding out how dividing it would affect its efficiency.[16] If by divisibility is meant merely the substitution of a smooth curve for the actual scalloped one, the substituted curve must at least be a reasonable fit to the one it replaces, and not involve an arbitrary assumption which carries it off on a tangent.

It may be added that in many cases where a factor *is* not divided, the reason may be, not that it is indivisible, but that to 'divide' it (by, let us say, sharing it part time with some one else) would entail a greater loss in efficiency than to have it standing idle a part of the time. In this case, using it as an indivisible unit *increases* efficiency.

In summary, it appears that indivisibilities play no part whatever in explaining economies of scale. Where all factors are perfectly divisible, efficiency remains nevertheless a function of size; so that the envelope curve, whether smooth or scalloped, descends to a minimum in its first phase. Where particular factors, or units of factors, remain fixed for substantial portions of the long-run average cost curve, and where this introduces scallops, the 'trend' will be the same, and for the same reason. And where the segments of the long-run average cost curve to which the fixed factor analysis applies are substantial, to attribute the economies (or diseconomies) within this range to 'indivisibility' is either tautological or meaningless.

3. Proportionality and Diseconomies of Scale

Let us turn now to the behavior of the *AC* curve to the right of its minimum point. Here again the proportionality thesis has

16. In the same way, if horses cannot fly, there is no way of finding out how *high* they could fly, if they could.

badly falsified the picture, both as to whether the curve rises, and, if it does, as to why.

The matter is of crucial importance for purely competitive theory [17] since, unless the curve rises, the number of firms is indeterminate, instead of being the 'large number' required for pure competition. Faced with this consequence of the sweeping proportionality thesis which divorces efficiency from size, Professor Knight, having just affirmed that 'these things (proportionality and size) must imperatively be kept separate,' finds, two sentences further on, that they cannot be, and so *postulates* the contrary [18]—an expedient which ought to indicate that something is wrong with the principle of separation.

Mr. Kaldor, up against the same difficulty, attempts to solve it within the proportionality formula. He asserts that, 'as diminishing returns to *all* factors together are not conceivable,' the optimum size of the firm cannot be determined unless at least one factor is fixed,[19] and therefore seeks a fixed factor such that '*only one unit* [of it] can do the job.' Analyzing the functions of entrepreneurship into uncertainty-bearing, supervision, and co-ordination, he agrees that the first two are variable, and settles upon the last as the fixed factor, holding that it is a unit because it involves a 'single brain.' Boards of Directors are almost a fatal rock and are finally admitted to be variable; but it is maintained that in spite of their plurality they conform to the requirement of a single brain. The firm is then defined as a 'productive com-

17. In contrast, it is of much less importance for the theory of monopolistic competition, in the sense that elements of monopoly will usually (but not always, cf. *Monopolistic Competition*, p. 78n. and p. 161) define equilibrium for the firm to the left of the minimum point on the production cost curve. However, the shape of the curve beyond the immediate vicinity of equilibrium must always be important as a part of explaining and understanding the economic system in the broadest sense.

18. 'For the competitive system to work, it is necessary to postulate . . . that an establishment of relatively small size in proportion to the industry as a whole is more efficient than a larger one.' *Risk, Uncertainty and Profit*, p. 98.

19. 'The Equilibrium of the Firm,' p. 66.

Professor G. J. Cady, in his *Entrepreneural Costs and Price*, seems to hold to this position so firmly that he mistakenly describes it (p. 7n.) as an 'implied assumption' of my own Appendix B (1st to 5th eds.).

bination possessing a given unit of co-ordinating ability.' [20] Yet if it has to be 'given,' it is fixed only by assumption, as any factor other than co-ordination might equally well have been.

But co-ordination, as white-headed boy destined to contain the firm within limits, fails us in the end, even with Mr. Kaldor, for it is finally discovered to be an 'essentially dynamic function,' which, with the approach of the stationary state, suffers a euthanasia, leaving us again with the size of the firm 'infinite (or indeterminate).' His final conclusion therefore is that 'long-period static equilibrium and perfect competition are incompatible assumptions.' How much simpler it would all have been if 'diminishing returns to all factors,' in the sense of rising costs when all are increased together, had not been barred as an absurdity!

Without accepting the proposition that a fixed factor is *necessary* in order to make the curve rise, it may be granted at once that if there *is* a factor which for some reason *is* fixed in any particular case, the curve will rise as in the plant curve analysis of Figure 1. 'Entrepreneurship,' however defined, appears to be variable; but if a particular entrepreneur does not *wish* to expand it in his own firm because he does not want to share with others certain functions which he performs, then the size of his firm will be limited by his ability to perform these functions, or by his available capital and borrowing ability, or by both, after the manner of the plant curve analysis.[21]

20. 'The Equilibrium of the Firm,' p. 69. (Italics supplied.) Mr. Kaldor labors to show that there must be a *single unit* at the top; but even granting this dubious proposition (Who is it in the corporation?), it would seem that all that is established is hierarchy within a variable factor. As the firm expands, resources are added to the Chief Accountant as well as to the mythical 'Chief Co-ordinator.' It would perhaps be as relevant to point out that they are also added to the tallest man in the organization, or to the one with the broadest grin.

The entrepreneur as a fixed and indivisible unit seems firmly imbedded in the theory of the firm in England. It is interesting to compare Mr. Kaldor's reduction of the variable factor co-ordination to the required unitary basis with Mrs. Robinson's similar conversion of an admittedly divisible entrepreneur (cited in *Monopolistic Competition*, 5th or later ed., p. 216n.3).

21. Mr. Kalecki's 'principle of increasing risk' (*Essays in the Theory of Economic Fluctuations*, Chap. 4) seems to come under this heading. With a *given* amount of owned capital, an individual entrepreneur may extend his

All factors being variable on the envelope curve, it is evident that the *general* explanation of why it rises cannot be in terms of a fixed factor. Yet there seem to be solid reasons why it should rise, and no reason to reject them merely because it is mathematically possible to subject the proportions at the minimum point to multiplication! The question is again: what does multiplication do to efficiency?

The plant curves which compose the average cost curve have, after a certain point, successively higher minima, and hence define an upward course for the average cost curve because of the greater complexity of the producing unit as it grows in size, leading to increased difficulties of co-ordination and management.

borrowings only at progressively higher rates of interest, as illustrated by the higher rate on second as compared with first mortgages, etc. But the extension of the argument to the corporation is not convincing. In seeking to show, as he must, that there is a limit to the *amount* of 'ordinary shares,' Mr. Kalecki only demonstrates that the promoters of a new company or the original shareholders of an existing (profitable!) one will not admit new shareholders on an equal basis with themselves, which is quite a different matter. The possibility of expanding common stock by offering to the *existing* body of stockholders rights to subscribe to the new shares is also ignored.

The 'principle of increasing risk,' combined with the fact that the private capital of various entrepreneurs is not the same, must certainly play a part, as Mr. Kalecki contends, in explaining the co-existence of large and small enterprises in the same industry. But in (correctly) dismissing imperfect competition as a factor contributing to the explanation of this diversity (p. 98), he has apparently committed the common error of identifying imperfect and monopolistic competition, and (incorrectly) dismissed the latter also. On this matter the reader is referred to *Monopolistic Competition*, pp. 209-10. Uniformity of conditions as between firms is of the essence of imperfect competition; diversity, of the essence of monopolistic competition (ibid. pp. 110-13). Under monopolistic competition, where different producers produce *different* products under *different* circumstances of cost and demand, the *expected* result would be firms of all sizes; and it seems most likely that the diversity associated with the different capital resources of different entrepreneurs would adapt itself to the more fundamental diversity arising from such 'product' heterogeneity. Thus an entrepreneur of small resources would establish himself in a situation where the market was limited, etc.

Incidentally, Mr. Kalecki, in his matter-of-fact statement that imperfect competition cannot account for diversity, has provided important corroborative evidence for my own interpretation of the nature of 'imperfect' competition, and therefore of the vital differences between Mrs. Robinson's theories and my own.

More elaborate systems of control are made necessary by impersonal relations. They are costly in themselves, and lead, furthermore, to a rigidity of procedure and the stifling of individual initiative. Mr. E. A. G. Robinson has used as an apt analogy from the army: 'A mistake made by a platoon commander demands only an instantaneous "As you were!" A mistake made by an army commander may require days of labor to set right.' [22] Again, this line of analysis is familiar [23] and need not be defended at length, especially since the proportionality thesis, in which our primary interest lies, has proceeded not so much by denying or criticizing it as merely by ignoring it.

It is important to avoid identifying the emergence of the problems of co-ordination arising from increasing complexity with the minimum point on the cost curve. Where they first become important will depend upon the product in question and the techniques and circumstances under which its production is undertaken at different times and places, but in general they will begin to appear for quite small outputs, as one element in the total picture of efficiency described by the AC curve. In the early stages they are submerged by the overwhelming gains from further specialization and more efficient techniques already discussed. But since these latter tend to exhaust themselves with larger aggregates, whereas complexity steadily increases, it appears certain that the diseconomies must *sooner or later* outweigh the economies, and beyond that point predominate. The forces making for economies and for diseconomies are in balance at the minimum point on the AC curve; the latter predominate to the right of it.

From this approach the central principle again emerges that there is no most efficient proportion of factors independent of output. If the descending curve had been explained by a failure to achieve the 'best proportions' because of indivisibilities, it might follow that when output was large enough the difficulties would be overcome, and that beyond that point there would a fortiori be no further problem. But our position, developed

22. *The Structure of Competitive Industry*, p. 44.

23. The reader may be referred to E. A. G. Robinson, loc. cit., and to J. M. Clark, *The Economics of Overhead Costs*, pp. 131ff.

above, has been that the proportion of factors corresponding to the minimum point on the AC curve is *not* the 'best proportion,' but only the best for that output. This is a very different thing, and gives no warrant for multiplying it. Already at this output the influence of complexity is playing a part; and because it is a force in itself making for higher costs at the minimum point, the other influences which make for economies must also be present in an offsetting role. From this point of view, since *both* forces are present in *both* directions from the minimum, there is no more reason to think that the conditions of efficiency which characterize the minimum could be extended to larger outputs than to smaller ones.[24]

4. CONSTANT PROPORTIONS AND HOMOGENEITY

We have now to inquire into the effect of holding the proportions of factors constant while varying their aggregate amount. It must be recalled that the envelope curve is characterized by complete variability throughout as to what factors are chosen, in what amounts, and hence in what proportions to each other. It gives merely the optimum for each output. If, to the right of

24. It is sometimes argued that a policy of decentralization may be adopted beyond the minimum point, reproducing the conditions there found in substantially independent units, and thus eliminating, almost by definition, the problems of complexity. The question is whether the firm, as the 'control unit,' can divest itself *completely* of control over its component parts; for unless it can, conditions are not duplicated. Decentralization and delegation of authority are well-known expedients of large (also of small) organizations; yet there must always be a residue of authority in central hands, including the vital one of choosing those to whom authority is to be delegated. In so far as decentralization is an effective means of combating the diseconomies of size, far from being denied, it is, of course, included by definition in the envelope curve at all points. Its importance will vary with techniques and circumstances, and its effect may often be to postpone net diseconomies far beyond the scales of production to be found in reality. It is contended only that the curve does turn up somewhere.

It should be noted that, in so far as the diseconomies are postponed, the conclusions of this line of argument are disastrous for purely competitive theory, since pure competition will result only if the curves *actually* turn up for scales of production which are small relative to total output. (Of course the product must also be homogeneous.) This is the difficulty which Professor Knight surmounts by merely assuming it away. (Above, p. 187.)

its minimum point, it rises when resources are applied *most effectively* to the overcoming of increased complexity, then a curve of unit costs, restricted by the arbitrary requirement that the proportions of factors which is optimum for the minimum point be maintained for the larger outputs, will rise still more rapidly. If, for instance, a 'managerial' or 'supervisory' or 'co-ordinating' factor is distinguished, and its proportion to the others increased with increasing size, the envelope curve will reflect this adjustment. Since cost per unit rises beyond the minimum with the managerial factor increasing more rapidly than the others (the envelope curve), it will rise even more steeply if the managerial factor is increased by the lesser amount necessary to maintain the proportions constant.

This curve of constant proportions, labeled CP, is shown in three different locations in Figure 4 (p. 174). Let us first consider CP_2 at the minimum point of the AC curve in its relation to the relevant plant curve PAC_2 and to the AC curve. As output is varied from OB, we know that PAC_2 in general rises as it does above AC in either direction because the restriction has been imposed that one complex of factors, the 'plant,' is held fixed at the amount appropriate to the OB output, whereas no restrictions whatever are imposed along the AC curve. A similar proposition may now be made for the CP_2 curve. As output is varied from OB, CP_2 will in general rise above AC in either direction because a restriction of another sort has been imposed: that the *proportions* of factors remain as defined for OB, whereas no such restriction is imposed along the AC curve. All three curves are tangent to each other at R. If along the envelope curve the proportions of the factors change very slowly with variations in output, CP_2 will diverge from AC on either side of R more slowly than will PAC_2, and will thus lie between PAC_2 and AC, as shown in Figure 4. If, on the other hand, the proportions of the factors change rapidly along the envelope curve, CP_2 will diverge from AC on either side of R more rapidly than will PAC_2, and will thus lie above PAC_2 as well as above AC.[25] There appears to be no a

25. I am indebted to Mr. Joseph Lerner for the suggestion of this second possibility. For a fuller treatment see his 'Constant Proportions, Fixed Plant

priori rule to indicate which of these two results is the more likely; only the first is illustrated in Figure 4.

These same curves may be drawn from any point on the envelope curve, and are drawn in Figure 4 for illustration also at outputs OA and OC. The relation of the plant to the envelope curve at each of these points has already been discussed. The CP curve will in each case lie above the AC curve on either side of their point of tangency, because the proportions which define it are those which are optimum respectively to OA and OC, but which are at all other points inferior to those given by the envelope curve. As before, it is drawn in each case below the plant curve, although the positions of the two might equally well be reversed, as just explained.

From the CP_2 curve drawn at the minimum point, it would now appear that when the proportion at that point is reproduced in smaller or larger aggregates, assuming this to be continuously possible, far from collapsing the envelope curve to a horizontal line, it would have an *opposite* effect, giving results which at all points other than the minimum would be inferior to the envelope curve (and perhaps inferior even to the plant curve from the same point).

There seems to be no reason why entrepreneurs should ever have any interest in maintaining the proportions of factors constant. With maximum flexibility, they will seek the conditions of the envelope curve. In so far as they are obliged to hold various complexes of factors constant in short periods, they will move on curves symbolized by the various PAC curves. In so far as factors may be varied slowly over intermediate periods, they will move along curves intermediate between the PAC and AC curves, expressing partially the full possibilities contained in the envelope curve. But unless they harbor an interest in the mathematics of homogeneous functions which submerges their ordinary entrepreneurial objectives, they will have no reason to pursue the possibilities illustrated by the CP curves.

The economist, however, is interested in the homogeneity of the production function as a part of the problem of distribution, and

and the Optimum Conditions of Production,' *Quarterly Journal of Economics*, August 1949.

in this connection it is the *CP* curves, not the plant or envelope curves, which are relevant. The firm will be in equilibrium under pure competition at the minimum point of the *envelope* curve; Euler's theorem will apply approximately at the minimum point of the *constant proportions* curve; and it is because these two points coincide that Euler's theorem applies to equilibrium conditions. In spite of the fact that entrepreneurs will not actually

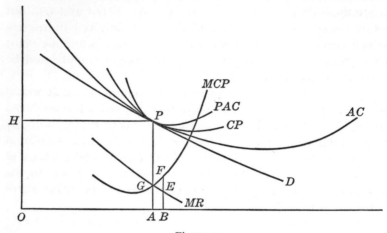

Figure 5

make adjustments along the *CP* curve, it remains true, nevertheless, that if each factor included in the cost curve is paid according to its marginal product at equilibrium, the total product of the firm will be exactly distributed among them without excess or defect.

A similar proposition will be true under monopolistic competition with marginal *revenue* product substituted for marginal product. However, for those whose knowledge of Euler's theorem is rudimentary or zero—in short, for those who take it on faith and associate it with constant cost, the fact that equilibrium for the firm involves conditions of decreasing cost is troublesome. Let us consider the case where demand and cost curves are tangent, as in Figure 5, equilibrium output being *OA* and equilibrium price *AP*. Plant, constant proportions, and envelope curves are drawn in, all tangent, as already explained, to each other and to the demand curve at P. The marginal cost curve to the CP curve, labeled MCP, has been drawn in, since this is the one which is significant for our purposes. It intersects the marginal revenue curve MR at G (as would the other two marginal cost curves also, were they drawn in). At equilibrium, total outlay for factors and total revenue product are both equal to the rectangle $OAPH$. If now a very small change in the outlay for factors were made, their proportions being held constant, the increase in physical product would be, say AB (magnified in the diagram in order to make it visible); the increase in outlay would be $ABFG$, and the increase in revenue product $ABEG$. If these increases are made smaller by letting B approach very close to A, the discrepancy EFG is sharply diminished, until for very small variations around G it may be neglected: the increase in revenue product is approximately proportional to the increase in the outlay for factors. Again, Euler's theorem is applicable under equilibrium conditions, although these conditions are defined without reference to the CP curve. It follows that if each factor included in the cost curve is paid according to its marginal *revenue product* at equilibrium, the total *revenue product* of the firm ($OAPH$) will be exactly distributed among them without excess or defect.

As an alternative, the curves might be redrawn, measuring along the x axis not physical product but revenue product: 'dollar's worth of product.' At equilibrium (output OA in Figure 5), the cost of producing a dollar's worth of product is exactly one dollar (since price equals cost), whereas on either side of equilibrium it is more (since cost is greater than price). The three cost curves would now all be tangent at their *minimum* points (equal to one dollar), and the demand curve would be horizontal and tangent to them at this point, since a dollar's worth of product will obviously always sell for a dollar. The case thus appears explicitly as one of approximately constant cost at equilibrium—constant cost of producing *revenue product*.

But suppose the curves are not tangent?—for I have myself insisted that the 'tangency solution' is of only limited applicability, the general situation being one of 'diversity,' including nontangency. By adding *all* actual profits (including the excess over the minimum) into the cost curve, equilibrium can always be identified with a condition of tangency; and although this would *certainly not be legitimate as a general procedure,* it appears to be unobjectionable for present purposes. Here the question is not one of the *determination* of equilibrium, since in the nontangency solution equilibrium must already have been defined before the new curve including total profits could be drawn. Thus *actual* profits are not being 'treated as a cost,' and the host of issues raised by that problem is avoided. We are interested only in knowing the relationship between what factors actually receive and their marginal revenue products. There is no doubt as to the income which entrepreneurship actually receives, and it may be treated for our purposes as the price paid for the factor in question. The conclusion is, as already developed, that under equilibrium conditions *all* factors, including entrepreneurship, receive their marginal revenue products to the firm, and that, by this rule, the total product of the firm is exactly used up.[26]

5. SUMMARY: PROPORTIONS AND SIZE

Let us now consider more specifically the central proposition that proportions and size are functionally related, and the nature of the errors which flow from treating them as if they were not.

The problems of proportions and size may be legitimately 'separated' only in the sense that a relative optimum may be formally defined for each, the other being held constant at an assumed value. Thus we have the optimum proportion for any given size (total outlay) and the optimum size for any given proportion, the former being discovered most effectively by the indifference curve technique but appearing as a point on the envelope curve; the latter being given by the minimum point of some particular *CP* curve, not in general on the envelope curve at all. Such partial solutions are 'legitimate' only in the sense of

26. The significance of this proposition for distributive theory and welfare economics has as yet hardly been touched, although a substantial literature has developed around the erroneous theme that the 'hired factors' are exploited by entrepreneurs. [1957] Cf. below, pp. 309ff., and other references there given.

being consistent with a recognition of the ultimate functional relationship between the variables in question. In the problem at hand each of them has only very limited meaning or value in itself. Certainly assent cannot be given to keeping proportions and size separate in the sense of stopping short with such partial analyses. Since in the general problem they are both variable, the optimum (minimum) cost conditions for the firm can be found only by bringing them together again.

Before proceeding with this *general* problem, it should be recognized that both proportions and size are variables in certain *partial* analyses as well. When one factor (or complex of factors) is held constant at an assumed amount while others are varied relative to it, movement along the 'plant' curve involves constant change in proportions and *also* in size (total outlay). This fixed factor analysis is highly important [27] (and certainly unobjectionable!), yet it would be ruled out by a strict interpretation of the dictum that proportions and size must be kept separate.

Our main concern, however, is with the general analysis, in which all factors are variable on the envelope curve. To rule, as is commonly done, that the 'best proportions' are a separate problem the solution of which opens the way to a second distinct problem of scale, defined as the reproduction of these best proportions for all aggregate outlays, is not to break up a complex problem into its parts, but to misconceive it completely. The reason is that the procedure which finds the best proportions yields also the best total outlay and vice versa, for it is the single procedure in both cases of finding the minimum point on the envelope curve. To define the question of scale, as is commonly done, in terms of reproducing these optimum proportions at other outputs (the CP curve) is to create a wholly artificial problem. To go further and rule, as is commonly done, not only that the best proportions are independent of size (coincidence of the CP and envelope curves), but also that (under the perfect divisibility of theory) they are no better at one size than at another (collapse of the CP curve to the horizontal), is to 'separate' the two elements

27. It is one of the deficiencies of the indifference curve technique, which by some seems to be regarded as having superseded cost curves, that in it this problem is lost from view.

involved by the extreme but effective expedient of liquidating one of them completely—thereby also wiping out the firm, and creating this time a whole host of artificial problems.

Historically it would appear that this state of affairs has evolved out of the very old practice of interpreting the 'fixed factor' approach to diminishing returns as one involving proportions alone, size being regarded as not changing, probably through unconsciously associating it with the *fixed* factor. For small changes in a variable factor the total outlay for which is in turn small, relative to that for the fixed ones, the error involved in this interpretation may not be great, but by extension it soon becomes prodigious. Thus, if management is 5 per cent, and all other factors 95 per cent, of the total outlay, a doubling of all others not only changes their proportion to management, but virtually doubles the total outlay. *Yet in all such cases, and indeed whenever a fixed element no matter how unimportant can be identified, the common practice has been to attribute the whole result to proportions.*[28] From this it has been an easy step to attribute the whole result to proportions even when there is no fixed factor, as on the envelope curve, so long as the proportions change at all with the changing total outlay.[29] Proportions have now won the day completely: since they explain all economies, it is evident that nothing remains to be explained by scale, and so we have

28. Examples abound; cf., for instance, Boulding, *Economic Analysis* (1941), p. 491; rev. ed., p. 677. Boulding's whole treatment is typical in its rigid insistence on the separation of proportions and size, with the usual result that proportions take over. 'Variability of returns to scale' are not absolutely denied, but are described as 'difficult to prove,' and when mentioned at all are always on the defensive. It is strange indeed that Boulding himself seems only faintly impressed by his own breath-taking example from nature (which ought to convince anyone) of a flea which, increased to the size of a man (proportions constant), not only could not 'jump over the Capitol,' but would collapse on the spot; his own cautious conclusion being only that 'the *possibility* of genuine departures from homogeneity in the production schedule must therefore be taken into consideration.' (P. 493, rev. ed., p. 678; italics supplied.)

29. In the flea example of Boulding this would mean that if the flea were increased in length and breadth by 100, but in height by only 99, its collapse would be attributed *entirely* to the change in proportions and not at all to size!

the dictum that economies (and diseconomies) of scale do not exist. The fact that they do has then been squared with the theory that they do not by the thesis that it is 'imperfect divisibility' which accounts for them by interfering with the right proportions at all outputs; and finally the whole preposterous structure is saved only by the happy expedient of turning it into a tautology.

How much better to have recognized from the first that when both proportions *and* size change, the effect upon costs is the effect of neither alone, but of both together! There is no element of the problem which does not fall readily into place once this has been done.

6. THE INDIFFERENCE CURVE ANALYSIS

The purpose of this section is not to add anything to the foregoing argument, but merely to interpret it in terms of the alternative indifference curve technique. A production function for two factors gives a surface in three dimensions, like a hill rising out of a level plain. It will be helpful to think of Figure 6 as a map, and of the various lines as roads or paths on this hill which rises to the northeast of O, the axes OA and OB being level roads in the plain. Quantities of the two factors are measured east and north along these two lines as indicated, and any point on the map northeast of O represents a certain combination of the factors. We may, for convenience, think of the plain as being located at sea level. The third variable is altitude; and the height above sea level of any point on the hill will represent the amount of product produced (under optimum conditions) by the combination in question. With larger aggregates of factors used as one moves to the northeast, the hill evidently gains in height. Contour lines, showing equal heights above sea level, are familiar to map readers, and the indifference curves labeled I_1, I_2, I_3, and I_4 are such lines, or paths, around the hill. From each of them may be read the different combinations of factors which will produce the same output, equal to the height at which the contour was drawn.

The prices of the factors are taken as given throughout, and we may now assume a given total sum of money and mark off the quantity of factors it will buy. Supposing the sum to be one thousand dollars, if it were spent entirely on factor A it would purchase (say) the quantity OA_1; and if it were spent entirely on factor B, it would purchase (say) the quantity OB_1. If we now draw the straight line A_1B_1 on the map, any point on it will indicate a combination of the two factors which could be purchased

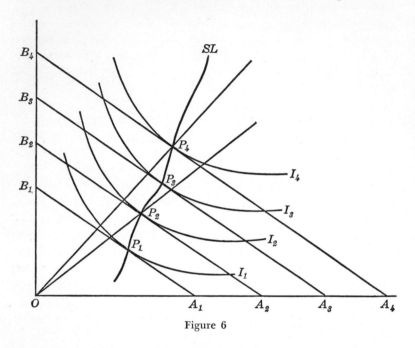

Figure 6

for the sum of one thousand dollars. This straight line will cut across many contour lines and will be tangent to the highest one it touches, the point of tangency giving the highest altitude reached on the path A_1B_1, that is, the largest amount of product which can be obtained for one thousand dollars. A_2B_2, A_3B_3, and A_4B_4, further out from the origin, are constructed similarly for larger total outlays, and similarly each will be tangent to a contour line at its highest point, indicating the maximum output obtainable for the total sum represented.

Since at each of these points of tangency the total product is a maximum for the outlay, and the total cost a minimum for the output in question, the cost per unit will evidently be a minimum, both for outlay and output. Any other point on the constant outlay line involved would give a smaller product for the same outlay; any other point on the indifference curve involved would give the same product for a larger outlay. Each point of tangency corresponds, therefore, to a point on the envelope curve, and the wavy line, labeled *SL* for scale line, which passes through all the points of tangency corresponds to the envelope curve. From it we can read off a series of optimum combinations of the factors for different outputs; and, the heights of the indifference curves on the production surface being known, we can associate each combination with the output it produces.

Since the application of a certain minimum amount of factors is necessary in order to obtain any product at all, one would not, in departing from *O*, begin climbing the hill at once. The scale line does not therefore pass through *O* (although one frequently encounters the conviction that it is 'mathematically' necessary for it to do so), but begins at a point discontinuous from it, as drawn in Figure 6. Nor is there any reason for it to begin in such a way that its extension backward would pass through *O*. This point is of major importance, since the belief that the line must pass through *O*, and the fact that it is usually drawn that way, must contribute substantially to the propensity to regard it as a line of approximately constant proportions, and from this to take the further step of treating the production function as approximately homogeneous.

Let us now consider straight lines from the origin through various points on the scale line. For illustration only two are drawn in Figure 6, through points P_2 and P_4. Each of these paths up the mountain involves a constant ratio between the factors (equal, of course, to that obtaining at its intersection with the scale line). They are the equivalent of our *CP* curves in Figure 4: just as any output except the one at a point of tangency of the two curves in Figure 4 may be produced more cheaply by moving from the *CP* curve to the envelope curve, so here any output on a constant proportions line, except at its point of intersection with the scale line, may be produced more cheaply by moving along an indifference curve to the scale line. Or, alternatively, the same outlay can be made to produce more product by moving along a constant outlay line of the AB type to a higher altitude at its intersection with the scale line. This will be true no matter on which side of the scale line the constant proportions line lies; that is, whether, in walking up the hill from O along the path OP_2, the scale line lies to the right (before P_2 is reached) or to the left (after P_2 is passed). The scale line is always the optimum.[30]

Since homogeneity involves the relationship of all three variables to each other, it is impossible to tell from Figure 6 whether its conditions are fully met, without knowledge of the altitudes involved. For homogeneity in the first degree, it would be necessary for the scale line, under every possible assumption as to the prices of the factors (hence the slopes of the AB curves), to be a straight line passing through O (as OP_2 and OP_4, not as SL), not only in the two dimensions pictured, but also in the third one of altitude. This would mean that, as one walked up the hill from O in any direction whatever, keeping a straight line on the map, the gradient of his path would never change. (It would, of course, in general, be different in different directions.) If this were true, it would follow that at any point (combination of factors) whatever on the surface, the total product would be exactly used up if each factor were paid according to its marginal productivity (Euler's theorem).

The condition is equivalent to constant unit cost, and we know from our earlier analysis that the production function of the

30. 'Plant' cost curves are derived, of course, from cross sections of the surface taken so that one factor is held fixed. Thus if factor B is the plant and factor A is variable, the plant curve tangent to the envelope curve at P_2 would be derived (as in Figure 1) from the factor prices combined with physical data given by the path on the surface traced by a line through P_2 parallel to OA (not drawn in the figure). If A were fixed and B variable, the line would be parallel to OB. The 'profile' of such lines, as seen from OA or OB, and usually divided through by the quantity of the variable factor for each output, is the curve common in presentations of the fixed and variable factor approach to diminishing returns. From any point on such paths (except their intersection with SL) it would evidently be advantageous to move along either an indifference contour or a constant outlay line in Figure 6 until SL was reached.

firm is not of this type. On the contrary, not only do the proportions of factors change in the scale line path, as in *SL* as drawn,
but the gradients of the constant proportions paths (as with most
hills in reality) rise slowly at first, reach a maximum, and then
decline. On the actual surface, as one travels on any path, say
OP_4, away from O, he will, after passing the steepest gradient but
before reaching the top of the hill, come to a point beyond which
he will be unable any longer, because of the curvature of the hill,
to see the point O. (The height of his eyes from the ground must
be neglected.) At this point the gradient of his path will momentarily be that of a straight line *through space* from O, and the
production function will be approximately homogeneous for very
small movements along the constant proportions path. There will
be such a point on each of the lines radiating from O, and their
locus (not shown in the figure) may be thought of as the path
which one would follow if he were to move along the hill in such
a way as just barely to keep O from passing out of sight; or alternatively, as the horizon if one stood at O and surveyed the hill. This
is the path of approximate homogeneity (constant cost), and its
intersection with the scale line gives the horizon point on that
line as well; in other words, the minimum point on the U-shaped
envelope cost curve of the firm. Let us assume this to be at P_4.
The constant proportions line OP_4 will now correspond to the
CP cost curve which is tangent to the envelope curve at the minimum point for both.

So far we have considered altitude as physical product, or as
physical product multiplied by a *constant* price, thus conforming
to the situation of the firm under pure competition. Under monopolistic competition the price varies with output, being lower
as the output sold by the firm increases. If each output is multiplied by the price at which it is sold, the resulting *revenue product* may be substituted for physical product in our analysis so far,
and a different surface will result. The contour lines (indifference
curves) of this surface will be the same as before, since the output
(altitude) for each is simply multiplied by its marginal revenue;
and therefore the scale line will not change. (The envelope cost
curve is evidently not altered by a change in the demand curve.)
But the *height* of each contour line is differently defined; and

since the price of the product steadily decreases with greater distance from O, the altitude of this surface (now defined by revenue product) will fall off earlier and more rapidly, with the result that the horizon viewed from O (that is, the line of approximate homogeneity) moves nearer. Let us suppose it to intersect the scale line at P_2, and we have here a point of momentarily constant (minimum) cost of producing, not a unit of product, but a unit of *revenue* product. In terms of our earlier Figure 5 where the base line measures physical product, this is the point of tangency of the demand and cost curves.[31] The constant proportions line OP_2 corresponds to the CP cost curve drawn tangent to the envelope cost curve for the output in question. At this point, the *revenue production* function being approximately homogeneous for small variations along OP_2, the total revenue of the firm will be exactly used up if each factor is paid according to its marginal *revenue* product.

REPLY TO MR. MCLEOD AND MR. HAHN [32]

The arguments of both Mr. McLeod and Mr. Hahn provide striking examples of the familiar and widely held thesis against which my earlier article was directed, and I believe that a complete and satisfactory answer to much of what they have said has already been given. But there are some misinterpretations of my own position to be cleared up, and some new lines of argument

31. Defining the cost curve for this purpose, as explained earlier, to include the remuneration of *all* factors, entrepreneurial as well as hired.

32. Reprinted from the *Quarterly Journal of Economics*, February 1949. The 'Comments' by A. N. McLeod and F. H. Hahn in the same issue should of course be consulted. But those of their arguments which are discussed here are sufficiently indicated so that most of the 'Reply' should be intelligible as it stands. It is reprinted because of new material it contains on the issues involved.

For further discussion of the issues (and defense of the position here taken) see T. M. Whitin and M. H. Peston, 'Random Variations, Risk, and Returns to Scale,' *Quarterly Journal of Economics*, November 1954, and Harvey Leibenstein, 'The Proportionality Controversy and the Theory of Production,' ibid. November 1955.

which afford the opportunity to strengthen and elaborate the case made earlier in several important directions.

One point of agreement should first be noted: we are agreed that the position I am attacking is held not merely by the few economists I was able to mention in my earlier article but very generally. Mr. McLeod speaks of it as 'more in accord with common usage' than my own, and as 'the customary approach'; Mr. Hahn twice links it with 'common sense,' describes it as 'unassailable,' and asserts that 'the only definition feasible is one which identifies perfect divisibility with constant returns.' Similar observations have been made to me by others, both orally and in written communications. Clearly it is not a straw man that is being attacked.

The issue of the real world versus a theoretical 'model' is raised by Mr. McLeod, who reproaches me, saying, 'In effect he simply defines his terms to include only those types of divisibility that are practicable in the real world, and he discussed no other possibility.' [33] To this I plead guilty, and with enthusiasm. I am sorry if I have, as he states later on, 'missed an excellent opportunity of bridging the gap between theory and practice,' for it was precisely my purpose to do something in this direction. My position was and is, in fine, that the theory of this subject is quite unnecessarily and absurdly remote from the real world, and that it should be brought into a closer relationship with it in order to be more useful in explaining this world instead of a world of ant-men.[34] The answer, then, as to whether I am 'speaking of the real world or of some particular theoretical model' is that I am speaking of (a) a 'particular theoretical model' which is (b) modeled closely on the 'real world.' Economic theory needs the firm, because the firm is very important in the real economic world. And it needs both the falling and rising parts of the firm's cost curve for the same reason; explained in terms of the forces *actually* at work, instead of by arbitrary assumptions resorted to in order to put the economies and diseconomies back after they have been made to disappear by still other arbitrary assumptions.

We are told by both critics that the issue is simply and solely

33. *Quarterly Journal of Economics*, February 1949, p. 129.
34. [1957] 'Ant-men' are used as an illustration of divisibility by Mr. Hahn.

one of definition (a common view); and whether or not this is so will be discussed further on. But first it should be observed that fundamentally they hold the much more positive view that there is really no choice in the matter: the very definition of a (homogeneous) factor as a prerequisite to analysis allegedly carries with it the denial of economies and diseconomies of scale. Thus, according to Mr. Hahn, 'the only definition [of divisibility] feasible is one which identifies perfect divisibility with constant returns,' [35] and my 'difficulties' arise simply from sidestepping this crucial matter of defining a factor.

This is at bottom the 'mathematical' argument: the 'formulation of divisibility' which I attack is described as 'a necessary premise [sic] on which such [mathematical] analysis must be based,' [36] and Mr. Hahn thus identifies himself with that school discussed in my article which seems to hold the strange opinion that the very use of mathematics commits one to some *particular* mathematical function. Mr. McLeod is less explicit, but in his last paragraph he speaks of my 'refusal to discuss increments in the amount of a factor used by a given firm on the assumption that the units are of unvarying unit efficiency,' [37] and clearly holds also that to resolve the problem of variations in efficiency as between the 'natural' units of a factor [individual laborers, for instance] by assuming a unit of 'standard efficiency,' is to be led inevitably to the 'customary approach' in which economies and diseconomies of scale vanish.

This is certainly a very common view, and involves a mistake at such an elementary level that it perfectly illustrates the prevailing state of confusion in the subject. But first let me explain why a factor of production was not more explicitly defined in my earlier analysis.

There is not, I think, universal agreement as to how a factor of production should be defined, and I purposely refrained from adopting any *particular* definition in order to leave the argument more general, and hence acceptable, to those holding different views in the matter. Hence the discussion of fractional units was

35. Ibid. p. 131.
36. Ibid. p. 133.
37. Ibid. p. 130.

rather fully developed in order to cover numerous possibilities under different definitions of a factor and different conceptions of 'dividing' it. The result was, as intended, that some of the discussion applies to one definition of a factor and of its division, and some to others. Its purpose, however, was always to look into the *actual* effect of divisibility upon efficiency under different circumstances and with different meanings given to the terms, and to show that there was *no* sense in which divisibility involved the collapse of the cost curve to a horizontal line—excepting, of course, when defined in a question begging way to include this result.

My own belief is that factors of production may be defined differently for different purposes, and that there is no single classification or definition of a 'unit' which is universally and uniquely valid or most useful. For present purposes it is necessary only to accept the definition of my critics, as developed especially by Mr. Hahn, and to show that it does not, as represented, wipe out economies and diseconomies of scale.

Mr. Hahn tells us that 'we must define a factor in a manner such that the marginal rate of substitution between its individual units is equal to unity for all levels of output.' [38] Agreed. But it does not follow from this that efficiency is independent of output. To my knowledge no one has ever held that because individual oranges are interchangeable at the margin, the law of diminishing utility is denied. Similarly, the fact that Smith can be substituted for Jones in any aggregate of factors without effect upon the total product tells us nothing whatever about the shape of the production function. To interpret units of a factor of 'standard efficiency' as meaning uniform efficiency *at all outputs* is as much nonsense as it would be to interpret it as meaning uniform efficiency *in all combinations with other factors*, i.e. as a denial of diminishing returns. One wonders why this latter has not been proposed.

Mr. Hahn would seem to agree, at one stage of his argument, that efficiency is not necessarily independent of output, when, in discussing fractional units of a single factor he points out explicitly that the fact that 'the marginal rate of substitution

38. Ibid. p. 132.

between $1/k$ the amount ka and a' is unity 'is, of course, perfectly compatible with either increasing, constant or diminishing returns to successive amounts ka of the category Fi.' [39] But with the addition of a second factor and the manipulation of a few more symbols, he concludes that 'it is easily seen that . . . there must be constant returns to scale.' In truth, all that the mathematics shows is that the ratio of (say) $1/3$ of factor a to $1/3$ of factor b is the same as that of a to b, which could hardly be disputed. It is also perfectly compatible with either increasing, constant, or diminishing returns to successive amounts of the two factors together (either in the fixed proportion a/b or, possibly, with varying proportions). Indeed, the cancellation from which emerged the equation $c/d = a/b$ even removes the earlier requirement that there be no loss of efficiency through dividing the factors. Such loss is consistent with the final result provided only that it be the same proportionally for both factors.

Mr. Hahn's argument in its various phases rests heavily upon the concept of fractional units, and it should be called to mind therefore that this may be a minor part of the whole problem. The argument is made in my earlier article [40] that without considering fractional units at all the curve is defined for practical purposes by the discontinuous series of dots at the unit breaking points. It may now be added that variations in the efficiency of the 'natural units' may in itself result in virtual continuity with respect to 'efficiency units.' A simple illustration is found in an analogy with dividing a sum of money. With only ten pieces of money: one half-dollar, one quarter, one dime, two nickels, and five pennies, any whole sum between one cent and a dollar may be had without resorting to fractions of coins. Similarly, if the efficiency of Jones is taken as unity, and we find that Smith is equal to 1.13 efficiency units, White to .84, Brown to 1.07, etc., etc., the finest gradations on the scale of efficiency units may be possible without ever dividing a natural unit at all. Such considerations are especially important where natural units *cannot* be divided in any meaningful sense, and therefore where it is futile

39. Ibid. p. 132.
40. Above, p. 180.

to discuss what the efficiency of a fractional unit would be.[41] In any event, the assumption of a standard efficiency unit as a measuring rod for quantitative analysis, when considered together with the actual heterogeneity of natural units, far from collapsing the cost curve to a horizontal line, will instead merely make it more continuous than before, and therefore reduce still further the already limited importance of the issue as to what dividing a unit does to its efficiency.

Perhaps considerations of this sort would spare us the ant-men, although I think we ought to be spared them on general grounds as well. My own earlier mention of division by meat cleavers and the like was expressly in order to turn attention away from such silly examples to economic realities. Yet Mr. Hahn appears to be quite serious, and from his excursions into ant-economics emerges with the conclusion that 'perfect divisibility leaves no room for increased specialization with increased size.' [42] Let me then be equally serious in pointing out what is wrong. There is no simple and single interpretation to be given to the 'division' of a factor; and if Blackstone the magician could establish the necessary link between the human and the ant world by causing Jones to disappear in a cloud of smoke from which would emerge 100 ant-men, this result would no more illustrate 'perfect' divisibility than would the use of the meat cleaver or the employment of part-time workers. In all these cases, including the ant-men, it is still necessary to inquire: *what does the division do to efficiency?* I have never met an ant-man, and therefore cannot give the answer, but I am very skeptical as to whether even 100 of them could do the work of Jones. The point is that such weird concepts do not illustrate perfect divisibility; they only serve as a device for begging the question by *assuming* unchanged efficiency as a part of the definition of an ant-man.

Mr. Hahn twice refers to the 'common sense' view that doubling all factors must double output, and adapts Adam Smith's example of pin manufacture to demonstrate that with twice as many workers and tools 'there is no possibility of increased specialization.' [43]

41. Cf. above, p. 186.
42. Op. cit. p. 134.
43. Ibid. p. 135.

Yet what could be more sensible and more in accord with the most elementary economics than this: that with more workers and tools the division of labor could be carried further? If an office staff expands from five to ten secretaries, always of equal efficiency, each complete with typewriter and desk, is there not typically a further division of labor between them, each acquiring an added proficiency in some particular part of the total work to be done? Again, ten carpenters, each with a standard kit of tools, could certainly organize the manufacture of chairs among themselves by division of labor so that the output would be more than ten times that of a single carpenter and kit. Of course in real life there are typically also qualitative changes in the factors to be taken into account with any substantial change in their amounts, but what 'common sense' is there in supposing that a restrictive assumption which would bar such changes would thereby remove *all* possibilities of specialization?

With reference to co-ordination and management, Mr. Hahn gives no criticism of my argument, but merely reasserts that 'increased complexity is due to the fact that management and entrepreneurship are not increased in the same proportion as are the other factors and to nothing else.' [44] Evidently he believes that an army is no more complex than a squad, no higher controls being needed to hold it together if only every squad is headed by its corporal. But if one grants that more 'co-ordination' relative to other factors *is* needed with a larger control unit, the conclusion reached in my earlier analysis, that failure to provide it by holding proportions constant only makes matters worse, is unescapable. At the close of his discussion of this problem it becomes clear that he is confusing the expansion of an *industry* by the addition of identical firms, with the expansion of the firm itself.

Both of my critics defend tautologies, and Mr. McLeod even finds that my own argument 'may also be dismissed as tautological.' [45] As I seek to discover why, it appears to be because I have rejected tautological definitions, and thereby 'exclude the

44. Ibid. p. 135.
45. Ibid. p. 129.

influence of indivisibility in the sense used by others.' Now if rejecting tautological definitions really is in itself tautological, I am bound to say that there appears to be no escape. But Mr. McLeod has confused two things: (a) the rejection of any definition of divisibility which *requires* that the efficiency of a factor be not affected, which I have done, and (b) the rejection of any definition which *permits* that efficiency be not affected (thereby assuring by definition that it *will* be affected), which I have not done. My inquiry was directed to the question: 'What, if anything, *does* divisibility do to efficiency?' [46] and the appeal is constantly to the facts of the real world. Among the conclusions is that it *may* do nothing at all, *the cost curve then remaining U-shaped for other reasons*.[47] There are no *assumptions* as to efficiency included in any of the several definitions discussed, and hence there is no begging of the question at issue.

Mr. Hahn comments that 'there is no harm in tautologies, indeed a great deal of modern economic analysis makes use of them —one need only look at modern welfare economics, the analysis of the firm or expectations. . .' [48] This, I fear, is only too true, and goes far to account for the emptiness and futility of a great deal that currently passes for 'economic theory.' However, it is not 'rigorous definition' which is at fault, but, in Mr. Hahn's own words, definitions which 'define whole problems out of existence.' This latter might serve as a rough description of 'tautology' in our present context; it is certainly not to be identified, as Mr. Hahn asserts, merely with 'definition.' In the matter at hand, the economist's responsibility is to explain the phenomenon of economies of scale; and in his standard reply he solemnly asserts that his study of the problem has led him to the conclusion that there will be such economies only if there are such economies. This, as I understand it, is tautological, and, although it may not be 'wrong,' it is singularly lacking in nourishment.

I am certain that some will share the view repeatedly expressed by Mr. Hahn that the 'whole problem' is one merely of defini-

46. Above, p. 179; see also top of p. 189.
47. Above, p. 181.
48. Op. cit. p. 136.

tion; and as an aid to the reader in deciding whether it is or not,
I should like to put before him a story attributed to Abraham
Lincoln. When visited by a delegation of clergymen in 1862 urg-
ing him to proclaim the slaves free, he replied by asking them
how many legs a sheep would have if you called its tail a leg.
'Five,' they replied at once. 'You are mistaken,' said Lincoln, 'for
calling a tail a leg doesn't make it so.' If some visiting Martian
should ask how many legs our animal the sheep had, it would
appear to me quite wrong to reply: 'It is simply and solely a
matter of definition; for instance, if the ears are included . . .
but on the other hand, if only the tail. . . etc.' Unless it can be
shown that 'perfect divisibility' (*in some non-question-begging
sense*) removes economies and diseconomies of scale, there would
seem to be nothing but error in attributing such economies and
diseconomies to 'imperfect divisibility.' To call them thus does
not make it so; and, as I hope to have shown earlier, it has actually led to wide ramifications of further erroneous analysis.[49]

49. I should like to add a word of comment on Mr. R. G. D. Allen's brief
discussion of the problem in relation to the formulations of Hicks and
Samuelson. (*Quarterly Journal of Economics,* February 1949, p. 116 and n.)
It is perfectly true, of course, that (a) if all factors are not included (Samuelson), or (b) if one factor is held fixed (Hicks), an explanation is afforded
of why 'doubling the use of all factors does not double the output.' But
to admit only these possibilities seems to me dangerous and misleading, for
it implies that *if* all factors were (a) included and (b) variable, the function
would be linear and homogeneous, which I maintain is quite without foundation. If such expedients as leaving out factors or holding some of them
fixed are necessary in order to make the curve turn up,' I predict that the
linear homogeneous production function, which we seem to agree should
be abandoned, will have a long and healthy existence; for such a position
constitutes a tacit admission that with all factors present and continuously
variable (which seems to be the most 'general' assumption) the function *is*
homogeneous. It evidently involves also a completely different explanation
of the *falling* part of the curve from that given in my analysis.

SPECIAL TOPICS

10

The Impact of Recent Monopoly Theory

on the Schumpeterian System [1]

THE chapter on 'Recent Development' in Schumpeter's *History of Economic Analysis* remained unwritten at the time of his death. It appears that he had, quite naturally in view of its content, left it for the end; and so we are deprived of the systematic evaluation of recent and prevailing trends which he was about to write. Yet he had, of course, already put into print many of his views, and I propose in this short paper to indicate and to comment upon his expressed evaluation of one 'recent development'—that of monopolistic and imperfect competition theories—as found in his two major works of 1939 and 1942. I shall maintain that, in spite of a definite hostility to what he saw as its impact on his own system, his later views on monopoly serve well to illustrate the fundamental compatibility between the two.

It is necessary first to look at the *Theory of Economic Development,* where the underlying structure of his system of thought is to be found. There will, I think, be general agreement (including my own) with the statement by R. V. Clemence and F. S. Doody in their recent book, *The Schumpeterian System,* that 'the circular flow is a model of a purely competitive system. . . . Despite all the theoretical contributions [in connection with mo-

1. Reprinted from the *Review of Economics and Statistics,* May 1951. The essay also appeared in *Schumpeter, Social Scientist,* S. E. Harris, ed., Cambridge, Mass., 1951.

nopolistic and imperfect competition] . . . the Schumpeterian circular flow in its most recent formulation remains essentially what it was in 1911.' [2]

There is only a minor qualification, but it is interesting to look at it. There is in fact surprisingly little insistence in the *Theory of Economic Development* on the competitive nature of the circular flow, and no statement that I can find that it is *necessarily* characterized by 'perfect competition' (the word 'pure' had not yet appeared). The primary concern is with an uninterrupted flow which steadily repeats itself in the absence of entrepreneurial innovation. It seems evident that such a flow *could* embrace monopoly of all kinds and degrees without in the least interfering with its static quality. On page 152 the possibility is explicitly envisaged of 'a permanent monopoly' (clearly, however, identified with the old *industry* concept) from henceforth embodied in the circular flow.

On the other hand, there can be no doubt that the analysis of the circular flow does commonly proceed by 'abstracting from monopoly' (p. 129), so that monopoly revenue becomes a phenomenon only of the innovations which for short periods bring about departures from it. 'Since the entrepreneur has no competitors when the new products first appear, the determination of their price proceeds wholly, or within certain limits, according to the principles of monopoly price. Thus there is a monopoly element in profit in a capitalist economy' (p. 152). Such a 'surplus' in the form of a monopoly profit is only temporary, however, for if it exists, 'a tendency to reorganization in the industry will set in, which will finally restore the rule of the law of cost' (p. 135). Indeed, one of the chief features of the circular flow seems to be the overwhelming tyranny of the 'law of cost' which forbids any surpluses. On page 31 it is proved, apparently with complete rigor by the logic of imputation, that in the circular flow 'net profit cannot exist, because the value and price of the original productive services will always absorb the value and

2. P. 21. For those unfamiliar with the concept of a 'circular flow' it may be explained that the phrase is used by Schumpeter to characterize the functioning of a static economy in the absence of 'development'; it may be taken as synonymous with a static state.

price of the product.' Yet the possibility of ubiquitous surpluses appears at once if only monopoly elements are admitted into the picture; and proof is unwittingly supplied for us by a later demonstration based equally upon imputation theory. On page 143 it is shown that the innovating entrepreneur may be constituted a third original productive factor, and that this factor may have imputed to it as a surplus 'the value of the new products minus the value which could be realized without it.' If we now recognize that the 'new' products, and in fact, *any* products in the system, are typically subjected to a competition of substitutes which varies in its effectiveness and may easily be insufficient to eliminate the monopoly profits, the possibility of such 'surpluses' very generally in the circular flow is established. And of course it is a familiar part of monopolistic competition theory that monopoly often exists without monopoly profits (under conditions of 'tangency'). In summary, imputation theory and the 'law of costs' dispose neither of 'net profits' nor of monopoly elements.

I believe it is fair to say that the chief concern of Schumpeter about the impact of monopolistic competition theory on the circular flow was the question of determinateness. This is foreshadowed in a footnote inserted in 1934 in the *Theory of Economic Development* (the English translation) on page 40: 'This [that an individual acts in one and only one particular way in adapting himself to given conditions] is universally recognized, indeed, only for the cases of free competition and unilateral monopoly in the technical sense of both words. Yet it is sufficient for our purposes. And it has been shown of late that Cournot was not wrong, after all, in holding that there are important cases of determinateness even in the field of "monopolistic competition."' The question of *determinateness* becomes the focal point of his whole discussion of 'Imperfect Competition' in *Business Cycles,* to which we now turn.

The possibility of 'monopoly gains' in the circular flow receives brief explicit mention on page 40; and it is soon stated (p. 41) that 'The first and foremost task of economic analysis is to explore the properties of that system.' 'What we want to learn before anything else' is whether it is determinate, and the proof that it is, is described as the 'magna charta of economic theory.' The 'special case' of perfect competition is first discussed, and it is concluded (p. 56) 'that—subject, it is true, to serious qualifications and reservations—there is a real tendency toward equilibrium states in a perfectly competitive world.' In then taking up 'imperfect competition' it is significant that he aims merely to reassure those who question such a tendency 'when we leave the precincts of the perfectly competitive case,' and comments that his 'sketch of an answer . . . may be omitted by those who feel convinced already.' The ensuing discussion turns mainly on whether and in what degree the various sub-cases under 'imperfect competition' give 'difficulties' on the score of determinateness.

Now it is easy to understand (though not to accept) this emphasis on determinateness if one is seeking to establish a theoretical norm characterized by 'equilibrium' as a point of departure for a theory of business cycles. But I must enter a vigorous protest on two grounds: (1) Even supposing that a case can be made for a generally determinate system which is sufficient 'for our purpose,' or 'for most practical purposes,' it remains true in Schumpeter's own words that *the first and foremost task of economic analysis is to explore the properties of that system.* It is held that a system of 'Universal Monopoly' may be determinate (p. 57), and it may be added that a variety of 'models' characterized by various types and degrees of monopoly elements and influences will also be determinate. But the *determinateness* of a set of equations, important as it is, is only a small part of what we want to know about them; we also want to know what they are if possible, or at least as much as we can about their form and properties. And it would seem that the properties of the economic system, in terms of monopoly and of competition as well as in other terms, would be of prime importance not merely in general, but with specific reference to the kind of 'evolution' it generates, including the cyclical process. (2) Supposing the system not to be determinate in certain aspects or in certain areas, it appears to me to be the job of the economist, as a scientist, to say so—in fact to insist upon giving full importance to the indeterminate properties as well as to the determinate ones. I am myself convinced that oligopolistic elements are very general, and that one of the prime subjects of economic study must be their influence upon prices and upon other economic categories. It appears likely that many situations are indeterminate when account is taken of only the *economic* variables involved, and that they are rendered determinate only by the influence of what would ordinarily be regarded as noneconomic factors. There is nothing surprising about this when we consider that economics deals with only one aspect of a much wider set of social relationships. The revelation that certain 'economic' problems, considered in their own narrow isolation, are 'indeterminate' may be a necessary preliminary to putting them into the wider context which will explain why in the real world they do in fact settle down into some form of stable relationship. To this extent economics simply is not an 'autonomous science' (p. 41) and will only lose in the end by pretending to be. It must seek out the indeterminate as well as the determinate, and carefully avoid the tempting expedient, currently so popular with the mathematicians, of adjusting the formulation of its problems with the *objective* of assuring a determinate answer.

Returning to the main argument, let us pass over the discussion of bilateral monopoly and oligopoly-without-product-differentiation, and examine the conclusions with respect to product differentiation. In view of a generally adverse judgment, it should not be overlooked that the possible seriousness of the impact of this factor upon economic analysis is envisaged with rare intuition, and that a number of the routes whereby it is often diminished or dismissed are carefully avoided. Thus, although there is some tendency to speak of the 'creation' of special markets by sellers as a mere strategic or 'short-run' device, there is also the statement that 'Differences in location and other factors which will induce customers to prefer, rationally or a-rationally, one firm to another, are of course unavoidable, irrespective of any intention to create them. And there is simply no such thing as a homogeneous commodity motor car or liver pill' (p. 63). A footnote at this point presents criticisms of prevailing treatments of 'irrational behavior of consumers' and of product differentiation as necessarily wasteful, either from the standpoint of buyers or of society, with which I heartily concur, and which I have myself criticized elsewhere [3] as features of the Robinsonian theory, not my own. Furthermore, in spite of a general disposition to pass off the phenomena of monopolistic competition as frictional, in the sense of disappearing in the long run, the statement is made that 'it is not denied that, where circumstances are favorable . . . the consequences predicated . . . may even in the long run prevail' (p. 66); and further that 'we do not think, as Mr. Hicks seems to do, that we can now contentedly return to the Marshallian apparatus' [4] (p. 66n.).

However, the general conclusion is that, although 'one corner of business reality is adequately taken care of by this theory,' 'In general . . . that is not so' (p. 64). The corner that is taken care of appears to be that segment of business reality where there is no 'oligopolistic difficulty,' and where we therefore have 'acceptable approximations to straight monopoly' (p. 64). The *general* case, *not* adequately taken care of by the theory, appears to be that of product differentiation combined with oligopoly, described in terms of the sales of one firm being 'a function of the behavior both of the firm itself . . . and of all the other firms in the field' (p. 64). I should like first to concur in the judgment as to the quantitative importance of this last case: the evidence seems overwhelming that it constitutes a major sector of the economy.

Yet the arguments by which it is disposed of simply do not dispose of it at all. The main one is that 'the demand curves for the products of individual firms will, in general and in the long run, display a high elasticity' which 'will enforce approximate realization of the results of perfect competition . . .' (p. 65), followed however by the comment (which must be obvious) that 'Strictly, this applies only to cases which differ from perfect competition in nothing else but product differentiation.' Thus are we brought back to the 'corner' already 'taken care of' because of the absence of the 'oligopolistic difficulty'—the case is simply

3. Essay 5 above.
4. The reference to Mr. Hicks is to his article, 'Annual Survey of Economic Theory: The Theory of Monopoly,' *Econometrica*, 3:1 (1935). But the fundamental reason for Mr. Hicks' position is found in *Value and Capital* (see above, p. 62n.10).

that of monopoly with the location of each seller's demand curve independent of his movements along it. An 'exception' is then made for what had *appeared* to be the case under discussion, viz. product differentiation plus oligopoly, with the conclusion that, although it may be important in particular industries, 'it is hardly ever important enough to interfere substantially with the working of the system as a whole' (p. 65), from which it would appear not to be the general case at all! The only addition made at this point to the general discussion of oligopoly elsewhere is that a demand curve thus conditioned (by oligopolistic interdependence)—'as brittle as that—had better be discarded altogether.' It is in fact 'discarded' in my own discussion of this case (*Monopolistic Competition,* pp. 100ff.) in that it becomes only a landmark indicating the lower limit of the range of oligopolistic solutions; and in some types of solutions it is completely irrelevant. Wherever oligopoly is a factor, with or without product differentiation, the demand curve of an individual seller is not in the nature of the case a datum, unless it has been made so by an appropriate subassumption as to the behavior of the oligopolists. Schumpeter, having taken the position that the demand curve should be discarded in this case of product differentiation plus oligopoly, certainly gives no indication of how the case is to be analyzed and fitted into the whole picture—except perhaps in the end to say, as was indicated above, that it is not very important anyway.

Let us now comment briefly on the proposition that the demand curves are highly elastic. (Let us assume that Marshallian curves are meant; my own—but never Mrs. Robinson's—are frequently of this type.) Clearly, the general theory of monopolistic competition, including as it does *all* sellers except those in purely competitive markets, embraces elasticities ranging from infinity to the lowest value to be found. And since there are all degrees of substitutes, both actual and potential, with conditions varying widely in different areas of the economy, it is quite impossible to make sweeping generalizations as to elasticities. This will appear at once when we bear in mind that monopolistic competition (but not Mrs. Robinson's imperfect competition) explicitly embraces *all* monopoly (my pp. 68, 74; Mrs. Robinson's position is discussed, pp. 208-12), and is not to be associated merely with those situations where 'close' substitutes are a possibility. But even if we restrict our attention to cases where demands are highly elastic, there are still two more observations to be made: (1) the results will be quite different from those of pure competition, if for no other reason because of the presence of two new and disturbing variables—the product itself and selling costs; and (2) even without these, although *price* may not be greatly divergent from what it would be with a perfectly elastic demand curve, outputs, profits, and other features of the system may be strikingly different.

Several other points are added, of which only one can be discussed: that problems of short-time strategy appear under monopolistic competition which would be absent under perfect competition, and which in particular constitute the correct explanation of excess capacity, 'rather than . . . any particular properties of normal equilibrium in monopolistic competition.' The emphasis on short-time strategy is important, especially when it is realized that what happens in the short run affects the long-run equilibrium itself; but what appears to be the conclusion, that on the whole the phenomena of monopolistic competition are *merely* short run (pp. 67 and 64n.), cannot be accepted. The particular matter discussed at this point is 'excess capacity,' which at once introduces major problems of definition. But what is at issue is not at all the phenomena discussed in *Monopolistic Competition* (pp. 100-109), but merely that of equilibrium under conditions of diminishing average unit cost for the firm. I believe it is not too much to say that the key to an understanding of most of Schumpeter's reluctance to accept the schema and conclusions of monopolistic competition lies in his *much earlier* rejection of descending long-period cost curves (cf. *Business Cycles,* p. 91 and n.). Such curves he attributes again and again merely to lumpiness of factors, and argues (p. 90) that 'disregarding the effects of lumpiness or smoothing them out by drawing a monotonic curve through the alternating stretches of rising and falling average costs, we should, strictly speaking, get a curve which would for a small individual firm, be parallel to the quantity axis, i.e. constant unit costs.' In accord with this view he also held that utilization of a *plant* at outputs less than that corresponding to the minimum point on its cost curve is not consistent with long-run equilibrium; and it is largely for this reason that he concludes that what 'is more than anything else responsible for our impression of a prevalence of decreasing cost . . . is innovation, the intrusion into the system of new production functions which incessantly shift existing cost curves' (p. 91).

Now there is no intention to deny this latter force; but it should not be given an artificially high value for what is certainly a false reason. What is at issue is the correct explanation of the descending phase of the long-run average unit cost curve of the firm. In a footnote on page 64, the distinction is made between a U-shaped long-run average cost curve and an envelope curve which I am unable to follow because to me they are the same thing, since the envelope curve merely involves the variability of all factors in the long run. My own views on these matters are developed at length elsewhere [5] and cannot be elaborated here. Whatever lumpiness exists in fact must be a part of the analysis of these curves, but it is easy to show that the long-run average cost curve has a descending phase even under the assumption of perfect divisibility (barring the usual tautological definition of divisibility, which simply removes the problem wthout answering it). The minimum points of the plant curves cannot lie on it except at its own minimum point. This is the old envelope curve controversy, and by now we know the answer.[6] One final comment: U-shaped cost curves are *incidental* to the theory of monopolistic competition in the same way that the shapes of cost curves generally are incidental to a theory of pure competition; they naturally affect the result when they are introduced, but the fundamental idea of blending monopoly and competition does not involve them.

Only brief space remains for a discussion of *Capitalism, Socialism, and Democracy*. For the most part the arguments appearing are the same as or similar to those already discussed, and attention will be directed to only a few points of difference. There are in the first place statements which contrast strongly with the basic defense in *Business Cycles* of perfect competition as the

5. Essay 9 above.
6. [1957] See above, p. 175.

theoretical norm. To quote: 'If we look more closely at the conditions . . . that must be fulfilled in order to produce perfect
competition, we realize immediately that outside of agricultural
mass production there cannot be many instances of it . . . [ex-
amples] . . . Thus we get a completely different pattern which
there seems to be no reason to expect to yield the results of perfect competition and which fits much better into the monopolistic
schema. In these cases we speak of Monopolistic Competition. . . .
As soon as the prevalence of monopolistic competition or of
oligopoly or of combinations of the two is recognized, many of
the propositions which the Marshall-Wicksell generation of economists used to teach with the utmost confidence become either
inapplicable or much more difficult to prove.'

However, in spite of this and similar statements, most of the
lines of argument by which the *un*importance of monopolistic
competition in the circular flow was argued earlier again put in
their appearance somewhere or other. What seems to have happened is a shift of emphasis away from statics to dynamics,
'. . . the problem that is usually being visualized is how capitalism administers existing structures, whereas the relevant problem
is how it creates and destroys them' (p. 84). It had been foreshadowed in *Business Cycles* that the area in which monopolistic
competition theory really came into its own was that of 'new
firms producing new commodities or old commodities by new
methods' (p. 67), and it is this problem which now moves into
the center of the stage. It is at once linked with the two new
variables introduced by monopolistic competition, the product
itself and selling costs: 'Economists are at long last emerging from
the stage in which price competition was all they saw. As soon
as quality competition and sales effort are admitted into the
sacred precincts of theory, the price variable is ousted from its
dominant position,' and we have 'the kind of competition which
counts,' . . . viz. that 'from the new commodity, the new technology, the new source of supply, the new type of organization.'
The new products enjoy a monopoly position—the familiar analysis going back to *The Theory of Economic Development*—and
monopoly comes in for a substantial defense as the engine of
economic progress. Into this thesis we cannot go in detail, and

especially the extent to which monopoly profits may be defended as an *incentive* to change and innovation. However, the general theoretical conclusion that 'the bulk of what we call economic progress is incompatible with [perfect competition]' (p. 105) would seem to be incontrovertible. And it follows that 'In this respect, perfect competition is . . . inferior [to the " 'monopoloid' species of capitalism"], and has no title to being set up as a model of ideal efficiency' (p. 106). The consequences for both economic dynamics and welfare theory are evident.

To many, certain features of the theory of monopolistic competition would indicate that it is *necessarily* a theory of change, to be associated with dynamics rather than with circular flows. Among these features are the constant change in the product which is implied by its recognition as a variable in the problem, the incessant shifting about of demand curves with the recognition of selling costs as an essential element in the structure of theory, and the fact that each change in the number of producers involves a corresponding change in the number of products in the system (by contrast with either pure or imperfect competition, where the number of products in the system is a datum). Nevertheless, it is clearly possible, and it is also essential, to define the *static* theoretical norm to include monopoly as well as competition, since it seems true beyond question that if the economic system were actually to 'settle down,' there would be nothing in the process to diminish the importance therein of either product heterogeneity or oligopoly.

In summary, while criticizing most of the grounds on which Schumpeter sought to diminish the importance of monopoly elements and to preserve perfect competition as the static norm, I have also sought to indicate his perception of their overwhelming importance in a theory of change. In spite of many—and important—differences between his system and my own, the two systems have always seemed to me essentially harmonious in the sense that their differences could easily be resolved, and that a marriage between them would be most fruitful, at least in congenial day-to-day living, and possibly even in the production of economically handsome offspring.

11

An Experimental Imperfect Market [1]

1. INTRODUCTION

IT is a commonplace that, in its choice of method, economics is limited by the fact that resort cannot be had to the laboratory techniques of the natural sciences. On the one hand, the data of real life are necessarily the product of many influences other than those which it is desired to isolate—a difficulty which the most refined statistical methods can overcome only in small part. On the other hand, the unwanted variables cannot be held constant or be eliminated in an economic 'laboratory' because the real world of human beings, firms, markets, and governments cannot be reproduced artificially and controlled. The social scientist who would like to study in isolation and under known conditions the effects of particular forces is, for the most part, obliged to conduct his 'experiment' by the application of general reasoning to *abstract* 'models.' He cannot observe the actual operation of a *real* model under controlled conditions.

The purpose of this article is to make a very tiny breach in this position: to describe an actual experiment with a 'market' under laboratory conditions and to set forth some of the conclusions indicated by it. The experiment has been carried out in a number of classes in economic theory, with the students offering

1. Reprinted from the *Journal of Political Economy*, February 1948. An added comment [1957]: From the fact that the market studied extends over time and that each transaction is 'dated' within the period of time, it would appear to me that the analysis and conclusions of this essay may have some significance for economic dynamics.

themselves up as the guinea pigs. It was actually designed to illuminate a particular problem which I had analyzed earlier in abstract terms,[2] viz. that of the effect of deviations from a perfectly and purely competitive equilibrium under conditions (as in real life) in which the actual prices involving such deviations are not subject to 'recontract' (thus perfecting the market), but remain final. It was designed also as a pedagogical experiment; and in my own experience has been found stimulating and instructive to students both (a) for their actual participation as buyers and sellers in a market mechanism and (b) for the many comparisons afforded, both of similarity and of contrast, between the laboratory market and its diverse counterparts in the real economic world. Pedagogy to one side, however, it has in its present form, yielded at least some 'scientific' results. It is evidently capable of substantial variations and might possibly be extended and adapted to other problems.

2. Description of the Experiment

The participants are informed that they are to take part in a 'market,' approximately half being buyers, the other half sellers. Under the simplest conditions, usually followed, each person deals in only one unit of the commodity. Cards are passed out on which are written either 'B' or 'S,' for 'buyer' or 'seller,' and a figure defined as the Marshallian demand price or supply price, as the case may be. Thus a person receiving a card marked 'B-36' would be willing to pay as high as 36 but no higher in purchasing his unit; 'S-20' would be willing to sell his unit for as low as 20 but no lower. Each participant will naturally not reveal the figure on his card but will bargain, seeking to obtain as great an advantage as possible. An interval is allowed within which the participants move about seeking to conclude bargains with each other, and a warning is given before the market ends, so that those who have been holding out for a better deal may come to an agreement, if possible. As rapidly as contracts are concluded, they are reported at the desk, tickets are surrendered, and the bargains are recorded in sequence. A convenient way to record

2. 'Note on Deviations from Equilibrium,' *Monopolistic Competition*, p. 25.

them is in three columns headed 'B,' 'S,' and 'P,' giving for each bargain the buyer's limit, seller's limit, and price. The last item of price has usually, but not always, been written on the blackboard as reported, so that this information (analogous to the ticker tape for the stock market) might have its influence on subsequent bargaining. When the market is declared ended, all tickets are turned in for those unable to conclude a bargain, since these are obviously necessary to complete the demand and supply schedules. The data may then be read back to the class with instructions to discover what the price and sales volume would have been had the market been perfect, and to compare them with the average of actual prices and with the actual sales volume.

With few exceptions, the problem has been presented in terms of straight-line demand and supply curves of the same slope but opposite sign. In the example here given, tickets for both buyers and sellers ranged from 18 to 104, taking even numbers only. Since there were more tickets than there were participants, the B and S cards were shuffled separately, and the requisite number of each was dealt off the top. This procedure leaves irregular random gaps without altering the essential symmetry of the schedules, and enables the instructor to say truthfully that he does not himself know in advance what the equilibrium price is.

3. ANALYSIS OF RESULTS

Let us now follow through an example. The figures are given in Table 1. Actual sales were 19 units, and the average of actual prices was 52.63. The perfectly competitive figures are obtained by arranging buyers' tickets in descending order, and sellers' in ascending order, and placing the two columns in juxtaposition, as at the right of Table 1. The schedules are shown graphically in Figure 1. Perfectly competitive sales are found to be 15, substantially less than the actual figure; and the equilibrium price is found to be indeterminate between 56 and 58, or, to take a single figure, 57, which is substantially more than the average of actual prices.

These divergences are clearly without significance when only a single example is considered, since they might easily have re-

TABLE 1

TRANSACTIONS			MARKET SCHEDULES	
B	S	P	B	S
56	18	55	104	18
54	26	40	102	20
72	30	50	94	26
84	34	45	90	28
44	44	44	86	30
102	42	42	84	32
80	20	40	82	34
60	28	55	80	36
48	40	45	76	40
76	36	45	74	42
94	52	55	72	44
68	58	62	68	46
66	46	55	66	50
82	32	58	60	52
90	72	72	58	54
104	54	54		
52	50	50	56	58
86	64	64	54	62
74	62	69	52	64
			50	66
LEFT OVER			48	68
			44	70
38	68		38	72
50	66		34	74
28	82		32	78
32	88		30	80
18	90		28	82
26	84		26	84
22	104		24	88
24	78		22	90
30	80		20	98
20	98		18	104
34	74			
58	70			

Equilibrium sales. 15

Actual sales. 19

Equilibrium price. 57 (56-58)

Average of actual prices. 52.63

sulted from mere chance. Let us therefore look at the summarized results of the forty-six times the experiment has been carried
out. In these forty-six experiments the actual volume of sales was

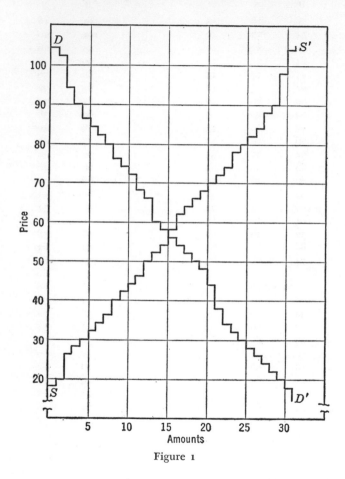

Figure 1

higher than the equilibrium amount forty-two times and the
same four times. It was never lower. The average price was
higher than the equilibrium price seven times and lower thirty-
nine times. The schedules used—hence the equilibrium values—
were different in each example, and no statistical computations

for the entire sample of forty-six experiments have been made. The simple figures given, however, clearly indicate divergences not to be attributed to chance. They require explanation.

The characteristic excess of actual sales over the equilibrium amount, as indicated by the demand and supply curves, is explained by the fact that imperfections introduce prices above and below the equilibrium figure. At prices above it some 'normally' excluded sellers may make bargains; at prices below it some 'normally' excluded buyers may make bargains. For instance, the seller whose limit is 58—and who would not make a sale if the market were perfect—has a good chance to make a bargain with *any* of the normally included buyers; sellers 62, 64, and 66 with any of the first thirteen buyers; seller 68 with any of the first twelve buyers, and so forth. Sellers 58, 62, 64, and 72 did, in fact, dispose of their units in the example before us. Similarly, buyers 56 and 54, normally excluded, can make a bargain with *any* of the normally included sellers; buyer 52 with any of the first fourteen sellers; buyer 50 with any of the first thirteen sellers, and so forth. Buyers 56, 54, 52, 48, and 44 did, in fact, make purchases in the example before us. Since every buyer and seller will, by hypothesis, make a bargain within his limit if possible, the volume of sales can never fall below the equilibrium amount; [3] and the bringing in of normally excluded buyers and sellers almost always carries it above this amount, as in the present example. The conclusion seems unavoidable that 'price fluctuations render the volume of sales normally greater than the equilibrium amount which is indicated by the supply and demand curves,' [4] a proposition which must be of substantial im-

3. In perhaps four or five cases out of the forty-six it was discovered—when the unused tickets were turned in at the close of the market—that a single transaction which could have been made had not been made. In other words, the highest remaining buyer's ticket was higher than the lowest remaining seller's ticket. In each of these cases the bargain was ruled as having been made at the midpoint between the two figures. This procedure was justified on the ground that there was pressure for time, and that the buyer and seller would, in fact, have found each other if the market had lasted longer. The reader may judge for himself the legitimacy of this procedure—the results would have been changed only slightly had it not been resorted to.

4. Since I reached this conclusion on the basic of abstract argument in

232 A MORE GENERAL THEORY

portance in applying theory to the real economic world, since all actual markets, whether purely or monopolistically competitive, are more or less imperfect.

Although no *pair* of normally included buyers and sellers can fail (by hypothesis) to make a bargain, individual buyers *or* sellers, normally included, may so fail, as did buyer 58 in the present example. In a perfect market he would have made a purchase; yet, before he actually did so, all those with whom he might have made a contract had committed themselves with others. Such exclusion has happened for a single normally included buyer or seller perhaps ten to twelve times out of the forty-six trials. It might conceivably happen for more than one (always on the same side of the market)—as, for instance, in the present example if seller 28 had made a bargain with buyer 50 instead of with buyer 60, in which case both buyers 58 and 60 would have been excluded at the end.

This possible exclusion (by imperfections) of normally included buyers or sellers was first revealed by the experiment, which thus served to correct an erroneous statement,[5] carelessly made on the basis of purely abstract analysis, that such could not be the case. This may be meager fruit from our 'laboratory' method, but it proved at the time exciting at least to the writer and to one particular group of students.

What now explains the characteristic tendency of prices to be

1933 (op. cit. p. 27), I have never seen it challenged, with the single exception of a brief critical comment by R. F. Harrod in the *Economic Journal* (December 1933, p. 666). Mr. Harrod believes that I have 'slipped into error' and that the argument 'would be appropriate to a simultaneous manifold of prices, but not to a variation of prices through time.'

It will appear from the latter portion of this present article how the argument does apply, at least under certain assumptions, to the variation of prices through time; but this phase of the matter was not made explicit in the earlier brief treatment to which he took exception. I believe that his point is not damaging but shall not attempt to discuss it in detail, since he himself might not make it against the argument as now developed. I might add that the time analysis below is entirely a by-product of the laboratory market.

5. Op. cit. (1st ed.), p. 27: 'Since none of the normally included buyers and sellers can by any circumstance be left out. . . .' The statement is corrected in subsequent editions.

lower than the equilibrium figure, as witnessed by the price average being lower thirty-nine times and higher only seven times out of the forty-six trials? By contrast with the characteristic excess of sales just discussed, there seems to be nothing in the problem as defined which would account for it—at least, neither the writer nor any one of hundreds of students who have participated in the experiment has been able to find anything. Several plausible explanations *not* related to the mechanics of the problem have indeed been advanced but, before stating them,

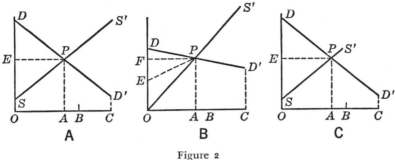

A   B   C

Figure 2

it will be instructive to note several ways in which a bias (upward or downward) *might* have been introduced into the conditions of the problem itself, as indicated by the shapes and lengths of the schedules. For this purpose simple diagrams are useful.

The demand and supply curves for the problem were always approximately as shown in Figure 2, *A*, where evidently—granted equal bargaining power and skill on both sides—one would expect *average* prices to show no systematic deviation from *AP*.

If the curves had been shaped as in Figure 2, *B*, the demand curve being much flatter than the supply curve, the midpoints between successive normally included buyers' and sellers' limits would lie on *EP*, and their average is evidently $(OE + OF)/2$, or less than *AP*. Taking in normally excluded buyers and sellers represented by *AB* and extending *EP* accordingly would raise this figure; but it would equal *AP* only when *all* excluded buyers and sellers were regarded as influencing the actual prices by their offers and attitudes. It seems clear that those farthest to the right would have, at best, an influence less than those normally included and, therefore, that curves of this shape would give a downward bias to average prices. Similarly, the manner in which a steep demand curve and a flat supply curve would indicate an actual average higher than AP is evident.

Again, if either curve had been shorter than the other, bias would have resulted. Thus if, as in Figure 2, C, the supply curve were cut short as shown—although there would be no bias if only those buyers and sellers to the left of B were considered—the presence of buyers from B to C would tend to pull prices down. Similarly, if the demand curve were shorter than the supply curve, there would be a tendency for the presence of more suppliers with higher limits to pull prices upward.

To repeat, however, the curves were generally symmetrical, as in Figure 2, A. How, then, can the downward bias in the results be accounted for? Three explanations have been given: (1) College students are, on the whole, more used to being on the buyer's side of the market than on the seller's. Those receiving buyer's tickets are therefore likely to feel more natural and to bargain more effectively. A corollary would be that, if the experiment were tried with a group of stockbrokers, who deal constantly on both sides of the market, the bias would be eliminated. (2) The markets with which students are mostly familiar (even though from the buyer's side) are retail markets, where, as a matter of market technique, there is no bidding on either side but a placing of prices upon goods by sellers. In the experiment the sellers therefore would have a strong tendency to look at what was formally defined as their lower limit, or *supply price*, as really a *price*. If they sold at anything at all above this figure, they would feel that they had done very well indeed and would be unlikely to press for a greater advantage. A corollary to this explanation would be that if the experiment were tried with a group of employers in an unorganized labor market, where prices (wages) are named by the buyers (employers) and accepted or rejected by the sellers (laborers), there would be an upward, rather than a downward, bias.[6] (3) In real life, buyers come into a market with money

6. Strictly speaking, it would be necessary for the market experience of the participants in this case to be dominated by the labor market rather

or general purchasing power which will still serve them in other markets if they fail to make a purchase in this one. Sellers, on the contrary, come into a market with goods for which, in general, they have little or no use themselves and which they are therefore eager to convert into money. Whatever may be the effects of such considerations in various markets in the real economic world, they may have unconsciously affected the participants in the experiment. A corollary would be that, if the problem had been defined somehow in terms of a barter of two commodities instead of in terms of a sale for a money price, there would have been no bias.[7]

It may be added that, in several instances, a first price either above or below the equilibrium was followed by others similarly above or below. Of course, no causal relation is proved by such sequences; but it is at least possible that—since no one knows what the equilibrium price is (incidentally, a very realistic feature of the laboratory market)—the first bargain was interpreted as near the equilibrium figure and hence mistakenly followed as a guide by others. This factor would evidently afford no explanation of bias in a large number of examples, since early prices would in repeated experiments occur both above and below the perfectly competitive figure.

All the sources of possible price 'bias' that have just been discussed would be quite without influence if the market had been perfect. This is true of both the shapes and the lengths of schedules (Figure 2, B and C) and of 'bargaining power,' the myriad aspects of which have been only suggested by the three possible explanations of a downward bias in our particular problem. The conclusion must be that important forces present in *actual* (always imperfect) markets may be wiped out by the perfectly competitive assumption—forces which produce not random deviations but systematic and predictable departures from 'perfectly competitive' norms. Such forces must be given their due importance in defining the norms toward which prices 'tend.' They would

than by other (such as retail) markets, in which they would also take part in real life. A similar reservation should be made under (1), above.

7. If any reader can offer other (plausible) reasons than these three, I should be interested to hear them.

presumably cause the same or similar deviations from the norms of perfect monopolistic competition as from those of perfect competition in the case at hand.

4. A 'MOVEMENT TOWARD' EQUILIBRIUM?

In Marshall's description of equilibrium in a corn market he says that "unless they [the two sides] are unequally matched— unless, for instance, one side is very simple or unfortunate in fail-

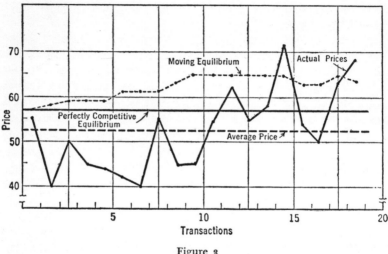

Figure 3

ing to gauge the strength of the other side—the price is likely to be never very far from 36s. [the equilibrium figure]; and it is nearly sure to be pretty close to 36s. at the end of the market.' [8] It may be of interest to note that no tendency for prices to move toward equilibrium during the course of the market or for the last price to be closer to equilibrium than earlier ones is discernible in the data of our experiment.

In Figure 3 the successive prices are plotted in relation to the equilibrium figure of 57 (also in relation to the average figure of 52.63 and to a 'moving equilibrium' to be explained shortly).

8. Alfred Marshall, *Principles of Economics*, p. 333.

The trend of prices during the market is evidently upward, thus correcting the earlier bargains at low figures. But, after what might appear to be a 'movement toward equilibrium' in the eleventh to fourteenth transactions (prices 55, 62, 55, 58), there are again wide deviations and a final price upon which the market closed, which, if anything, is striking for its divergence from equilibrium. Among the other forty-five examples, the most diverse patterns appear, with no apparently predominant tendencies to be noted.

It may be recalled that prices were sometimes written upon the blackboard as deals were completed and sometimes not; and it might be thought that a tendency toward equilibrium could be expected only when this information (analogous to the stock-market ticker tape) was provided for the remaining buyers and sellers in the market (as it was in the case before us). This view, however, reveals an all-too-common confusion between actual prices and the equilibrium price. All that can *ever* be known—either before, during, or after any *real* market—is the actual prices; for no buyer or seller can know any limits other than his own, and data on the mental attitudes of the various buyers and sellers are never available to the economist who would like to construct the schedules. Our laboratory market is of particular significance in that the schedules *can* be constructed after the market has ended, although they are, quite realistically, unknown to the participants during its existence. Actual results can therefore be compared with the hypothetical ones. Information during the market as to the *equilibrium* price would help establish a trend in that direction, but information as to *actual* prices may do the opposite, in so far as they are divergent from equilibrium and are falsely interpreted to be near it. (This was possibly the case in the first half of the market before us.)

My own skepticism as to why actual prices should in any literal sense tend toward equilibrium during the course of a market has been increased not so much by the actual data of the experiment before us—which are certainly open to limitations—as by failure, upon reflection stimulated by the problem, to find any reason why it should be so. It would appear that, in asserting such a tendency, economists may have been led unconsciously to share their unique knowledge of the equilibrium point with their theoretical creatures, the buyers and sellers, who, of course, in real life have no knowledge of it whatsoever.

5. THE SHORT-TIME COMPONENTS OF LONG-TIME MARKETS

Our analysis enables us to compare a 'long-time' market with various types of shorter-time ones contained within it. Such comparisons arose out of the experiment and will be introduced here in the order in which they actually evolved from it.

In the first place, it appeared that there might be recomputed after each transaction the new equilibrium price for the market as it then stood. In this way we recognize what is evident upon reflection—that in any market situation the bargain which has just been completed is no longer a part of the market, the situation henceforth being described by the demand and supply schedules remaining rather than by the initial ones. If the bargain in question was made between a buyer and a seller both of whom were intra-marginal, they would cancel out, and, in spite of their disappearance from the schedules, the equilibrium price for the remainder would be unaffected. But if either the buyer or the seller was either marginal or extra-marginal, the intersection of the schedules would be affected, and, in general, a new equilibrium would be defined. The procedure for discovering the new equilibrium is as follows: remove from the demand and supply schedules—as arranged in Table 1 on the right—the tickets for the first transaction (B-56, S-18), move up the buyers' tickets below 56 and the sellers' above 18 to fill in the gaps, and read off at the margin the new equilibrium figure for the second transaction; then remove the tickets for the second transaction (B-54, S-26) to discover the equilibrium price for the third; and so on. This has been done in Table 2 and is plotted in Figure 3 as the 'moving equilibrium.'

It now appears that the equilibrium, as defined for a market by the original conditions and ordinarily identified with it throughout its entirety, may be quite out of line with a substantial portion of it. In the present example the equilibrium price of 57, indicated by the curves, holds only for the first trans-

TABLE 2

Transaction No.	Limits of Equilibrium Price	Equilibrium Reduced to Single Figure
1.............	56–58	57
2.............	58–58	58
3.............	58–60	59
4.............	58–60	59
5.............	58–60	59
6.............	60–62	61
7.............	60–62	61
8.............	60–62	61
9.............	62–64	63
10.............	64–66	65
11.............	64–66	65
12.............	64–66	65
13.............	64–66	65
14.............	64–66	65
15.............	64–66	65
16.............	62–64	63
17.............	62–64	63
18.............	64–66	65
19.............	62–66	64

Average of successive equilibria..... 62.32

action. It rises steadily thereafter until, when the market is half over (after the ninth transaction), it stands at 65, eight points above the initial figure, and its final value (for the last transaction) is 64. Its average is 62.32, more than five points above the conventional conception of equilibrium for the market. It would seem that, whatever the 'tendencies' one might expect toward equilibrium, they would be toward this constantly 'corrected' moving figure rather than toward the initial one. In this sense its average of 62.32 is much more significant than the 'perfectly competitive' 57. On the other hand, the path and average value of the moving equilibrium cannot be discovered from the original conditions alone—it is the product of the actual unfolding of the market.[9]

A second and more important type of submarket arose out of an attempt to discover the supply and demand schedules which set the limits for the *individual* transactions, since these are evidently not governed by the limiting prices in the larger market. Thus the limits set by the original schedules (Table 1) are 56-58, and only one of the actual transactions took place within them— the fourteenth, at the price of 58. The type of submarket just obtained—by narrowing down the original market through removing, one by one, the completed transactions—does not advance us in our quest, for here again only one transaction took place within the limits indicated for it by Table 2—the next to the last one at the price of 64 (limits 64-66). Even the very last transaction, in whose market 'equilibrium sales' are only *one unit,* took place at a price (69) outside the limits (62-66) set by its own schedules! How can such things happen? Cannot some type of submarket be defined which will obey the law of supply and demand within itself?

Let us look for a moment at a real market, such as the stock exchange, where it seems evident that the transactions of a year, regarded as an annual market, may be broken up into months, weeks, and days, and even those of a day into hours and minutes. A market extending for *any* period of time—even ten minutes, as in our classroom problem—is in some sense a summation of markets of still shorter duration. In such a succession of markets, prices change because conditions change. Not only are buyers and sellers constantly dropping out because they have completed contracts, but new buyers and sellers are constantly being added. Also buyers' and sellers' limits are constantly changing as they re-evaluate their willingness to buy or sell in view of changing moods and new information, including the behavior of the market itself. Schedules are constantly shifting, and we now see that

9. Just as no reasons were found in the 'mechanics' of the problem itself for the downward bias in actual prices as compared with 'equilibrium,' so there appear to be no reasons for systematic bias in the relationship of the moving equilibrium to the initial one: its movement upward and its higher average value in the present example are not to be taken as typical.

what appear to be 'imperfections' over any substantial period may alternatively be regarded as a succession of prices under a succession of different demand and supply conditions.

In these respects our classroom example was highly realistic— it was actually composed of a succession of submarkets, in each of which only a fraction of those in the more general market were to be found. Bargaining was going on not only over a period of time but also in numerous places at the same time, between groups ranging from two to half a dozen. There was a continual shifting about of individuals, and each momentary grouping constituted a market in a very real sense, with schedules and limits of its own. May it not now be said that each price was necessarily within the limits of these smaller markets, even though outside those defined by the larger ones?

The answer is 'No,' since (in the absence of recontract) these smaller markets are also imperfect. In the vagaries of bargaining, it is always possible that an actual offer made by someone at a figure outside the limits set by the schedules will be accepted by someone else before it is replaced by a competing offer nearer to or within the limits. For the same reasons as in the larger market, therefore, the actual price or prices in these smaller ones need not lie within the range which, according to their schedules, equates demand and supply.

Let us therefore proceed to a third type of submarket: the still smaller momentary one in which each transaction is made. Before any contract can be closed, *actual* bids and offers must be made. Such bids and offers give us still another set of schedules, whose nature at any moment must be that all bids lie *below* all offers so that the demand and supply curves do not meet and no contract can be made until the curves change. When a bid is raised or an offer lowered to a meeting point so that a contract is closed, this 'market' includes momentarily *within the margin* only a single buyer and seller, both of whom then drop out, leaving again a demand curve (bids) lying at all points below the supply curve (offers). Schedules for such a market are illustrated in Figure 4, where the highest bid is 64 and the lowest offer 66.

This 'market' of actual bids and offers is in a sense more real than any of the others, since the limiting prices which make up its schedules are the only ones which ever receive objective expression. A familiar example is the schedule of bids and offers in the hands of the specialist in charge of each security on the stock exchange. One is tempted to conclude that only when we

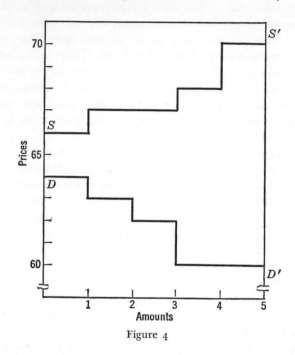

Figure 4

have reached this ultimate and irreducible 'market' will particular prices conform with certainty to the range within which supply and demand are equated, the range in this case being always reduced to a point; but, in fact, the conditions are not quite so severe as this.

The conditions necessary in an imperfect market to assure that a particular price lies within the limits where supply and demand are equated are (a) that all demand and supply prices within the margin be marginal and (b) that they constitute the effective limits to price, the first extra-marginal items lying outside them. The first condition allows for the possibility of what might be called a 'multiple margin' with several sales;[10] more usually, however, the equilibrium volume would probably be limited to a single transaction. If this first condition were not met, a contract might be made with an intra-marginal buyer or seller at a price beyond that of the marginal buyer's or seller's limit. If the second condition were not met, a contract might be made with a marginal (or intra-marginal) buyer or seller at a price beyond the limit set by the first extra-marginal seller or buyer.[11] The market of actual bids and offers is a particular instance under these more general conditions, in which the marginal demand price and marginal supply price are equal at the actual price.

The strange case of the last transaction in our original problem is now seen to be explained as an instance of the failure of the second of these conditions. The market for it may be reconstructed from the leftover tickets in Table 1 plus B-74 and S-62, who made the last bargain. With buyers 74 and 58 (plus others lower) and sellers 62, 66, 68, and 70 (plus others higher) the limits were set by the marginal seller (S-62) and the first extra-marginal seller (S-66). Yet the actual bargain, made by S-62 and B-74, was at the price of 69. In the market of actual bids and offers, either S-62's offer of 69 was accepted by B-74 or the other way around; and clearly, *in this market,* the *actual* offers of S-66 and S-68 were either above 69 or lacking altogether, thus giving conformity to

10. As an example of a 'multiple margin,' there might be five buyers with identical limits of $2.00 and five sellers with identical limits of $1.00 and no other buyers or sellers. The market price would then lie between the limits of $1.00 and $2.00. There might be five different contracts at different prices, but none of them could lie outside the limits set by the market.

11. To illustrate the first possibility, assume buyers 52, 50, and 46 and sellers 46, 48, and 52 (limits 48-50, set by the marginal buyer and marginal seller). Either included seller might contract with B-52 at 51, or either included buyer might contract with S-46 at 47, in either case outside the limits within which supply and demand are equated. To illustrate the second possibility, assume buyers 52 and 48 and sellers 46 and 50 (limits 48-50, set by the first extra-marginal seller and first extra-marginal buyer). Either seller (marginal or first extra-marginal) might contract with B-52 at 51, or either buyer (marginal on first extra-marginal) might contract with S-46 at 47, in either case outside the limits within which supply and demand are equated. The reader may find it helpful to work out these cases for himself in simple graphs.

our second condition. In the *more general market,* however, S-66, the first extra-marginal seller, defined the upper limit to price; the second condition, therefore, was not met. In terms of this larger market the contract at 69 was made possible only by the inactivity of both S-66 and S-68, who were either trying to make a bargain somewhere else at the time or, if immediately present, were holding off, hoping to do better in a moment. (It must never be forgotten that in the problem, as in real life, both the equilibrium price and the remaining number of possible transactions are quite unknown to the participants.)

The phenomena here described in abstract terms are quite familiar in real life, and examples are not hard to find. Suppose A is willing to pay $50\frac{1}{2}$ for 100 shares of a security, but, the last sale being at 50, he enters a bid at that price, hoping to save half a point. Suppose, now, that another buyer, B, whose upper limit is $50\frac{1}{4}$, makes the next purchase at $50\frac{1}{8}$ and that all subsequent sales are higher than $50\frac{1}{2}$ indefinitely, thus excluding A. B was clearly the first extra-marginal buyer at the time he made his purchase (except, of course, in the market of actual bids and offers), and his upper limit of $50\frac{1}{4}$ was the lower limit to the price. Yet the actual sale took place below this at $50\frac{1}{8}$, and he was the one to make the purchase instead of A. This sort of thing must happen over and over again daily on the great exchanges, and I should hazard the guess that many a reader will recognize himself in the unhappy role of *ex ante* included, but *ex post* excluded, buyer A.

Again, let us suppose that a man is willing to go as high as $25,000 for a house but actually bids only $20,000, expecting to get it for this figure. The owner offers to sell at $22,000, but the prospective buyer still thinks he can get it for $20,000 and decides to hold out for a few days more. Meanwhile, the seller's offer of $22,000 is accepted by someone else.[12]

6. An Experiment with Submarkets

Actual data have not been recorded for submarkets of the second and third types discussed above, since such markets have

12. A true case, in which a friend of the author's was the victim.

not, in fact, been determined experimentally. Yet it may be instructive to consider how this might have been done—for example, in the case of the second type (consisting of smaller groupings within a given aggregate)—and to carry through an approximation to the experiment. It would have been possible to create the smaller markets, after the tickets for the larger market had been distributed, by designating a series of smaller groups and recording the data for each. The fact that the demand and supply prices of the participants in such markets would not, in general, be the same as for the larger market (although necessarily lying within the latter as limits) could be taken into account by having the participants submit their individual limits for the smaller market (in secret) to a central authority in each case before the bargaining began. An approach to this procedure, which will indicate in a general way what is involved, may be achieved under somewhat more restrictive assumptions by mechanically dealing out the cards after the manner of solitaire and reading off the results.

For this purpose let us assume (a) that the limits for the larger market (i.e. the figures on the tickets) are also those of the smaller markets; (b) that the smaller markets consist of a succession of subgroupings from the larger one, taking buyers and sellers at random and removing those who make bargains as fast as they are made; and (c) that the equilibrium price indicated by the submarket schedules actually obtains in each case. The rules followed might be subject to further variation in detail, but the example given will illustrate the possibilities.

The same schedules were used (right of Table 1), except that they were shortened by cutting off some of the extreme excluded buyers and sellers: buyers at 30 and below and sellers at 80 and above. This leaves twenty-four buyers and twenty-four sellers. Both the B and the S tickets were well shuffled, and three of each were dealt off to compose the first market, as shown in Table 3. Two transactions resulted at a price of 55 (assumed to be midway between the limits of 48 and 62). Tickets for these two transactions were removed, and those for the excluded buyer and seller (B-48 and S-62) were put back into the pack, which was then reshuffled and the process repeated. There were fourteen markets as indicated in the tables and summarized below them. There was an

TABLE 3

Market 1		Market 2		Market 3		Market 4		Market 5	
B	S	B	S	B	S	B	S	B	S
94	26	84	20	102	58	60	50	76	62
82	40	74	34	—	—	—	—	68	66
—	—	72	64	58	66	52	66	—	—
48	62	—	—	56	68	32	74	66	68

Market 6		Market 7		Market 8		Market 9		Market 10	
B	S	B	S	B	S	B	S	B	S
104	44	56	36	52	42	66	18	86	32
90	70	54	54	—	—	50	28	—	—
—	—	—	—	50	52	—	—	44	46
58	72	34	78	48	68	34	68	32	52

Market 11		Market 12		Market 13		Market 14		Left Over	
B	S	B	S	B	S	B	S	B	S
80	46	—	—	44	30	58	52	48	68
—	—	48	52	—	—	—	—	38	72
44	52	44	68	38	52	48	68	34	74
34	78	38	74	34	72	34	72	32	78

Summary

Market No.	Sales	Price
1	2	55
2	3	68
3	1	62
4	1	56
5	2	67
6	2	71
7	2	54
8	1	51
9	2	42
10	1	45
11	1	49
12	0	....
13	1	41
14	1	55
Total	20	....
Av. price (weighted)	....	57.05

aggregate of 20 sales, which should be compared with a volume of 15 if the same sellers with the same limits had made up a single perfect market, as shown in the schedule at the right of Table 1. The average price was 57.05, which happened in this case to coincide almost exactly with the equilibrium price in the perfect market (taken as midway between the limits).

The same method was tried, taking six buyers and six sellers at a time, with resulting total sales of 19; it was tried again, taking twelve each at a time, with resulting total sales of 17. Again, moving in the opposite direction from the original three each, taking two each at a time was tried, with resulting total sales of 21; and taking one each at a time—a succession of bilateral monopolies—with resulting total sales of 23. It seems evident that, as the number in the submarkets increases from two (the minimum of one buyer and one seller) to forty-eight (twenty-four buyers and twenty-four sellers), where it equals that of the larger market, sales tend to diminish until, when all buyers and sellers are present at once, they equal 15.

A conclusion of some practical import is indicated by this experiment. If, instead of trading continuously in the stock market (for example), buyers and sellers submitted bids and offers hourly to a central authority who would arrange them in schedules and announce the equilibrium price, the volume of sales would be substantially reduced without (it would appear) greatly interfering with anyone's legitimate purchases or sales of securities.[13] If such bids and offers were submitted once a day, the volume would be still further reduced.

As an added factor in reducing volume, it appears likely that manipulation would in some measure be interfered with by such a procedure, since the common technique of making prices move by control over a quick succession of momentary submarkets (consistent with much less or no control in the longer-time market) would be impossible. That part of total sales which is manipulative would therefore be reduced. On the other hand, there

---

13. There would be nothing really novel about such a procedure, since it is, in fact, followed each day for the accumulated bids and offers at the ten o'clock opening of the market in New York.

seems to be no reason why speculation arising out of legitimate differences of opinion as to the relation between present and future values would be interfered with in any degree.

No attempt will be made to give a detailed summary of conclusions, but a final word of caution is necessary. All the analysis above has been carried out in terms of curves of falling demand prices and of rising supply prices, and its conclusions may evidently not be generalized beyond these conditions. The important cases of a fixed (perfectly inelastic) supply, of constant cost, and of decreasing cost have not been touched upon; and, indeed, further considerations (especially in relation to the short run versus the long run) would arise in the interpretation of our curve of rising supply prices as a cost curve. Some slight beginnings have been made in looking into these cases, and it is evident that they pose problems of their own. For instance, in the case of a fixed supply, sales *could* not, by hypothesis, be greater than the equilibrium figure (what happens then?); and in the case of constant cost (indeed, in *all* cases of cost) the familiar problem is raised of the nature of the costs appropriate to the short-run (submarket) and long-run (total market) conditions and of their relations to each other. But consideration of these problems is not included in this paper.

One final comment: an objection may be made to this general line of analysis to the effect that it yields only the expected results of its special conditions—that 'no one would ever have thought that if a market were broken up into a series of individual pairs of buyers and sellers, and dealings run in successive contracts through time, there would be any tendency toward the market-clearing price of a perfect market.' [14] But is this not precisely what *has* been thought? It cannot be overstressed that all *actual* markets are, *in fact,* a succession of contracts separated in time; and actual markets have been thought by generations of economists to be approximately described by the device of a perfect market, which assumes that they are not separated in

14. Specific comment made to the writer.

time. If it seems that strange results have been derived here by subjecting market schedules to arbitrary manipulations, it is replied that the 'manipulations' are intended to be realistic and not arbitrary. Perhaps it is the perfect market which is 'strange'; at any rate, the nature of the discrepancies between it and reality deserve study.[15]

15. [1957] A conclusion drawn from the earlier analysis on which this article was based (see Note 2, above) was that speculation, instead of stabilizing prices, as commonly argued, is more likely to cause 'more and greater fluctuations.' (Op. cit. pp. 28-9.) This conclusion has since been confirmed by elaborate empirical studies of floor trading made by the Trading and Exchange Division of the Securities and Exchange Commission. See especially the Report on Floor Trading, dated Jan. 15, 1945, which concludes in part (p. 35) that 'the tendency for floor trading to be "with the trend" and, therefore, to create or accentuate the trend, is the most typical and most persistent trait of such trading.' The report also deals at length with the way in which floor traders make incomes out of the advantages they are permitted to enjoy over the public; and it recommends (p. 44) 'the prohibition of floor trading in stocks on the New York exchanges.' The recommendation was not enacted, and the report is now out of print. But it may still be consulted in libraries.

12

The Monopoly Power of Labor [1]

ORGANIZED labor in the United States at the present time [1950] numbers about 15 million in round figures. This is a far cry from the three million of 1933 and the still smaller number over a long earlier period during which the ideas and attitudes of both ordinary citizens and economists toward collective action by laborers were being formed. Organized labor can no longer realistically be described as the 'underdog,' or as an 'underprivileged' element of the population. Among labor unions are to be found some of the largest and most powerful organizations in the country, both politically and economically. Professor Slichter has coined the phrase 'a laboristic economy' to bring home to those with a time lag in their thinking the tremendous shift in relative power between labor and 'capital' which has taken place in recent years.

Allowing for families, organized labor as an element in the population is roughly one-fifth of the total. There are in addition millions of unorganized laborers, including agricultural workers, white-collar workers, government and institutional employees, farmers and small businessmen, members of the professions, students, old people, insurance beneficiaries, and receivers of pensions and of interest and dividends. Among these last are many of small incomes, as well as endowed institutions, educational and other, endeavoring to carry out various types of disinterested ac-

1. Reprinted from *The Impact of the Union*, David McCord Wright, ed., Harcourt, Brace & Company, New York, 1951. Reissued, Kelley and Millman, New York, 1957.

tivity. All of these have their real incomes reduced when the prices of commodities produced by organized labor are increased by a rise in labor costs. It may seem strange that such banalities should have to be said. But it is even stranger that anyone saying them should risk being labeled as a person of no social sympathies. Verily, Henry Simons was right in his much-quoted observation that to criticize unionism is like attacking motherhood or the home. Large segments of the American public seem to accept uncritically that what is good for organized labor is good for everyone, and that no one can claim to possess any feeling for his fellow man who does not ally himself completely with the cause of unionism. One wonders in what degree this general attitude may contribute to explaining the fact that the typical university course in 'Labor Problems' is a course in trade unionism, with little, if any, attention paid to the unorganized sector and to the possible means of alleviating the lot of the *really* underprivileged by means other than collective action.

Labor in a broader sense, including unorganized labor and all those who receive 'wages' as the term is ordinarily defined in economics, is clearly a majority of the population (again allowing for families), and it is this fact which no doubt serves most often as a rationalization for the proposition that labor's interest and that of society are one and the same, via the specious identification of the majority with the whole. It is again strange that in these days when we are generally so sensitive to the political and economic oppression of minority racial and other groups, it should need to be asserted that no group, whether a majority or not, has unlimited rights over other elements in society, and that therefore it becomes the duty of every good citizen (including every good economist), in the interest of promoting the *general* welfare, to seek to define reasonable limits for particular elements and to become 'anti' whoever attempts to go beyond them.[2]

2. The standard of 'reasonable limits' in the present paper is not the familiar competitive one; for, in accord with the general theory of monopolistic competition, it involves a recognition of ubiquitous monopoly elements in product markets and of possible monopoly elements in the labor market. It should be said, however, that the chief purpose of this paper is analytical—to examine the extent to which collective bargaining is correctly described as monopolistic. Where policy implications emerge, they involve

This latter appears to me to be such a reasonable position that it is of interest to contrast it with that of Henry Simons, whose famous indictment of 'labor monopoly' is preceded by solemn affirmations of concern only for this segment of society. 'My central interest,' he says, 'and the criterion in terms of which I wish to argue, is a maximizing of aggregate labor income and a minimizing of inequality. If unionism were good for labor as a whole, that would be the end of the issue for me, since the community whose welfare concerns us is composed overwhelmingly of laborers.' [3] Professing less partisanship than Simons, I shall nevertheless emerge with conclusions less sweepingly hostile to collective bargaining than his.

Similarly, Machlup, in an article which is lavish in its praise of Simons, says: 'If monopolistic wage policies "exploited" only the business man and stockholder, but *no one else,* these wage policies would have my blessing. Since there are not even a million business men and stockholders in this country earning $5,000 or more per year, we should recognize that what is good for the sixty million jobholders and job seekers (and their families) constitutes the interest in the nation.' [4]

It is such a professed lack of concern for anyone *but* laborers—and on the ground that nonlaborers are a mere minority—that seems profoundly shocking to me; and I believe I may claim a more fundamental concern for labor than either Simons or Machlup: if there were less than a million laborers, and sixty million businessmen, I should still hold that the laborers deserved protection from overreaching policies on the part of the businessmen. In brief, I see no reason whatever to identify the

mainly a prejudice in favor of allowing labor as much monopoly as anyone else, but not any more.

The general position that the welfare ideal must contain a substantial element of monopoly is developed more at length (with particular reference to product markets) in Essay 5 above.

3. 'Some Reflections on Syndicalism,' *Journal of Political Economy*, March 1944, p. 1.

4. 'Monopolistic Wage Determination as a Part of the General Problem of Monopoly,' in *Wage Determination and the Economics of Liberalism* (Chamber of Commerce of the U. S., 1947), p. 61.

interest of labor with that of society merely because labor is a majority.

Obvious as such a proposition may be, there can nevertheless be no doubt that what I am proposing constitutes a major departure from a strong prolabor bias in traditional liberalism. This being the case, it is of interest to inquire how the liberal tradition, so strongly against monopoly in general, could at the same time have so warmly espoused the cause of collective bargaining. Indeed, this is only one of the many avenues by which one may approach the issue of whether and to what extent collective bargaining *is* monopolistic. It seems to me very clear that traditional liberalism did not regard it as monopolistic and that we must find out the reason why.

On this issue, as on many others, F. W. Taussig may be taken as the embodiment of the best of the liberal tradition. His textbook [5] was widely used and the views it expresses have been of tremendous influence. It was characterized by great sympathy for 'reform' in general, a consistently 'public' point of view, and at the same time an especial concern about the problems of labor and the improvement of the lot of the laboring class. Collective bargaining was in general approved because of the belief that it could not obtain for labor more than a 'competitive' wage, meaning by this the wage at which the existing body of laborers could be absorbed into the system according to the familiar principles of marginal productivity. The overwhelming consideration, here, was undoubtedly the *number* of laborers, and the fact that their *numbers,* either in the aggregate or in any particular trade, would not be changed merely by collective action. Wherever union policies *did* take the form of restricting numbers, as directly in the closed union or indirectly by high initiation fees, etc., such actions were condemned as roundly as were the corresponding restrictive actions on the part of business monopolies. Restrictive union policies were labeled for what they are—actions designed to benefit a particular group at the expense of society in general, and in particular at the expense of other laborers. But collective action as such appeared to be something different from

5. *Principles of Economics,* Macmillan, 1912. Last edition 1939.

restriction. The distinctive feature of this view, and what gave it an appearance of consistency, was its identification of monopoly with the *literal* restriction of output. The error is a simple one, as we now know, but since it is still highly prevalent it had better be made explicit.

A monopolist in any field may seek to increase his total profits by adjusting either the quantity he sells or the price at which he sells it. If he had perfect knowledge of his demand curve the two types of adjustment would blend into one, for he would be able to announce both his higher price and his smaller sales with precision. Since he does not in any case have such perfect knowledge, he must either restrict his output and look to the market to discover at what price it will be taken, or raise his price and look to the market to discover how much he can sell. The two actions are equally monopolistic. The second is the one almost universally followed. The monopolist is able to raise his price because he *controls* the supply, but not because he literally restricts it: within the area of his monopoly there is no one who can undercut his price for the reason that there is no one else who has any supply to offer at a lower price. His sales are less at the higher than at the lower price but, far from restricting his supply in any *literal* sense, he is always eager to sell more than he does, and in the typical case even spends money on advertising in order to do so *(vide* those indisputable monopolies, the public utilities). With these considerations in mind it is easy to see how far astray one may go if one identifies monopoly with restriction of supply in any literal sense. In the labor field, as elsewhere, it is the market which does the 'restricting' in response to the higher price (wage), and the unsold supply (labor services) either joins the unemployed, or drifts away to some other area, or may be absorbed by the reduction of hours or working days, by institutionalized work stoppages as in coal mining, or by other work-sharing devices.

Returning to the liberal position, it seems clear that, monopoly being generally condemned, it was a colossal error to suppose it to be present in the labor field only to the extent that the common varieties of restrictive practices could be observed. A union which achieves a higher wage rate and lets the market do the restricting for it is on equal terms with one which engages in restriction of the direct and observable variety. The time is past when the economist who wishes to be friendly to organized labor and critical of monopoly at the same time does not at least have something to explain. He can no longer retreat into the comfortable position which I have identified with traditional liberalism.

One ground on which collective bargaining has always been defended is the allegedly weak 'bargaining power' of the laborer when acting as an individual. Again it is interesting to note that in traditional liberalism (1) this defense is standard, and (2) it was never imagined that 'increasing bargaining power' could do more than assure the laborer of the 'competitive wage,' defined, as will be recalled, with reference to his numbers. The term bargaining power has, as we know, an extremely ambiguous meaning, and has been subject to a variety of interpretations. One of its primary meanings has reference to an indeterminate range of prices, any one of which will equate supply and demand so that competition within this range is inoperative as a determining force. Such a range may appear with discontinuous demand and supply schedules as in the typical analysis of the Austrian school; the range is automatically compressed to a point where the schedules are continuous, as, for instance, in Marshall, where 'natura non facit saltum.' The limits to such a range, if it exists, are set by competition, and beyond them no bargaining takes place. Conversely, within them there is bargaining but no competition. *Any* wages within such limits would be 'competitive' wages, and in theory they would be nearer the upper limit as labor's bargaining power was stronger, and nearer the lower limit as it was weaker. Is it not highly probable that such a frame of reference, an integral part of the then prevailing theory of value, contributed consciously or unconsciously to the view, still highly prevalent, that bargaining power has nothing to do with monopoly power? And is it not equally obvious that such an analysis has virtually no relevance to a modern wage negotiation where each side is acting as a unit and where the problem is therefore one of bilateral monopoly with the bargaining strength on each side being inseparable from its *monopoly* position?

Who is the weaker in bargaining power under these circumstances? There is certainly no simple answer to this question, but several aspects of it may be laid open for examination. It has frequently been urged that the individual employee is only one of, say, a thousand in a plant, and that therefore his threat to quit work is as nothing beside his employer's threat to discharge him. In the one case the employer is left with 99.9 per cent of his labor force; in the other the employee is left with zero per cent of his job. By such logic, for all workers to walk out together merely re-establishes the balance, and leaves the two sides precisely equal in this type of bargaining power. This appears to me to be both valid and important. The objection may be made that *mere* disparity of numbers does not *necessarily* put the more numerous group at a disadvantage; and this is true. A retail grocer, for instance, has many customers, and there would hardly seem to be a case for the customers to organize and to deal with him collectively in order to equalize bargaining power. Yet in fact there is. It is only under the artificial assumption of pure competition—a homogeneous product and a very large number of grocers at the identical location—that it would be a matter of no consequence to consumers that their numbers were, say, a thousand times greater, so that the conclusion would be warranted that there was no case for their organizing into groups of a thousand, equal in number to the grocers. (Even here one would have to conclude also that there was no case *against* their organizing into such groups; for, since the number of groups would still be large, no one of them would have any monopoly power.) But when we drop pure competition and recognize that, in spite of a great deal of competition, generally speaking, between retail grocers, there remain substantial elements of monopoly which attach customers in some degree to one grocer rather than to another, there *is* a case for customers' organizing, in the sense that they could in this way offset some of the monopoly power in the hands of the individual grocer and drive a better bargain. To be sure, the case is evidently not strong enough, considering also the difficulties, to be exploited by an organizer. But in the labor case, where a particular job is a means of livelihood (in contrast to a source of obtaining a retail good), and where a worker 'takes roots,' not only with reference to the job itself, but to the community in which he lives, the element of 'immobility' is typically much greater, and the power in the hands of the employer may be great indeed if he deals with each laborer individually. There is, I believe, a genuine and compelling case on this score for collective bargaining within the firm, and it is not to be put off by demonstrating that it puts monopoly power in the hands of the union. So far there is no reason to suppose that this power would be any greater than it already and necessarily is on the side of the employer.

But this argument deals only with the situation within a single firm; no case has been made as yet for collective bargaining on an industry- or trade-wide basis.

Let us pass over with only brief comment such considerations as the alleged perishability of labor and the alleged lack of reserves which put the laborer under pressure to find work or to go back to work with a minimum of delay. As to the first, labor *services* which are unsold today produce no *goods* for the employer to sell, so that these latter 'perish' equally with the services; and it should be added that the loss of good will may extend into the indefinite future, far beyond the period of actual work stoppage. To the extent that goods already produced may be sold, the depleted stocks must be replaced later, which replacement requires labor, so that the labor is no more nor less perishable than the goods. Where a concern produces services, as in the case of public utilities, there is again equal perishability on both sides. As to lack of reserves, the argument first appeared at an earlier period, when wages and the level of living for laborers were much lower than they are now, and when the 'reserves' on the other side were more often the bank account of an individual capitalist employer. In any event, although it remains true today that the average representative of management has more money in the bank than the average laborer, it is not *his* reserves that are relevant, but those of the firm. Firms range from those that could hold out for a very long time if they were willing to swallow the losses to those on the verge of bankruptcy, and evidently no generalization can be made. On the other hand, workers who are already receiving good wages may be able to cut back their expenditures severely, postpone all purchases but food, run up bills, borrow, get help from friends, from the union, and from relief, and take terrific punishment before they give in. It does not appear to me that any safe generalization can be made as to which side is at the greater disadvantage for want of ability to hold out. In some cases it will be the firm; in others the striking laborers.

In fact it is this very ability to hold out on both sides that is so alarming, for it opens up the possibility of the long-drawn-out strikes which we now seem to take as a matter of course. Occasionally a strike is won or lost by one side exhausting the staying powers of the other. But more often it is settled long before such exhaustion, and the appropriate measure of relative bargaining power seems to be, not relative ability to last, but the relative ability of each side to inflict damage upon the other. Certainly this is a major factor, in the first place, in deciding whether there shall be any strike at all; and it must be in the forefront throughout the duration of any actual conflict. Again, ability to inflict damage is bound to vary with circumstances, and I see no possibility of generalizing as to which side is the more powerful in this type of warfare. It seems much more relevant to say that nowadays the power on both sides is so great that there is not much point in comparing them. It has become a commonplace that in warfare nobody wins. And it seems clear that in warfare, whether international or industrial, 'bargaining power' is no longer an appropriate term to apply once war has actually broken out.

The fact that strikes are a form of warfare needs to be stressed, because to many they seem to be regarded as a natural and inevitable concomitant of collective bargaining; and since this latter is taken to be a *sine qua non* of 'democracy,' they take their place, in the minds of such people, as a necessary feature of the democratic way of life. Yet the Bureau of Labor Standards has estimated that before the last war nine out of ten union agreements were renegotiated each year without interruption of work and without arbitration. The goal is ten out of ten. It is no more desirable to settle industrial relations by putting the ultimate strength of the two sides to a test than it is to settle international relations in this way. In either case there is confession of failure in the peaceful means of negotiation and compromise. It can be said flatly that a strike, being a test of strength, implies victory by the stronger, and hence could hardly be expected to yield results bearing any relation to standards either of justice or of desirable economic policy (except, of course, that the conflict is finally terminated). Yet strikes take place within a larger framework of law and social restraint, which might as reasonably be expected to prevent them as it is expected to prevent people from burning down each other's houses, or from fighting any other kind of private war which involves the infliction of material damage on one another and on innocent third parties.

It might be held, however, that in this particular type of economic issue the most 'workable' social policy would be to permit the two parties to settle a disagreement by inflicting as much damage as possible on each other until one of them gave in, *provided* no one else were involved. But surely there is no need to expand on the familiar complexity and interdependence of the economic system, and to point out that third parties are *always* involved in some degree and often in overwhelming degree. It is easy to understand why unions should try to persuade both themselves and the general public that to deny or in any way to qualify the so-called 'right' to strike is to establish 'involuntary servitude.' Since no one favors involuntary servitude, there can be only gain for the labor cause by such a confusion of issues. But where is the 'servitude'? Workers are always free to leave any occupation individually. And what is at issue is not even the freedom of any *group* of workers to leave their occupations collectively, for no one expects to leave them at all. If anyone did he would find work elsewhere, and would offer no obstacles to someone else moving in and taking his job. Whatever may be said against the legal injunction in a case of emergency—and I hold no brief for it if a better method of protecting the public interest can be found—economically considered, it merely aims to compel a collective body of men for a limited period of time *actually* to work at the jobs they have freely chosen, jobs which they claim the right to prevent others from taking, and jobs to which they expect soon to return. The essential problem is one of protecting the public interest against an aggregate of private power which puts it in jeopardy. It is hard to believe that the public will in the end be persuaded that the restrictions on *collective action* necessary to achieve this end constitute in any sense a re-establishment of that 'involuntary servitude' to which the Thirteenth Amendment to the Constitution sought to put an end.

Most of the traditional arguments as to the weak bargaining power of labor seem to apply, if at all, within the firm, and the disparity they indicate would be corrected if the laborers within each single firm bargained as a group with their employer. As has already been indicated, I see no case against collective bargaining per se within the firm as monopolistic. The employer is already a single unit, and for employees to become one through collective action only restores the balance, whether we think in terms of the hardship caused to the other by either side terminating the work contract, or whether we think in terms of monopoly power in the labor market, possibly already enjoyed by the employer, and now offset by a similar monopoly power on the employee side. In this latter case we now have a bilateral monopoly in the labor market, one more or less restricted by competitive elements on both sides: alternative employers for the employees; alternative employees for the employers. In short, whatever the power gained by labor within the firm, it can at best no more than offset similar powers already in the hands of management.

If the firm is making monopoly profits in the sale of its product, the question of labor sharing in these gains arising from the product market must also be raised. I have argued elsewhere that such monopoly profits exist very generally throughout the economy; and it is quite possible, of course, that members of a particular union may be able in some degree to share in the monopoly profits, if any, of the enterprise by which they are employed. One may well ask why the laborers in one firm should be paid more than those in another, and the 'orthodox' answer to this question is that they should not. But it appears to me that the case for labor sharing in the extra profits in question is no better or worse than that for the entrepreneur himself making off with them; *as long as the monopoly profits are tolerated,* it seems not to be an objection to labor's getting a part of them to point out that this is possible only because labor too has some monopoly power in the situation. When and if the monopoly profits are disallowed by appropriate social action, the case for labor having any share in them will no longer arise. It should be mentioned that all of the above is reasoned on the assumption that labor is not accorded any special weapons in bargaining, such as the right of intimidation or of preventing others from taking over jobs left vacant. This is obviously a major qualification, and will be discussed further below. But so far it would appear that for laborers within a firm to bargain collectively with their employer is quite defensible so long as there is no collusive action among laborers beyond the firm. Evidently this would mean no industrial or trade unions, but it is a substantial departure from the sweeping condemnation of all collective bargaining as monopolistic.

Beyond the firm it would appear that the considerations by which collective action by labor over a wider range such as an industry or a trade are to be judged are strikingly similar to those whereby collective action by businessmen over such an area are judged. There are no problems of weak bargaining power, except in the sense that, generally speaking, *anyone* can strengthen his economic position by acting in concert with those who otherwise would appear in the market as his competitors. Of course, to the extent that businessmen may enter into agreements, actual or tacit, to keep wages down, there is a similar case for the laborers in more than one enterprise acting together as trade- or industry-wide unions against their collective employers. But in this area the organizations of labor which extend beyond the firm appear to be far ahead of those of employers, so that the actual power is on the side of labor, whose industry-wide organizations can play one employer against another by tying up either the entire industry at once, or particular units of it in succession, all in accord with the most advantageous strategy as it appears in the larger perspective.

In this wider struggle the odds appear to me to be heavily with the labor unions. The first and chief reason is that public sympathy is fundamentally with the unions. For this there is a variety of explanations: (1) A majority of the public consists of laborers, in the broad sense, who regard particular unions as representing the interests of labor in general and hence their own interests. (2) Labor is regarded as the 'underdog,' and though the public may be very angry with John L. Lewis it will never be angry with coal miners, even when they earn $15 a day [1950], at which rate there appear to be only about two hundred days a year of employment for the existing body of workers in the industry. (3) The public is unaware of any connection between unduly high wages and unemployment, because such a connection involves long-run considerations to which the public almost never pays any attention. This natural human propensity, against which economists have fought for generations, has now been fortified by the depression economics of J. M. Keynes, presented in the garb of a 'general theory' in which the long run doesn't matter. (4) The public does not (usually) deal directly with labor, and, being unfamiliar with the theory of value, readily believes that high wages come out of profits instead of out of its own pockets through the influence of higher costs upon prices. For all these reasons and others public sympathy is with labor. And public sympathy is of vital importance in this type of warfare, since the public determines the rules under which it takes place, and since in the last analysis it could not take place at all without public sanction.

A second and related reason why the odds are with labor is the political one. In any major conflict, government participation as an umpire of some sort is inevitable, and the attitude and policies of the government may be of primary importance. A prominent labor economist said to me of the recent coal strike, 'Don't forget there's lots of votes in those coal-mining districts.' The point does not require elaboration.

A third reason arises from the principle that the prices of commodities tend to express their cost of production, including an appropriate allowance for profit. This is a principle which operates with many refinements and qualifications, of course, but by and large it means that the more fundamental clash of interests in any particular labor dispute is between labor and the consumer of the product involved, and not between labor and the businessman or corporation who employs it. The laborer is bargaining about his own income, whereas the businessman can usually in some measure, and perhaps entirely, protect his own income by a price adjustment. To the extent that he *can* protect it by a price adjustment he will be more ready to give in; this gives us another important reason why the pressure to increase wages may not be matched by an equal opposing pressure. To understand the importance of this factor we have only to ask if the businessman's position in a wage dispute would not be transformed in a regime of price fixing where he was forbidden by law to increase his prices. Who can deny that it would be?

This last consideration has its application chiefly to warfare conducted over a broad front, and including a number of firms in substantial competition with each other in the product market. To the individual firm, although higher costs mean a recomputation of its maximum profit position, the possibilities of a price adjustment are severely limited if its rivals, not subject to the same pressures, hold their prices at the same level. The extreme of this situation would, of course, be pure competition, where the individual firm could not change its price at all merely because its own costs had changed. In any event, wherever a *general* upward adjustment of costs has taken place among firms in substantial competition with each other, a *general* price adjustment will be a natural result, since no individual firm will have reason to fear any substantial loss of business to competitors. This contrast points up again the difference between the case which may legitimately be made for collective bargaining within the firm and the illegitimacy of extending it uncritically to areas beyond the firm.

A final reason why the greater power is on the side of labor in struggles beyond the firm arises from the fact that, although the laborer retains his freedom to seek other employment, the employer does not effectively retain his freedom to hire other laborers. Indeed he usually does not even retain the freedom to continue operations with that portion of his working force which, if not intimidated, would prefer to work. The techniques by which this result is accomplished are several, including the key one of picketing, which the American public for some curious reason continues to associate with 'free speech.' (It is heartening to record that the American Civil Liberties Union, one of whose primary objectives is the preservation of free speech, has issued strong protests against mass picketing.) But the fundamental fact appears to be that the public sanctions the proposition that when persons stop work collectively they may legitimately prevent from working, not only a minority of their own numbers who would prefer to continue, but also others working for the same enterprise whom they may successfully intimidate, and, more to the point, still others who might be glad to take their jobs either temporarily or permanently. It is certainly by public sanction that violations of the most essential freedoms of other citizens are tolerated in order that a group of organized laborers may press its case more effectively. We have here only one more instance of the importance of public sympathy and support.

The significance of this peculiarity of 'bargaining' in the labor area seems to me hardly to have been noticed. In earlier discussions of bargaining power, collective action used to be defended by making a contrast between the position of a single worker in a large plant and, for example, an individual housemaid who bargains supposedly on equal terms with the individual householder. If the mistress discharges the maid, the maid is put to the trouble of finding another job; if the maid quits work, the mistress is similarly put to the trouble of finding another maid. Here bargaining power appears truly to be equalized. But suppose now that the maid were to be given the power to quit and at the same time to prevent the householder from employing anyone else. Even the individual worker in a large factory might have great 'bargaining' power indeed if he could similarly threaten to quit and prevent the company from having anyone else do his work as long as he chose to stay out. The corresponding power in the hands of an employer would seem to be not only to deprive a worker of his job, but also to prevent him from taking any other until he comes to terms. The 'right' to strike is certainly not to be discussed in terms of the right of workers collectively to quit their jobs. There is no question of quitting their jobs at all. It is a question of *keeping* them absolutely, but of not working at them, and of preventing anyone else from working at them either. As has been brought out above, such a power greatly unbalances in favor of labor the relative position even within a firm. But it becomes vastly more significant in industrial warfare conducted over the wider area at present under discussion. This is partly because what is involved is mass coercion or, possibly, mass violence; and the magnitude of the forces which array themselves against the police power of the State is a matter of primary consequence. It is evidently easier to quell a riot of ten people than of ten thousand; and similarly it is easier to protect ten people from intimidation than ten thousand. But, on the economic side, the wider the area of conflict the smaller become the possibilities in realistic terms of replacing workers, either temporarily or permanently. Herein must lie a substantial part of the explanation of why such replacement is no longer a realistic possibility in an industrial conflict of any magnitude. 'Something new has been added' to the idea of bargaining—the power in the hands of one party to prevent the other from considering any alternative offers from others who might like to make a contract with him. And such a power in the hands of labor seems to be commonly regarded as not merely compatible with, but by many as even essential to, a 'free' society!

A number of special circumstances have now been mentioned which strengthen the hands of unionized workers in exerting pressure for wages higher than those they would be able to obtain if organized only within each firm to offset the unit opposition of their entrepreneur-employer. I suggest that the wages obtainable by merely intra-firm organization, with a strict prohibition of any collusive action by labor beyond the firm and of any action of intimidation to prevent the firm from making an alternative contract with nonstriking laborers, might be described, by a variation of Professor J. M. Clark's terminology, as 'workably competitive wages.' Such wages would still involve substantial elements of monopoly, but, as pointed out above, no more substantial than those that the owners of individual firms already have, either in the labor market or in the product market. And to the extent that monopoly profits in monopolistically competitive product markets were found socially undesirable and subjected to regulation, a corresponding check would be put upon any participation in these profits by labor.

It is of interest to recognize that the possibilities for monopoly income through collusive action beyond the individual firm, although usually associated with the profits share of income, are equally open to labor. In fact they may be open *only* to labor if competition in the product market is effective in keeping down profits. For example, an industry-wide union may first obtain higher wages for any or all of the various reasons already given. With higher costs, prices are adjusted upward to cover them, but competition in this case keeps *profits* at the 'competitive level' in the industry. At the higher price what has happened is that a portion of the area of possible monopoly profit for the industry has been taken over by labor. The process may be repeated, and by a series of such adjustments the monopoly income forbidden to enterprise by the antitrust laws may be enjoyed by labor as the sole factor with the privilege of selling its factor services under unified monopoly control on an industry basis.[6]

A similar argument is equally valid for labor organized on a trade basis, the upward pressure on prices here being merely exerted in several industries at the same time. There is no reason to think that such is not the general situation—in fact there is every reason to think that it is. Economists as well as the public are fooled by the fact that the adjective 'monopoly' is always attached to the noun 'profit' and never to the noun 'cost.' But economists at least should not be fooled in a matter as straight-forward technically as this appears to be.

One final observation. It has been an objection to analyzing labor unions as monopolies that they do not aim at maximizing total income, or that there is at least a good deal of uncertainty as to what it is they are maximizing—whether it is the income of *all* members, of those actually employed, of older members with seniority rights, who will be the last to be laid off, or of those in some other preferred position (politically within the union, etc.). Also it has been pointed out that the problem of labor monopoly varies in important detail from that of industrial monopoly: for instance, by the necessity of adding into the pic-

---

6. If neither competition nor the antitrust laws are effective in preventing unreasonably high profits over the area in question, I see no case against labor having a share in them. The argument is identical with that for monopoly profits within a firm (cf. above, p. 260).

ture in this case the influence of political factors within the union —the necessity of recurrent wage demands for internal political reasons, etc. But all these considerations merely indicate that the monopoly problem is not simple. If a monopolist, industrial or labor, moderates his policy for fear of an unfavorable public reaction, or if a union leader presses his advantages more vigorously because he must maintain his prestige as an officer, he is nevertheless in each case a monopolist. The economist will have to learn that there is more to the theory of monopoly than the simple maximizing of profits. Indeed, the behavior of monopolists in different circumstances is certainly one of the most fruitful fields for economic investigation.

The reaction of many to the above, or any similar, analysis will be that it is 'unrealistic,' and that 'labor unions are here to stay' because it is 'politically impossible to abolish them.' I think the first reply to such a position is that made by D. H. Robertson in discussing a similar problem: '[Before we talk about politics], let us get the analysis right.' [7] To this I may add a second observation: If the above analysis turns out to be reasonably 'right,' it seems to follow that the problem of labor monopoly is not one of a simple 'yes' or 'no' to collective bargaining. Rather, it appears possible to limit and restrict labor monopolies in a variety of ways and degrees, and to find workable solutions in appropriately adjusting their powers.[8] Perhaps it is not too much to hope that, even in a democracy where pressure groups are disconcertingly powerful, such an objective may be achieved.

7. 'A Revolutionist's Handbook,' *Quarterly Journal of Economics,* February 1950, p. 13.

8. [1957] It should be noted that this essay is mainly concerned with analyzing the issues of monopoly power, and makes no specific policy recommendations. Thus the nature of collective bargaining within the firm is contrasted with that of collective bargaining which extends beyond the firm; but there is no proposal to 'abolish' industry-wide bargaining. This statement is made necessary because of misinterpretations.

Part

V

_____

CRITICAL

13

'Full Cost' and Monopolistic Competition [1]

MR. ANDREWS's recent account of the pricing process [2] as a variety of the 'full cost' principle and the ensuing discussion of it in the *Economic Journal* [3] have raised a major false issue which, as an interested party, I should like to correct. The issue has to do with the relation of the full cost principle to the theories of imperfect and of monopolistic competition. No attempt will be made in this note to evaluate either the full cost principle itself or Mr. Andrews's particular interpretation of it.

There can be no doubt that Mr. Andrews thinks he is presenting, and means to present, a theory of pricing which is antithetical to 'modern economic theory,' identifying this latter with imperfect and monopolistic competition; and Professor Robinson appears to view it as such, for he describes Andrews's 'attempts to construct alternative theories' as 'powerfully destructive not only of the newer accretions of imperfect competition theory but also of the whole body of economic reasoning.' [4] Likewise, Mr. Farrell's contribution to the discussion [5] takes place under the rubric

1. Reprinted from the *Economic Journal*, June 1952.
2. P. W. S. Andrews, *Manufacturing Business*, London, 1949.
3. Austin Robinson, 'The Pricing of Manufactured Products,' *Economic Journal*, December 1950; M. J. Farrell, 'The Case Against the Imperfect Competition Theories'; Aubrey Silberston, 'The Pricing of Manufactured Products: A Comment'; Austin Robinson, 'The Pricing of Manufactured Products and the Case against Imperfect Competition: A Rejoinder,' ibid. June 1951.
4. Op. cit. December 1950, p. 771.
5. Cited above.

'The Case Against the Imperfect Competition Theories.' One may go back even farther to Hall and Hitch in whose well-known article the principle of setting prices in accord with full cost is also presented in sharp contrast to 'current doctrine' including specifically my own work.[6]

It seems to have been overlooked by all concerned that the principle in question, far from being at odds with the theory of monopolistic competition, has been from the first an integral part of it. Unless I have badly misunderstood the principle, it is clearly (if briefly) described and contrasted with the principle of maximum profits on page 105 of *Monopolistic Competition*,[7] and is the basis, together with several closely related factors such as custom, traditional mark-ups, etc. (also oligopolistic influences), of my analysis of the important phenomenon of excess capacity.[8] In so far as the full cost principle is an acceptable part of price theory there is no difficulty whatever about assimilating it into a system of monopolistic competition—it is, in fact, a further development of the theory.

Since I have for years taught the full cost principle as one phase—and I think a very important one—of monopolistic competition theory, it may be understood how profoundly shocking

6. 'Price Theory and Business Behaviour,' *Oxford Economic Papers*, 1939. 'Current doctrine' is always identified with the concepts of 'marginal cost and marginal revenue' (p. 17 and *passim*), and such identification seems to me lamentably correct (cf. *Monopolistic Competition*, 5th or later ed., pp. 191-3) both in general and, I must say, especially in England. But these concepts, offensive to so many, are almost totally absent from monopolistic competition (as explained below); and the attack upon 'current doctrine' draws so heavily on oligopoly theory and other elements from the theory of monopolistic competition that a more careful examination of the issues would seem to reveal that it is *imperfect* competition which is being criticized, and (in spite of the reference on p. 30) *monopolistic* competition which is being defended! The authors are in fact generous in their acknowledgments, and I venture to think and hope that they might even agree with this interpretation.

7. I certainly do not mean to assert that nothing has been added to this by Hall and Hitch, by Andrews, or by others. Nor do I make any claim to have been the first to state the theory (cf. references to Cairnes, Wicksell, and Mill, loc. cit.).

8. Not, by the way, to be identified, as it usually is, with departures from the minimum point on the cost curve.

it is to see it advanced as something in opposition to it and designed to disprove it. One naturally seeks an explanation, and I think it lies in good part in the very common confusion between the theories of imperfect and of monopolistic competition, so that propositions true of one of them are carelessly assumed to be true of both. This has happened so continuously since 1933, and continues to happen so regularly, that it is one of the most predictable of economic phenomena. I have written at length on this question already,[9] and although there is still much more to be said, I limit myself here to those aspects of the matter which seem to be particularly relevant.

The main issue raised by the full cost principle, as I see it, is that of a price determined on the one hand by cost, in the sense of being set by the producer at a figure arrived at by a cost computation including a margin of profit defined by custom, convention, or what is thought just or 'reasonable' (as opposed to a maximum), or on the other hand by maximum profits. In their pure form, these are analytically quite different principles leading to different price results (even when the amount of profit involved is the same in both cases), although, as Professor Robinson has shown, a great deal of profit maximization lurks in Mr. Andrews's exposition of pricing by the full cost principle. The conflict with 'the imperfect competition theories' appears only in so far as these theories have identified themselves narrowly with the profit maximizing principle, so that any other principle could not be a part of them. Such identification is complete under imperfect competition, and therefore the conflict exists; it is absent under monopolistic competition, and therefore the conflict does not exist.

That the identification is complete in Mrs. Robinson's *Imperfect Competition* is revealed at once by the crucial role played by the marginal revenue concept. In Mrs. Robinson's own words, the marginal revenue curve is 'the heart of the whole matter,' [10]

9. See especially the Preface and Chap. IX of the 5th or later edition of *Monopolistic Competition*. Chapter IX is a revision of an earlier article: 'Monopolistic or Imperfect Competition?', *Quarterly Journal of Economics*, August 1937. Cf. also Essays 3 and 5 above, and [1957] 16 below.

10. *Imperfect Competition*, p. 8.

and her book 'arose out of the attempt to apply it to various problems.' [11] The point to be made is that the technique itself effectively excludes any other entrepreneurial objective than the maximization of profits and infallibly gives the answer in these terms. An equilibrium situation in which an entrepreneur decided to be content with something less than maximum profits, or to charge a customary price, or a price based on 'full cost,' or a price in the short period which corresponded to Marshall's 'true marginal supply price for short periods,' [12] could hardly be depicted in terms of marginal revenue and marginal cost curves. Moreover, it is perfectly clear that Mrs. Robinson regards any admission of overhead costs into the pricing process 'in a given situation' as a 'confusion of thought.' [13] The equation of marginal revenue and of marginal cost is of the essence of *Imperfect Competition*. The full cost principle cannot lie down in peace with this theory.

By contrast, my own book arose, not out of the marginal revenue curve, but out of the attempt to combine the two theories of monopoly and of competition into a single one which would come closer to explaining the real world, where, it seemed, the two forces were mingled in various ways and degrees. This idea does not appear in Mrs. Robinson's *Imperfect Competition,* except on pages 4 and 5, where it is briefly considered and abandoned. In my own attempt to blend monopoly and competition, the marginal revenue curve was discovered at an early stage and seen for what it is—a piece of pure technique unrelated to the central problem. It actually enters into my own exposition as a separate curve at only two points (pp. 14 and 77), and in both cases parenthetically as an *alternative* way of saying what has just been said in terms of average curves. To Mrs. Robinson the marginal revenue curve is 'the heart of the whole matter'; to

11. Ibid. p. vi.

12. *Principles,* p. 374.

13. Ibid. p. 48. How 'confused' was Marshall in his description of the extent to which supplementary costs enter into prices in the short run, *Principles,* pp. 374-7, including the observation (p. 376) that 'the analytical economist must [view the problem as does the producer] if he would keep in touch with actual conditions'!

me the heart of the matter is something else and the marginal revenue curve is a red herring.

The idea of monopoly does not carry with it any necessary assumption as to how the monopolist behaves, although it is usual in the main to assume that he maximizes his profits. If he does something else (and we need to know more about what he does), he none the less controls the supply of his particular product and sells it in competition with others; and he is probably also in some measure an oligopolist in his relations with others. Thus the fundamental structure of economic society is one of monopolistic competition no matter what kind of a policy the monopolist follows, and there is no trouble whatever in fitting full cost, or other principles in addition to profit maximization, into the system. Even if the principle of setting prices according to cost had not in fact been included in the theory of monopolistic competition, it would never have occurred to me that there was any difficulty about including it. Indeed, it would seem to be only under a regime of monopolistic (instead of pure) competition that problems of price *policy* could arise at all.

The point has been made above that the marginal revenue technique itself effectively eliminates (in *any* time period to which it is applied) any objective on the part of the businessman other than profit maximization. But it may still be said that the actual development of the theory of monopolistic competition is predominantly in terms of profit maximization, and that within this part of it, the equation of marginal revenue and marginal cost is merely a matter of geometry (or of algebra). This is perfectly true. But I think we have here a good illustration of how a mathematical formulation can influence, unexpectedly and adversely, an economical explanation. A major deficiency in the marginal revenue technique is that it does not by itself reveal the price. This means that the discussion of equilibrium takes place primarily in terms of *output,* the category so neatly determined by the intersection of the two marginal curves, instead of in terms of *price,* the category with reference to which business decisions are most usually taken. This is abundantly illustrated in Mrs. Robinson's book, and on looking up the two places in my own, cited above, where the marginal revenue curve is introduced, I find also that *output* is described as 'chosen' or 'adjusted' first, and the price at which this output would sell is discovered afterwards. Elsewhere in my own exposition the businessman is described as deciding upon, or adjusting, his *price*. In looking back, I have no doubt that the lack of realism in the marginal revenue technique played an important part in leading me to use it hardly at all and to explain everything in terms of the average curves, where the graphics do not seem to get in the way of describing what really happens. There can be no doubt that the picture of businessmen computing and adjusting marginal revenues has been a major factor in alienating many from the theories of imperfect (and of monopolistic) competition, and has even sparked a sizable revolt against 'marginalism' in general. When two economists of the high competence of Messrs. Hall and Hitch can make the statement that 'for the above analysis (the "current doctrine") to be applicable it is necessary that entrepreneurs should *in fact* . . . attempt to equate estimated marginal revenue and estimated marginal cost,' [14] such a revolt becomes easier to understand. The propensity to make literal translations from geometry back into economics seems to be very general.

I am much concerned about this matter of realism, and in general about the danger, so widespread today in economics, that the mathematics of a problem may literally replace the economics of it. This may have happened for a time in the area of analysis with which we are concerned, and about which Professor D. H. Robertson wrote: 'Geometry ascended the throne left vacant by philosophy and commonsense; and ingenuous youths and maidens, beguiled into the belief that here at last was a true picture of the real world, spent the best moments of their young lives in memorizing (generally wrong) endless fantastic patterns of tangencies and intersections.' [15] It is hard to know just what my own contribution to this corruption of the youth has been, but I can certify that at least my avowed purpose was the contrary— to construct a theory which would be more closely oriented to-

14. Op. cit. p. 18 (italics added).
15. 'A Revolutionist's Handbook,' *Quarterly Journal of Economics*, February 1950, p. 8.

wards economic reality than the old one. I do not think that Mr. Andrews is correct when he observes that 'the result (of the theories of monopolistic and imperfect competition) has been a greater gulf between theoretical analysis and practical thought than can have existed during any other period since before Mill.'[16] Impressive evidence to the contrary is offered by Joe Bain,[17] who cites the fact that recent industry studies have tended to accept the new theory 'at least as an orientation for investigation and sometimes as a specific formula for verification,' and who believes that 'the many writings on the theories of monopolistic and imperfect competition since 1933 have been a fruitful source of new hypotheses for empirical study.'[18] It may be noted that the long list of books and articles cited by Bain is without exception from the United States.

It was said earlier that the explanation of the false opposition between full cost and monopolistic competition theory lay in part in the common confusion of the latter with imperfect competition. It also lies in a substantial number of misunderstandings on the part of Mr. Andrews as to the nature of monopolistic competition itself, several of which may be listed.[19]

16. 'Industrial Analysis in Economics,' *Oxford Studies in the Price Mechanism*, p. 139.

17. 'Price and Production Policies,' *A Survey of Contemporary Economics*, pp. 129-73.

18. Ibid. pp. 142, 153.

19. Professor Robinson has discussed two specific matters from the viewpoint of imperfect competition in its 'Cambridge origins' (op. cit. p. 773). I am grateful to him for making this distinction, because in good part what he says does not apply to the non-Cambridge theory, and it is possible that after all these years progress in separating the two is being made. He says first that 'it was of the essence of those theories that one was dealing with a situation in which entry was assumed to be sufficiently free and competition sufficiently effective to reduce profits to a "normal" level and to insure that average revenue did not exceed average cost including "normal" profits.' Far from being the essence of my own theory, this possibility is no more than a small fragment of it, and mostly an intermediate step in its development. A few key references are: *Monopolistic Competition*, pp. 8-9, 71-3, 82-3, 100, 110-13, 149-50, and 172-3.

He says secondly (in rebutting the idea that as a *modus operandi* prices were maintained by restricting output) that the analysis was 'by intention at least, an analysis of a highly competitive, though not perfectly competi-

(1) He objects to describing the monopolist as 'restricting output' (pp. 23, 174), maintaining that he should be regarded as 'quoting a price.' But I do not believe that the monopolist is even once described in *Monopolistic Competition* as restricting output. On the contrary, the general view is that he sets a price, and that at this price he is willing to supply more than the market is willing to take (pp. 13-15).[20]

(2) He—also Mr. Farrell (and dozens of others)—conceives the theory as 'much too short term' in its outlook (pp. 148, 270). But the theory, really independent of time, is actually developed primarily in terms of the long period. Relevant passages in *Monopolistic Competition* are on pages 21 note, 50-53, 81, and 139-40.[21] I must in passing record agreement with Mr. Farrell when he says that 'maximizing profits in each of any sequence of short periods is not in general consistent with maximizing profits over the longer period composed of these short periods.'[22] On this point I consider myself a good Marshallian.

(3) Mr. Andrews often speaks of monopoly and competition as if they were mutually exclusive (p. 23, for instance) and describes his theory as developing from the realization that 'manufacturing industry must be in some ways more competitive than is generally recognized' (p. 170). But highly competitive situations are part and parcel of the theory of monopolistic competition, and from this point of view at least there is no need for a new theory.

(4) Mr. Andrews's discussion of advertising (pp. 188-204) again separates monopoly and competition and seems to me a nest of misconceptions, certainly of my own theory of the subject. Unfortunately time cannot be taken to discuss them in detail. He

tive, situation.' Such a statement could not possibly apply to monopolistic competition, since *all monopolies are a part of it* and hence demands of all elasticities are included. A few key references are: Ibid. pp. 68, 74, 110-13, 172-3.

20. In fact, I have long insisted on the point here made by Mr. Andrews; as indicated above, I do not believe that the matter is one merely of geometry. The distinction in question has ramifications which are of the greatest import. Some of these are discussed with particular reference to the labor problem in Essay 12 above, p. 254.

21. Cf. also above, pp. 11-15.

22. Op. cit. p. 424.

seems concerned mainly in refuting the proposition that advertising is the 'handmaiden of monopoly,' and in establishing that it probably 'facilitates prices being lower than they would otherwise be. Certainly,' he says, 'there is no question of [its] being used to bolster up a pricing policy of the kind described in the modern theory of monopolistic competition . . .' (p. 204). But it is made very clear in my own analysis (p. 167) that advertising may lower the price. And although advertising is inevitably linked to monopoly in the sense that it could not take place under pure competition, it is a perfect illustration of the paradox of 'monopolistic competition': it is a leading means whereby monopolists compete with each other.

In spite of these criticisms, I should like to say again in closing that I think the full cost principle, properly conceived, is one of substantial importance in economics, and emphatically not in conflict with monopolistic competition theory. I join Professor Robinson in the hope that more of the materials which lie behind Mr. Andrews's researches may be analyzed and made available to us. I should like to add the hope that they might be discussed within the framework of the theory to which they belong.

14

Mr. Harrod's Recantation

IN his recently published *Economic Essays*, Mr. Harrod has 'revised' his views on 'excess capacity' and related matters,[1] taking a
strong and even vehement stand against doctrines to which he
had subscribed earlier in his conspectus of the 'Doctrines of Imperfect Competition.'[2] His recantation has naturally aroused interest; and especially because he now finds the doctrine in question 'altogether wrong,' and issues orders to all and sundry economists that they should 'cease to use,' 'discard,' and 'finally reject'[3]
the principles in question, some discussion of his arguments is
called for. Since, under the heading of 'current doctrine,' he deals
with issues quite other than those on which my own analysis is
based and therefore contributes nothing to refuting this latter, I
feel justified in issuing preliminary counterorders, viz. that economists should 'continue to use,' 'embrace,' and 'finally accept' the
doctrine in question—at least that which is presented as a part of
the general theory of monopolistic competition.

It seems very clear that Mr. Harrod's major quarrel is with an
alleged 'current doctrine' that businessmen pay attention only to
short-period marginal revenue, whereas they should and do, he

1. R. F. Harrod, *Economic Essays*, 1952, Essay 8, 'Theory of Imperfect
Competition Revised.'
2. *Quarterly Journal of Economics*, May 1934, reprinted in the *Economic
Essays* as Essay 7. Page references are to the book.
3. Op. cit. pp. 140, 152, and 157.

holds, pay attention only [4] to the *long period*. It is argued that
since the entrepreneur sets up his plant with reference to the long
period, he *must* give equal importance to the long period on the
revenue side if he is to 'avoid the charge of schizophrenia.' This
is the proposition which is advanced repeatedly and defended
throughout. But when it comes to pinning it down in terms of
the essentially static norms involved, it is difficult to find out just

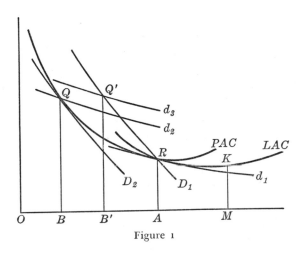

Figure 1

what Mr. Harrod is abandoning and what it is that he wishes
after all (p. 140) to retain. I must confess that I have spent hours—
even days—trying to find out and I am still uncertain. Perhaps
the best I can do is to set down some of these uncertainties.

A diagram seems virtually essential in order to discuss the issues
in this highly complex type of analysis. Figure 1 is an adaptation
and a composite of Figures 14 and 15 (pp. 91, 92) in my own
Monopolistic Competition. As has been explained above,[5] the
analysis in that book is fundamentally 'neutral' with respect to
time, but what was clearly in mind for the most part was the

4. Op. cit. p. 150 and *passim*. Although there are some minor exceptions,
the 'only' is justified both by the main argument and by the sweeping character of the conclusions.

5. Pp. 11-15.

long period, and so *LAC* in Figure 1 is a long period average
cost curve for a firm in a group characterized by the 'uniformity
assumption' (p. 82). Its minimum point is *K*, and *OM* is the corresponding output. A plant curve *PAC* is drawn tangent to *LAC*
at *R*. If output per firm is *OA*, price is assumed to be *AR*, and
d_1 is a demand curve showing the sales of a firm at different prices
on the assumption that all other firms are holding to the price of
AR. The curve D_1 shows the sales of the firm on the assumption
that all other firms are always charging the same price as this
firm; d_3 is like d_1 except that here all other firms are charging
B'Q'. If more firms enter the group, the demand curve when all
are varying their prices together becomes D_2. Again d_2 is like d_1
except that with the larger number of firms it is drawn through
the point of tangency *Q* and assumes that as one firm adjusts its
price all others hold to the price *BQ*. It should be noted that
there are no short-period demand or marginal revenue curves of
the type used by Mr. Harrod.

A major uncertainty may now be stated: it is as to what Mr.
Harrod means when he says 'no excess capacity.'

The distinction between the *D* type and the *d* type curves in
Figure 1, which is fundamental to my own analysis, is not made
by Mr. Harrod, but in its place we find short-run versus long-run
demand curves. Long-run demand curves are always more elastic,
he says, and his major argument is that they are the important
ones; yet nowhere does he argue that they are *perfectly* elastic
which is the only condition under which (with tangency) the firm
would operate at *K* (Figure 1) and thus without excess capacity
(in his sense). It may be significant that he does in fact show such
an equilibrium at a later point in his analysis ('Increasing Returns,' pp. 174-87), where he forgets all about the long-run demand
and marginal revenue curves. I say 'forgets' because he does not
dispose of them either by assumption or by argument—he simply
fails to mention them at all. In his Figure 3 (p. 180) and the accompanying analysis, there are nothing but short-period demand
curves, whereas with the long-period curves playing their part the
whole case which he develops for an equilibrium at minimum cost
(and hence for the '*independent*' influence of increasing returns

as distinct and separate from 'monopoly') falls to the ground.[6] In the straw man he has here set up, 'monopoly' has no influence for the simple reason that it is not there (except what might be called, 'short-run monopoly,' which vanishes by the Harrodian principle that entrepreneurs pay no attention to it). But since elsewhere he repeatedly speaks of long-run demand curves as if they had some finite elasticity, must we not assume that this is his general position as to long-run equilibrium?[7] We cannot be sure. In favor of this assumption is his insistence that 'long-run equilibrium is compatible with there being too many sources, that is, too many centres with a core of permanent equipment, and every one or many of these centres working below their optimum capacity' (p. 140, with a reference to p. 84). Although great stress is laid in this connection on *decreasing cost conditions* (his italics)[8] there seems to be no reason to accuse Mr. Harrod of holding that decreasing cost *to the firm* is compatible with perfectly elastic demand.

I therefore proceed on the assumption, in spite of the conflicting evidence, that Mr. Harrod does hold that long-run equilibrium with sufficiently free entry to give tangency is characterized by both long-run and short-run decreasing cost (as for the cost curves LAC and PAC at R in Figure 1). Does equilibrium at this point involve excess capacity or does it not? In the argument developed beginning on page 148 and culminating on page 152 he says it does not; and again on page 162 (second full paragraph)

6. H. R. Edwards presents a similar diagram (with no long-run demand curves) and interprets Harrod as holding for 'no excess capacity' in the sense of constant cost. ('Price Formation in Manufacturing Industry and Excess Capacity,' *Oxford Economic Papers*, February 1955, p. 103). He finds Mr. Harrod 'undoubtedly correct' and thus joins Mr. Harrod in falsely identifying my own position with short-run demand curves.

7. On page 151 (and elsewhere) he clearly distinguishes between the long-run equilibrium point and the minimum, or social optimum.

8. Mr. Harrod's *explanation* of (long-run) decreasing costs in this connection escapes me. It seems to be based (p. 84) on the presence, even in the long period, of some elements of overhead, such as 'immaterial elements of organization and goodwill'; yet elsewhere (p. 117) it appears to be the conventional envelope curve with all factors variable. It does not appear to me, however, that this set of issues plays a part in his argument.

he says it does not.[9] Yet it obviously does by any of his own definitions: it involves 'too many centers' (compared to his own optimum, which is K), and each is 'working below optimum capacity.' Furthermore, how is this different from my own solution in the case of large numbers and sufficient ease of entry to give tangency, which identifies equilibrium with R and which Mr. Harrod is now supposedly *abandoning* (p. 141)?[10] The only explanation I can give to this puzzle is that Mr. Harrod is doing battle, not with excess capacity at all, but with one particular explanation (out of many) as to how excess capacity might be *increased;* it is this explanation, and not the 'doctrine of excess capacity,' which is 'altogether wrong.'

Professor Hicks, in discussing Mr. Harrod's more recent analysis, praises his 1934 paper and remarks that this 'prop and stay' is now taken from us.[11] But it is not. So far as I can see, nothing whatever is lost from the earlier article if only the demand curves in it are interpreted as long-run curves.[12] The envelope and plant curve analysis remains, and it would seem that this is what Professor Hicks must have had mainly in mind as a 'prop and stay,' for the article contains no distinctions whatever on the demand

9. Mr. Kaldor, whose 'line of thought' Mr. Harrod is developing (see p. 145) also concludes that 'foresight' of the entrepreneur in choosing a 'low profit' so as not to encourage entry 'will, or at any rate may, prevent him from being driven to a state of "excess capacity"' (a footnote contains a minor qualification), and he too describes this foresight as merely increasing the elasticity of the demand curve, not as making it infinite. ('Market Imperfection and Excess Capacity,' *Economica*, February 1935, pp. 40-41.) Apart from this equivocal position in which both are in agreement, it should be noted that Mr. Kaldor's argument is based on oligopoly, which Mr. Harrod rules out (p. 151). It also deals with the result *'if'* a producer is 'foresighted,' instead of asserting that he *will* be, as does Mr. Harrod.

10. Comparison with Mrs. Robinson's solution is waived. Although, as usual, the two of us are lumped together as holding the 'same conclusion in regard to excess capacity,' the definition given by Harrod at this point is certainly not my own, and it is not easy to know how Mrs. Robinson would define it, since it is not found in her index and I cannot recall her ever using the term at all.

11. 'The Process of Imperfect Competition,' *Oxford Economic Papers*, February 1954, p. 41.

12. It is indeed disturbing, in the attempt to interpret Mr. Harrod's 'recantation,' that this is so.

side. It does not, for instance, make the vital distinction between the d and D type of curves in my own analysis (although it is specifically concerned with this analysis); [13] nor does it even suggest any of the arguments with respect to long-run versus short-run demand curves which Mr. Harrod now discusses. Like a substantial part of the literature of this area, it follows and perpetuates the Robinsonian tradition of simply drawing 'the' demand curve and proceeding, without bothering too much about what the curve means.[14] Yet in the problems of this area, where interfirm relationships are of the essence, it is impossible to make progress at all without specifying what kind of a demand curve one is talking about. Mr. Harrod did not specify in his earlier article, but since it is primarily concerned with an equilibrium on the envelope or long-run cost curve, it would seem fair to interpret the analysis as implicitly long run—in which case, how is it different from Mr. Harrod's new position?

Whatever the correct interpretation of Mr. Harrod's conflicting position on the *existence* of excess capacity, there can be no doubt that he is mainly concerned with one particular *process* by

13. It may be added that in discussing what he regards as the 'principal points of significance for economic theory' in the *two* books, Mrs. Robinson's *and* my own, Mr. Harrod does not say anything in this earlier article about: (1) oligopoly, nor about either of the two aspects of nonprice competition, (2) the 'product' as a variable, and (3) selling costs. His stress on the 'downward sloping demand curve' leads him in other directions, just as it did Mrs. Robinson; and as with her almost of necessity excludes these subjects. (Cf. above, pp. 28-9.) He is entitled, of course, to his judgment as to what is important. I mention the above omissions simply as added evidence of how completely Mr. Harrod followed (1934) and still follows (1952) the Robinsonian conception of the problem, so that, when he treats the two theories of Mrs. Robinson and myself as if they were one (p. 140 and *passim*), my own becomes (with one minor exception, pp. 141-2) simply Mrs. Robinson's, and a caricature of itself.

14. Mrs. Robinson's initial haste in this matter in order to get on with 'marginal revenue' (cf. my own contention that the marginal revenue curve is a mere piece of technique, *Monopolistic Competition*, 5th or later ed., pp. 191-3, and above, pp. 273-5), actually led her to a definition of the demand curve (*Imperfect Competition*, p. 21) which she has more recently disavowed as a 'fudge.' (*Economic Journal*, September 1953, p. 584). It thereby becomes difficult to draw more than geometrical, as distinct from economic, conclusions from her earlier theory.

which it allegedly comes into existence or is increased. The movement begins with restrictions of output by entrepreneurs under the lure of *short-run profits* made possible by a relatively inelastic short-run demand curve; these profits lead to the entry of new producers, smaller outputs per firm, and finally the return of profits to normal through higher costs and diminished demand per firm. Mr. Harrod's position is that no firm would be attracted by such a 'fleeting' profit (p. 147 and *passim*), so that the excess capacity in question would not come into being, and he defends it in terms of both conventional profit-maximizing theory and the full cost principle. Apart from other issues, what are the merits of this particular 'line of thought'?

It is strange indeed that he rules out oligopoly (p. 151), for it appears to me that any validity the argument may have derives logically from oligopolistic influences with respect to entry. The argument that price policy may in some circumstances be moderated in order not to encourage entry is well known,[15] but why should it ever happen in the 'large numbers' case where by definition a single firm is *without influence?* [16]

There can be no doubt that the summation of higher profits now plus normal profits later exceeds the summation of merely normal profits for the same period. Mr. Harrod's answer is that the entrepreneur will charge a low price from the beginning in order to make his own market 'less vulnerable' (p. 151). Of course he may (apart from entry considerations) charge such a price if his demand is elastic. But the argument contains a fundamental confusion between volume and vulnerability. To sell more for a period at a 'low price' implies nothing necessarily as to the

15. See, for instance, Joe Bain, 'Conditions of Entry and the Emergence of Monopoly,' in *Competition and Monopoly and their Regulation* (E. H. Chamberlin, ed.) and other bibliography there given.

16. My own theory of excess capacity is not confined to manufacturing industry, but is formulated in general terms and with a variety of examples, including the professions (cf. *Monopolistic Competition*, p. 106). Although high incomes by lawyers no doubt play some part in attracting young men into the law, who could imagine a particular lawyer charging a low fee on the ground that a higher one would encourage 'entry' and thus after a time lower *his* income anyway? Or a college professor turning down an increase in salary on similar grounds?

vulnerability (interpreted as demand elasticity) of the market temporarily acquired. The typical entrepreneur wants in some degree to attach his customers to him, but the kind of *price* policy which will do this is not obvious. The objective seems to imply making his demand less elastic, and this may best be achieved by leaving his price alone and concentrating on a better product, including service, or on advertising. In any event, how can it be argued that he will sacrifice profits in order to discourage entry if the magnitude of his own profits has no effect on entry?

Since Mr. Harrod takes a firm position that 'the analysis does not imply oligopoly' (p. 151), it becomes important to raise the question of his *(short-run)* demand curves whose relative inelasticity is so important to his argument. The steeper D curves in my own analysis are *not* short-run curves. They do imply either (a) some oligopoly, or (b) other forces (including full cost) which dampen or eliminate price competition; or both. It is forces of this kind which allow prices higher than AR (Figure 1) without a corrective movement back to R. Mr. Harrod clearly gives importance to full cost, but as a destroyer, not a generator, of excess capacity; and lack of vigor in price competition does not seem to figure in his analysis. Why then are his short-run curves so inelastic?

Mr. Harrod does not tell us—he seems merely to produce this particular curve out of an 'accepted doctrine' hat—which supposedly includes my own theory (identical of course with Mrs. Robinson's). But in the absence of oligopoly (or the other forces mentioned above which characterize my own D curves), an entrepreneur must adjust his price as though he were going it *alone*— in other words, moving from R, to the left along d_1. Such an adjustment would obviously be unprofitable and hence would not be made.

It is sometimes said that long-run demand curves are more elastic than short-run curves because of imperfect knowledge, inertia, etc. There is certainly some truth in this, especially for a downward price adjustment, where the gain in sales must come mainly from buyers other than the firm's present customers, buyers who may learn of the price cut and break their old ties only after an interval. But the situation is different for a price increase, where it is the existing customers who are the ones primarily affected—they know about it at once. Prevailing opinion (might I say 'accepted doctrine' as I know it?) seems to regard the demand curve for the firm (under the d assumption) as characteristically *elastic* for an upward adjustment. This is particularly in evidence in the literature of the kinked demand curve, which, as Hall and Hitch have pointed out, is merely a combination of my own d and D curves,[17] with the more elastic d portion lying *above* the ruling price. Even allowing for inertia it would seem that *in the absence of oligopoly, etc.*, Mr. Harrod's short-run demand curves, if they relate to anything longer than a few days, must fall into the d category, and hence indicate no movement whatever away from R in Figure 1.[18]

It is more difficult to be sure as to his long-run demand curves, for they are defined to include some questionable items which go beyond demand itself, such as 'potential competition' (p. 150) and even the losses of a potential price war (pp. 150-51). (It is perhaps significant that no long-run curves are drawn in the two figures presented.) They are held to be more elastic than short-run curves and 'consequently' to lead to planning for a '*larger* fixed equipment' (p. 151, his italics), although one might think that since they include potential competition whereas short-run curves do not, the reverse might be the case. But the inclusion of 'potential competition' really comes home on page 161, where the 'long-

17. 'Price Theory and Business Behaviour,' *Oxford Economic Papers*, No. 2 (1939), p. 29n.

18. Introducing oligopoly for a moment, there is a sense in which a time contrast *inverse* to Mr. Harrod's might be made between d_1 and D_1, with d_1 a short-run curve, and the less elastic D_1 a long-run curve. It is that one seller might raise his price knowing that he would lose sales temporarily along d_1 until the others followed him, but knowing also that if and when they did, in the long run, he would enjoy the larger sales at the new price which are indicated by D_1. Similarly, for a downward adjustment, a seller may lower his price knowing he will gain sales temporarily along d_1 until others follow him, and even hoping that this period may be long, perhaps indefinite. Thus the short-run demand curve may be more elastic than the long-run curve in this direction too. This argument seems especially important when considered with reference to imperfect knowledge and inertia among sellers, and to situations where the overlapping between markets is loose and uncertain.

period *demand* curve (my italics), which takes account of the vulnerability of his market if he charges a higher price,' by his description of it, simply becomes the long-run average *cost* curve *LAC*. For clearly the entrepreneur, considering what his demand will be at some higher price after the entry induced by this price has taken place, will find that the amount is always that given by the average cost curve for the price in question. Here is 'tangency' with a vengeance! Did Mr. Harrod really mean to scramble demand and cost curves in this way?

It remains true that the process for which Mr. Harrod argues is important in some degree, and where present works to diminish (not destroy) excess capacity. Wherever a businessman thinks *his own* profits will contribute to encouraging entry which will affect *him* adversely, he is likely to moderate his price policy. It must be clear by now, however, that the argument in question is not of such universal applicability as to warrant the conclusion that excess capacity is 100 per cent wrong and therefore to be 'discarded.' Perhaps 3 per cent 'wrong' would be closer.[19]

To define the circumstances under which, with oligopoly forces present, potential entry may influence prices, and in what degree, is a complex matter.[20] Certainly oligopoly is not to be thought of in terms of the simplified model, comparatively unusual in real life, in which three or four firms occupy a sharply defined 'market' (thus literally 'small numbers'). When conceived in the sense of the ability of one seller by his price (or nonprice) policy, to influence appreciably the sales of another, it is evidently very general.[21] Very general too (and not merely in the manufacturing industries but throughout the economic system) is an aversion to carrying (price) competition 'too far,' sometimes called a 'live and let live' policy, and perhaps explained ultimately in part by a subtle awareness of oligopolistic forces. (To this must be added,

19. It must never be forgotten that the forces in question are *general* in nature and not restricted to the 'big business' segment of the economy (see above, p. 286n.16). It should also be said that, as indicated by the argument so far (i.e. without oligopoly), the correction is zero per cent.

20. Cf. Joe Bain, op. cit. and *Barriers to New Competition*, Harvard University Press, Cambridge, Mass., 1956.

21. See *Monopolistic Competition*, pp. 102-4, also above, p. 61.

of course, actual and tacit agreements of great variety and abundance.) Indeed, one may well hazard the guess that since, as Mr. Harrod has argued (esp. pp. 153-6), entrepreneurs are extremely vague in their ideas about demand curves anyway, they often think and act (in so far as they think at all about the influence of *price* on sales) in terms of some sort of vague compromise between the *d* and *D* types of curves (Figure 1). After all, these two curves (in their present use) are quite rigidly defined, one depicting the complete *absence*, and the other the full *presence*, of 'price competition' as that term is usually understood. Any conduct, however explained, which fell between these two extremes, would, by now familiar reasoning, make for more excess capacity than at *R* in Figure 1.

Another consideration which mitigates the line of argument advanced by Mr. Harrod is that one may well get entry anyway, even without the flaunting of *actual* high profits before the prospective entrepreneur. It seems to be a sound generalization that what this latter is really interested in is the *prospect* of profits for himself after he enters, rather than the actual profits being enjoyed by someone else now. A prospective entrant into some area of economic activity may be led to enter it by the fact that a number of others are making a satisfactory living in it and that he may reasonably expect to do as well. Indeed this possibility was specifically envisaged as a part of my own original explanation of how excess capacity might come into being.[22] If a certain line of activity promises good prospective incomes, it may well be questioned whether even such an abhorrence of actual current profits as Mr. Harrod envisages would succeed in putting the lid on entry.

Another major factor which can only be mentioned is that even conspicuous success by an entrepreneur in some type of activity will not necessarily bring entry which would reduce *his* profits. Thus a successful supermarket does not necessarily lead to another one across the street. It is much more likely to lead to

22. Cf. *Monopolistic Competition*, p. 105, where reference is made to 'the persistent efforts of others to find a place for themselves in business' and a process by which excess capacity may develop *without transitional high profits* is described.

one in another part of the city—or in another city. The argument must evidently be extended beyond this spatial example to *all phases* of product differentiation. It calls seriously into question the extent to which any entrepreneur will imagine that present self-denial will protect him from potential competitors. The main point is that the competitors will come anyway if the future prospects are there. The presence or development of excess capacity is not conditioned on a transitional phase of high profits.

A part of Mr. Harrod's case rests on a line of argument which appears to me methodologically illegitimate, and it must now receive some attention. In Essays 1 and 7 above and elsewhere, I have commented on the problems encountered by monopolistic competition itself, of 'entry' into the field of economic theory, in view of the entrenched position of perfect competition; and have cited Keynes on the difficulties of assaulting 'habitual modes of thought.' [23] Mr. Harrod is such a good example of these difficulties that I must try his patience further by citing him and pointing to some of the internal evidence in his essay.

Mr. Harrod is fundamentally a 'perfectly competitive' economist. In his Presidential Address before Section F of the British Association, 1938, he refers to a 'map or model' which economists have constructed and which he identifies with the 'theory of perfect competition.' [24] 'Recent theorems relating to Imperfect Competition,' according to him, do not call for a change in the map; on the contrary, they show 'how real markets are *distorted* by comparison with those of the map.' Their significance is that they raise problems of 'what interferences might be introduced to make the real world *more like the map.*' [25] All this, of course, is quite in fashion. I wish only to say that for me the map itself is one of monopolistic competition. Since it involves many dimensions it can only be conceived as a map by analogy; I have tried to picture such a map in a two-dimensional space analogy above (pp. 47ff.). Another analogy would be that of a surface of water, a lake on which drops of water are falling and sending out rings.

23. Cf. above, pp. 13ff. and 139.
24. 'Scope and Method of Economics,' *Economic Journal,* September 1938, p. 392.
25. Op. cit. pp. 394-5. My italics.

The drops (and rings) are both large and small; they are irregularly spaced, and of course break into each other very generally. For a static analogy it would be necessary to photograph, or 'freeze,' the lake at some moment of time. Of course such a comparison cannot be pressed far, but it does serve to present a picture of endlessly overlapping products, with no more than limited opportunities for marking off areas which might be treated as 'industries,' a prerequisite of (purely) competitive markets. And it places the stress on the limited and overlapping markets of the *firms*, and on a *network* of relationships between them, rather than sweeping away all this aspect of the system by the 'homogeneity' and 'large numbers' assumptions necessary to perfect competition.

A perfectly competitive economist naturally regards monopoly elements as aberrations in some sense, since the 'fundamental forces' are those of perfect competition. He therefore (perhaps unconsciously) 'starts from' perfect competition. And where there are frictional obstacles to change, he may thus present an argument against the alleged 'aberrations' which is a simple begging of the question. Thus Mr. Harrod argues that there could be no excess capacity because the entrepreneur, *having installed* a large plant in accord with 'long-run considerations' (which include a highly elastic demand curve),[26] would not then underutilize it. If he were going to produce less, he asks, 'Why not plan to have [the smaller plant]?' Why not, indeed? Why should we *assume* that he has installed the 'large plant' in the first place? One might equally well picture the entrepreneur as foreseeing a smaller demand, and therefore as building a smaller plant. One could then ask why he would initiate a price war in order to *over*utilize it, since if he had expected to produce larger outputs he would have built a larger plant from the first? The question of the *initial* plant simply cannot be introduced without begging the question, for the size of the plant which will be built is a part of the answer.

26. It should be held in mind that the envelope curve analysis indicates some degree of underutilization of whatever plant is built, unless the demand curve is perfectly elastic. Here again, there is the recurring problem of what Mr. Harrod really means by 'no excess capacity.'

In fact, a more realistic picture would give recognition to the fact that plants are adaptable, so that the type of 'plunge' pictured by Mr. Harrod is quite imaginary. A typical enterprise (at least in the United States) will start with a modest plant and expand as increased sales warrant. But in so far as plants cannot be altered or adapted, entrepreneurs will surely build those which in their best judgment correspond to *future sales*. *All* market potentialities, including that of possible excess capacity, must enter into this judgment.

Another way of putting the matter is to point out that, in shifting one's 'mode of thought' from perfect competition to monopolistic competition, the danger to be averted is of imagining that the economy too must make a corresponding shift. There is no such necessity, for the economy is and has always been one of monopolistic competition. There is therefore no problem of how such a state might evolve out of pure competition. Of course conditions change, and certain areas become more, others less, monopolistic over time.[27] But the main point is that to argue against the possibility of monopolistic competition *on the ground* that there are 'frictions' in *escaping* from perfectly competitive commitments *already taken*, is simply to beg the question.[28]

27. In one respect, at any rate, it might be argued that change towards excess capacity is easier than change away from it: the former change may well—and in Mr. Harrod's case does—involve a transitional period characterized by 'extra' profits, whereas the latter involves losses and the painful process of failure and elimination for some of the redundant firms. (Cf. *Monopolistic Competition*, p. 93. The statement, line 2, that 'the situation is unstable' applies to large numbers. Its stability under certain oligopoly assumptions is affirmed on p. 105, l. 3.) For any particular entrepreneur, the fear that he may be one of those eliminated may well deter him from starting the process of moving from a situation of excess capacity to one closer to 'perfect competition.'

28. This is such a familiar dialectic that at least one other instance should be mentioned. Thus Sherrard, of the Chicago School, attempts to make monopolistic competition appear absurd by dwelling at length on the problems of its coming into being. 'Imagine,' he says, 'a great day of transformation when the idea of product differentiation dawns . . . curves are instantly tilted . . . abnormal profits become universal . . . Are new firms spawned in every industry, thus causing overcapacity? That is hard to imagine, since there are presumably no idle entrepreneurs or resources at the outset . . . the government might embark on inflationary schemes . . . etc., etc.' ('Ad-

Finally, it must be pointed out that, even allowing for the uncertainties already discussed as to his own meaning, Mr. Harrod and I clearly do not mean the same thing by excess capacity; and when he advised economists to abandon the 'doctrine,' this difference should have been indicated. I do not now refer to the fact that my own theory rests (in part) on oligopoly, which he excludes. This has been discussed above, and in 'so far as his line of argument may be *adapted* to the oligopoly explanation, it has been answered or allowed for. Nor do I refer to the fact that my own theory rests (in part) on numerous forces other than oligopoly which lessen the importance of 'price competition' or possibly eliminate it. It has been argued above that since oligopoly is necessary to his argument (even though he denies it), these latter forces are not touched by the argument. I do refer to the difference in definition of the welfare optimum from which excess capacity is presumably measured. For Mr. Harrod (and Mrs. Robinson) the optimum is perfect competition, K in Figure 1; for me the optimum involves product heterogeneity, and it was identified in *Monopolistic Competition* with R.[29]

Monopolistic Competition was primarily a theory of the economy, and said nothing specifically about welfare economics as such. But (fortunately) it contained a reference to 'a sort of ideal,' [30] with an accompanying bit of analysis, which makes clear

vertising, Product Variation, and the Limits of Economics,' *Journal of Political Economy*, April 1951, p. 139.) After much more of the same, he concludes that 'nothing will be gained by pursuing this giddy process further . . .' I agree, and suggest as an exercise for Mr. Sherrard that he try his hand at depicting the cataclysms which would accompany the transformation of a world of monopolistic competition into one of pure competition.

29. See references to the 'ideal,' *Monopolistic Competition*, pp. 104-5. (A neglected article by J. M. Cassels, 'Excess Capacity and Monopolistic Competition,' *Quarterly Journal of Economics*, May 1937, in which he corrects Mr. Kaldor's initial misunderstanding, will also be helpful.) The case of nontangency was never dealt with specifically in this connection. Its great frequency and importance in general are argued in *Monopolistic Competition*, pp. 110-13 and 172-3. See also ibid. p. 78n.1, and above, pp. 52-3.

30. P. 94. See also pp. 104-5. There was discussion of welfare economics in my 1937 article, now Chapter IX of *Monopolistic Competition* (esp. pp. 213ff.); and the subject is carried much further in Essay 5 above, with the general conclusion that oligopolistic interdependencies militate almost fatally

that at no time was the ideal identified with the minimum point on the cost curve, K, or with perfect competition. K is a tenable optimum for the firm only if its sales are *not* a function of price. If firms have demand curves of finite elasticity, these curves must play a part along with cost in defining the welfare ideal, just as such demand curves for broader commodity categories play their part in conventional welfare theory.

These differences in fundamental conception of the problem render treacherous any instructions to economists that they must abandon forthwith something which is called the 'doctrine of excess capacity.' I do hope that in the preceding pages enough has been indicated as to the shaky foundations of Mr. Harrod's case so that the 'doctrine' in question may continue to receive the attention and importance it deserves.

against a satisfactory definition of the welfare optimum under monopolistic competition. On this latter point, see esp. pp. 100ff.

15

The Chicago School

A 'CHICAGO SCHOOL' of thought, with particular reference to economic policy, is familiar to economists, and has been frequently referred to as such. For example, M. Bronfenbrenner speaks of 'the so-called Chicago School of economic policy, whose intellectual parent is Frank H. Knight, but whose best-known publicist is Henry C. Simons.' [1] Such a school is recognizable too in the field of economic theory. As with the school of policy, its 'intellectual parent' is undoubtedly Professor Knight, to whom must be added Milton Friedman, George Stigler, and a number of others.[2] It believes in 'competitive theory,' but such a belief is widely held and would not in itself distinguish a Chicago school. It is distinguished by the zeal with which the theory of monopolistic competition has been attacked, and in particular by the extraordinary set of misconceptions as to the nature of this theory which have emerged in the process. I shall therefore call it the Chicago School of Anti-Monopolistic Competition.

The purpose of this essay is mainly to indicate the existence of such a school. Several of its preconceptions have already been discussed in Essay 1, and especial attention will be turned here to some of its more important lines of attack on monopolistic competition theory. Of these there are many—'Any stick

1. 'Contemporary American Economic Thought,' *American Journal of Economics and Sociology*, July 1950, p. 487.
2. All of whom have taught or studied at the University of Chicago, and whose interpretations of the theory of monopolistic competition reveal this common intellectual origin.

will do . . .' and sometimes the stick is grabbed by the middle while both ends are used. But it would certainly bore the reader to go into too much detail—to deal separately, for instance, with each one of the misstatements and misunderstandings in Stigler's major blast, 'Monopolistic Competition in Retrospect.' [3] It will be more helpful to stay close to a few of the major issues.

What characterizes the Chicago School is not its belief that the economy is 'highly competitive,' but its apparent conviction that monopolistic competition denies this and must therefore be up-rooted, cast in the fire, and burned. The starting point is surely Professor Knight's extreme views on the nature of 'economic theory' as being literally identical with, and restricted to, the theory of 'perfect competition.' Professor Knight's views are well known, but a convenient and characteristic statement of them, 'Knight in a Nutshell,' will be found in a paper given at the meetings of the American Economic Association in December 1945.[4] At this point, I can do no better than to reproduce that portion of my own 'Discussion' of Professor Knight's paper which deals directly with monopolistic competition theory:

The axiomatic law which is to govern all the highly complex market situations in real life, according to Professor Knight, is that of the 'perfectly competitive' market. This is another 'must' of theory.' It requires getting rid of monopolistic competition (a good beginning is made by calling it 'imperfect' competition) and, what is still more gratuitous, of monopoly itself, 'one of the older . . . branches of price analysis.' Professor Knight wavers, and in one place grudgingly admits monopoly as a (supplementary) 'law' (ruling otherwise, however, for monopsony, and other allied categories); but, since *really* to admit it to a co-ordinate place would raise havoc with 'perfect competition,' which to him is synonymous with 'theory,' his general position in this paper is as it has always been—to relegate it to the category of 'imperfections,' not really a part of 'economic theory' at all.

This position is always in the background, but it emerges clearly in

3. *Five Lectures on Economic Problems*, Lecture 2.

4. 'Immutable Law in Economics: Its Reality and Limitations,' *American Economic Review*, May 1946, p. 93. The paper is general and devotes only a few paragraphs to 'imperfect competition.' My knowledge of Professor Knight's teaching on the subject, however, has a much broader basis than this limited source from which quotation is possible.

the extended discussion of 'theory versus reality.' 'Reality' is identified with 'mechanical imperfections,' 'various forms of "imperfect competition," especially *monopoly*, itself a genus of many species.' Monopoly, then, and its cousins, are descriptive of reality, but not a part of 'economic theory.' It is now clear why 'theory' is to Professor Knight virtually a finished subject—any new development (and monopolistic competition is only one example) which is not a part of the theory of a perfectly competitive market simply is not a part of the subject!

It is difficult for me to refrain from offering some 'laws' from the field of monopolistic competition as candidates for [his] category of 'economic axioms.' Some of them are indeed quite self-evident—to any who are familiar with them. But I must state bluntly what seems appallingly evident to me, that in awareness of the theoretical problems of this field, Professor Knight has not, in his own words, reached 'the point where real discussion should begin.' Witness his dismissal of them as mainly due to imperfect knowledge! And the reason is not difficult to find. He is interested in 'economic theory,' and these matters are not a part of the subject. This will seem strange to many, but apparently there is nothing to be done about it. To Professor Knight, that is just the way 'theory' is.

To summarize my own criticism, the subject of *economics* is changing rapidly. I believe that *economic theory* should change along with it.[5]

The tradition of 'theory versus reality'—that the less economic theory has to do with the economic world we live in the better— is strong in the Chicago School and has been further developed by Friedman (see below). But our concern for the moment is with the proposition that there *is no* theory excepting that of 'perfect competition.' It follows from this view that the phenomena of monopolistic competition are 'unsystematic,' and merely an indistinguishable part of a great jumble of deviations from perfect competition which cannot be generalized about at all. In this matter Stigler followed Knight closely in his first treatment of 'imperfect competition' in the *Theory of Price*, 1946 edition, where he refers to 'the literally infinite number of possible deviations from perfect competition' and observes that 'we

5. Ibid. pp. 141-2. The earlier part of my 'Discussion' (beginning p. 139) deals with a number of other alleged 'theoretical requisites' and exclusions, all of which lead to Professor Knight's almost uniquely narrow view of 'theory.'

do not possess the practical knowledge to select for detailed study those cases which are empirically important.' [6] He also followed him here in attributing the phenomena of monopolistic competition to consumer ignorance,[7] but in a later edition (1952) this particular misconception seems to have been abandoned.

'Perfect rationality' is one of Professor Knight's prerequisites to economic theory, and the explanation of 'imperfect competition' by the phrase 'imperfectly economic behavior' [8] must be interpreted in part in terms of irrationality. The clearest statement on this issue is by Henry Simons, who has described the analysis of monopolistic competition as 'fundamentally irrational; no sane enterpriser would ever behave in accordance with the Robinson-Chamberlin prescriptions for maximizing profits—and on their own premises would lose his shirt if he did.' [9] The quotation is reproduced with approval by Bronfenbrenner.[10] An obvious comment seems to be that if the entrepreneur would lose his shirt by *maximizing* profits he would risk losing other even more important garments by doing anything else. I cannot recall anyone outside the Chicago School who has represented the theory as fundamentally based on imperfect knowledge or as fundamentally irrational.

A major mystery to me is a line of argument presented by both Stigler and Friedman, which appears in each case to play a de-

6. *Theory of Price* (1946), pp. 197-8. The interested reader may like to refer to my strongly worded criticism of his treatment of the problems of monopolistic competition in a review, *American Economic Review*, June 1947, p. 414.

7. According to Knight, 'Imperfect competition . . . and monopoly itself [sic] is closely connected with buyer ignorance of products, often fostered by deception . . .', op. cit. p. 104. Cf. Stigler, *Theory of Price* (1946), pp. 214, 329n.

8. Op. cit. pp. 103-4.

9. 'Some Reflections on Syndicalism,' *Journal of Political Economy*, March 1944, p. 12n.

10. 'Imperfect Competition on a Long-Run Basis,' *Journal of Political Economy*, April 1950, p. 81. For years I have puzzled over Simons' statement, until the context in which it was cited by Bronfenbrenner suggested as a possible explanation that he may not have been discussing, as stated, 'their own premises' at all, but a very different premise of his own—that the analysis is 'short run.'

cisive part in their rejection of the theory. According to Stigler, '. . . by the uniformity assumption Chamberlin has implicitly defined the group as a collection of physically homogeneous products. The identity of costs and demands is otherwise *meaningless*, and so also is the demand curve he proceeds to draw for a firm on the assumption that "competitors' prices are always identical" (p. 90). We simply cannot attach meaning to the statement that physically diverse things have the same price.' [11] Similarly, Friedman says, 'In one connection Chamberlin implicitly defines an industry as a group of firms having identical cost and demand curves. But this, too, is *logically meaningless* so long as differentiation of product is, as claimed, essential and not to be put aside. What does it mean to say that the cost and demand curves of a firm producing bulldozers are identical with those of a firm producing hairpins? And if it is *meaningless* for bulldozers and hairpins, it is *meaningless* also for two brands of toothpaste—so long as it is insisted that the difference between the two brands is fundamentally important.' [12] The idea is virtually the same, and I am unfortunately unable to identify its origin as between the two writers cited. Stigler thinks monopolistic competition is 'temporarily destroyed' by this consideration; and Sherrard has a reference to 'a special case . . . . which verges on pure competition' [13] which seems clearly from its context to refer to the same argument and hence to have had the same origin, whatever it is.

Surely better sticks than this could be found. No one outside the Chicago School has to my knowledge interpreted the 'uniformity assumption' to mean homogeneity of the products involved; and since it is clearly explained [14] what is meant by it and why this is not so, there is no excuse for anyone to proclaim such an absurdity. Stigler would appear to argue that for two students to receive the same course grade is meaningless because the men are different. Or that it is meaningless to say that they are of the same height (unless they are identical twins and hence

11. 'Monopolistic Competition in Retrospect,' p. 16. My italics.

12. *Essays in Positive Economics*, p. 39. My italics.

13. 'Advertising, Product Variation, and the Limits of Economics,' *Journal of Political Economy*, April 1951, p. 137.

14. *Monopolistic Competition*, pp. 82-3.

homogeneous). I have no difficulty whatever in attaching meaning to the statement that a number of brands of coffee sell for the same price, or that a number of laborers who are heterogeneous as to race, religion, disposition, or even efficiency, receive the same wages. Why is it meaningless even to say that a pound of coffee and a theater ticket sell for the same price? What is it all about? Yet this and related arguments are described by Stigler himself as so 'devastating' that on the basis of them he announces: 'The first attempt has failed.'

Friedman's contention is limited to uniformity of the *curves,* as distinct from *prices,* and thus does not go so far; but why is such uniformity (of curves) 'meaningless'? No one has said that, *literally interpreted,* it would ever be found in real life, and even Friedman's brief footnote about 'transformations' does not assert that it *could* not exist. It is of course an unrealistic but simplifying assumption, of the kind which Friedman himself advocates as a means of obtaining 'useful results,' and one would think that, in view of his own statement that 'the more significant the theory, the more unrealistic the assumptions,' [15] its very lack of precise 'realism' might commend it.

Without doubt the 'uniformity' assumption is a rigid and extreme one, and I sometimes think that if I were doing it over again today some variety of carefully defined 'representative firm' might be substituted. (In *Monopolistic Competition,* p. 111, it is suggested that the preceding analysis might be interpreted as for an 'illustrative' firm.) Such a firm would obviously have to express all the monopoly elements in the picture on a 'representative' basis, and therefore could not in any way be associated with a purely competitive analysis for the group. Most likely *each* of the two approaches would contribute something, so that neither needs to rule out the other. Another point: the uniformity assumption itself is a device which must be used with care and flexibility. Specifically, 'uniformity' *must* be temporarily relaxed in order to describe a competitive *movement* in which one seller precedes others.[16] For example, if one seller lowers his price from

15. Op. cit. p. 14.
16. In this respect it is no different from pure competition, where the principle of uniform price may be relaxed during a price movement.

$B'Q'$ along d_3 (Figure 1, p. 281), while the others keep their prices steady at $B'Q'$, the others will sell less than before at this price, which means that their d_3 curves have temporarily moved to the left.[17] The diagram describes the situation for *all* sellers only when all prices are in fact uniform. In short, it appears to be a useful device mainly for *simplifying* the more realistic picture which would be given by drawing a separate diagram for each seller. In any event why its use should be such an enormity that monopolistic competition must pay the full penalty remains a mystery.

Another leading feature of the Chicago School is its repeated assertions that monopolistic competition theory has 'failed' and that the 'failure' is total, complete. According to Friedman 'it possesses *none* of the attributes that would make it a truly useful general theory,' and it 'offers *no* tools for the analysis of an industry.' [18] (Strange indeed that so many industries have in fact been analyzed in terms of its 'tools'!) Stigler repeatedly asserts its 'failure' as *fact*—the theory is obviously a corpse and his purpose is merely to explain how it met its death. Sherrard, after elaborating on its substantial success, sets out to show that anyway it is a *'scientific* failure.' [19] Bronfenbrenner describes it as 'under growing attack,' [20] and according to Nutter, the economist 'is bound . . . to be disillusioned' by it.[21] And so on. The theory has of course been widely discussed, and in the course of this discussion has received a fair amount of criticism. But the verdict that it has, for all these years, already been under six feet of earth is unique to the Chicago School.

There is finally the dismissal of monopolistic competition on grounds of methodological principle. Here the chief contribution seems to be that of Friedman; [22] it is his ideas and phrases which

17. See *Monopolistic Competition*, pp. 90-92, for a description of this movement.

18. Op. cit. pp. 33, 39. My italics.

19. Op. cit. p. 127. His italics.

20. 'Imperfect Competition on a Long-Run Basis,' op. cit. p. 81.

21. G. Warren Nutter, 'Competition: Direct and Devious,' *American Economic Reveiw*, May 1954, p. 69.

22. 'The Methodology of Positive Economics,' op. cit.

are repeated by others, in particular by Stigler and Sherrard.[23] Friedman's plea for 'important and significant hypotheses' which 'abstract the common and crucial elements from the mass of complex and detailed circumstances,' [24] and his black-and-white contrast between perfect competition and monopolistic competition on this score, are strongly reminiscent of Knight, as discussed above. The general idea is to identify monopolistic competition with the detailed and special, the unsystematic and even 'descriptive,' the 'photographic reproduction'; whereas the meaningful and important generalizations are those where 'the firms can be treated *as if* they were perfect competitors'—or perhaps as Marshallian monopolists. According to Stigler, monopolistic competition 'cannot make a single statement about economic events in the world we sought to analyze.' [25] Sherrard quotes this with approval,[26] and adds a line of argument to the effect that the results of both product variation and selling activity too are 'unpredictable.' [27] He lists five major assumptions of Marshall (p. 129) and holds that 'every one of them has been abandoned [by monopolistic competition] and that no new assumptions have been introduced in their place' (p. 133): the result is an appeal to 'raw reality' (p. 134). What nonsense! Monopolistic competition is full of 'assumptions,' and on Sherrard's own list for Marshall, only the first (product homogeneity and 'large numbers') has actually been 'abandoned.' [28]

23. Stigler in fact attributes his specific remarks on methodology to Friedman. (Op. cit. p. 23.)

24. Op. cit. p. 14.

25. Op. cit. pp. 18-19.

26. Op. cit. p. 138n.

27. Ibid. pp. 134-6. Much of what he says could be applied (although he denies it) equally to prices, and would show that the results of price variations by entrepreneurs are 'unpredictable' in the same sense. Cf. above, p. 116, esp. n.10.

28. Indeed, the theory as presented in 1933 actually progresses through a *series* of assumptions (see above, p. 68 for a summary), so that I have often thought it a very good example of Marshall's own description of the 'one bit at a time' method, involving 'partial solutions' which are at last combined 'into a more or less complete solution of the whole riddle . . . The more the issue is thus narrowed, the more exactly can it be handled; but also the less closely does it correspond to real life. Each exact and firm handling of

The Chicago School speaks *ad nauseam* about finding 'the important common elements' of phenomena,[29] and about 'simplicity' and 'simplifying.' [30] It does not seem to occur to them that there might also be simplifying assumptions other than those identified with perfect competition.[31] Monopolistic competition to them is the 'abandonment of theory,' since it does not 'direct attention toward significant and observable relationships.' [32] According to

a narrow issue, however, helps towards treating broader issues, in which that narrow issue is contained, more exactly than would otherwise have been possible. *With each step more things can be let out of the pound . . .' (Principles,* p. 366, my italics).

29. Stigler, op. cit. p. 23; and Friedman, cited above.

30. Cf. especially Sherrard, *passim,* who concludes that monopolistic competition is not 'really a theory' because it does not 'simplify' (p. 133). Cf. also Nutter, op. cit. p. 70.

31. This addiction to the particular 'simplifications' of perfect competition can easily lead to a begging of the question when the issue is monopoly. Thus Arnold C. Harberger, in discussing 'Monopoly and Resource Allocation' (*American Economic Review,* May 1954, p. 77) makes so many 'competitive' assumptions that he inevitably comes out with the competitive answer. The problem is the 'welfare effects of monopoly.' *Constant returns* is assumed for both *firms* and industries, thus eliminating *all* monopoly distortions related to cost as a function of output. *'Monopoly'* is then identified merely with *profits,* (so that with universal tangency of demand and cost curves, there would be zero 'monopoly distortion,' no matter how inelastic the demand curves). It is moreover identified with deviations, plus or minus, of actual profits from a statistical average (whose monopoly content is not discussed). The deviations are those of an *average industry* rate for each of 73 manufacturing industries, from the average for all, thus wiping out all 'monopoly' ($=$ profits) *within* each industry, except what fails to cancel out and thus remains in the industry *average.* (To make this point clear, the broader and fewer the industry classifications, the less the monopoly; at the extreme of a single industry called 'manufacturing,' monopoly would be zero by definition.) This is only the beginning. With the help of numerous other 'simplifying assumptions,' he emerges with a figure for welfare loss due to 'monopoly distortion' of $1.50 per capita, refines this figure up to $2.00, back down to $1.40, and finally to $1.50 again. Taking this figure very seriously, he 'confesses' that he is 'amazed' at the result. The 'study' convinces him that 'our economy' is *'in fact* [my italics] . . . awfully close to being' competitive and that monopoly distortion is much less than the 'literature of the last twenty or so years' would indicate (pp. 86-7). But Ruth Mack, adding many other points to those here made, queries (p. 88) 'how can the calculations of this paper support any general evaluation of the impact of monopoly?' and I join her.

32. Sherrard, op. cit. pp. 140, 127; see also Stigler, op. cit. p. 22.

Friedman it is 'too narrow to be of great interest . . . too broad to permit meaningful generalizations.' [33] Is not all this again the same obsession that there *is* no theory excepting that of perfect competition and that all else is chaos? Perfect competition is being 'abandoned,' yes. But is this the same as abandoning *economic theory?*

The result, says Stigler, is *'ad hoc* empiricism,' and Sherrard quotes this with approval.[34] Yet is not any application of theory to particular situations necessarily *ad hoc?* At one point Stigler describes 'the effect of diversity of demand and cost conditions' as 'even more devastating: there may be monopoly profits throughout the group at equilibrium—and then again, there may not.' [35] But what of the ordinary and familiar theory of monopoly, to which Stigler would presumably have no objections? Certainly monopoly profits may be large or small or possibly zero, depending on demand and cost conditions in any particular situation. What is there that is so devastating about this? In what way, it may be asked, is monopolistic competition any more *ad hoc* than Marshall's time analysis? Again, on defining a commodity, Friedman quotes Marshall with approval: 'The question where the lines of division between different commodities [i.e. industries] should be drawn must be settled by convenience of the particular discussion,' and himself continues, *'Everything depends on the problem;* there is no inconsistency in regarding the same firm as if it were a perfect competitor for one problem, and a monopolist for another.' [36] Stigler echoes that 'different theories, each with its particular assumptions, can be applied to the same phenomena to answer different questions.' [37] What could be more *ad hoc* than this? People who live in *ad hoc* houses should be more indulgent: after all, is it any criticism of monopolistic competition theory that particular features of each situation to which it is applied must be taken into account?

In his discussion of methodology, Friedman has described the

33. Op. cit. p. 39.
34. Stigler, op. cit. p. 22; Sherrard, op. cit. p. 140.
35. Op. cit. p. 18.
36. Op. cit. p. 36. His brackets; my italics.
37. Op. cit. p. 23.

process of 'constructing hypotheses and testing their validity,' and I should like to quote from his description. The process 'involves comparison of the implications of an earlier set of hypotheses with observation; the contradiction of these implications is the stimulus to the construction of new hypotheses or revision of old ones.' [38] There could not be a better description of how the 'hypotheses' of monopolistic competition came into being.

38. Op. cit. p. 13.

16

Mrs. Robinson's Recent Visit

to Monopolistic Competition

AFTER twenty years, Mrs. Robinson has finally acknowledged in print [1] the fact that I have during most of that time insisted that her theory is very different from my own; and the occasion deserves to be noted.

Her brief comment begins with the statement that she has 'never been able to grasp the nature of the distinction between *imperfect* and *monopolistic* competition.' But the distinction has not been merely asserted—it has been extensively documented.[2] Would it be too much to ask Mrs. Robinson to meet the issues instead of merely asserting an inability to grasp them? Where, if at all, has she been misquoted or misrepresented?

As for the distinction between the two theories, I believe there is in the minds of many a fundamental confusion arising out of a certain similarity in the *subject matter* with which they are both concerned.[3] But surely the subject matter which a theory is

1. 'Imperfect Competition Revisited,' *Economic Journal*, September 1953, p. 579n.1.

2. The chief references are: *Monopolistic Competition* (5th or later ed.), Chap. IX (specifically section 2; but section 1, entitled 'Some General Misconceptions' also discusses major issues between the two theories); and above, pp. 26-30, 64-7, 73-5, 95-7, 141-43, 273-77.

3. Thus the fact that Robert Triffin, in his *Monopolistic Competition and General Equilibrium Theory*, displayed passages from Mrs. Robinson's book and from my own on opposite pages to show their similarity, has been taken

designed to explain and the theory itself must be carefully distinguished. The nebular and planetesimal theories both deal with the same subject, the origin of the solar system, but this does not make them the same theories. An examination of Mrs. Robinson's all-too-brief remarks in the light of this distinction between subject matter and theory should clarify just wherein the differences between us lie.

In explanation of her inability to grasp the distinction, Mrs. Robinson says that '. . . where we dealt with the same question, in our respective books, and made the same assumptions we reached the same results (errors and omissions excepted). When we dealt with different questions we naturally made different assumptions.' These statements are incontrovertible. In fact, it could be said with equal truth of *any* two people and of *any* two theories that if their assumptions are the same, and if there are no errors, they should reach the same results. The case that the theories are basically different, then, consists in pointing out that the *assumptions* are different. Before we proceed, however, Mrs. Robinson's statements should be completed by adding (in accord with the distinction between subject matter and theory, just made) that when we dealt with the same question *and made different assumptions,* we naturally got *different* results.

Different assumptions are the key. And since I can think of no place where *all* of the assumptions are the same, it can safely be said that in no place are the conclusions of the two theories the same. 'What of the tangency solution?' some will say at once. A sufficient (though not complete) answer is that since both (1) the demand curves and (2) the cost curves, which are tangent to each other, are differently defined (and in quite important respects),

by some (who evidently read no further) as indicating that he for one thought the two theories were essentially the same. (Cf., for instance, above, p. 106n.3.) The compared passages, however, have to do with only one out of four questions (p. 36) which he asks about the two books, viz. '*Are both writers tackling the same problem?*'—and after the explicit elimination, even from this limited comparison, of product variation and selling outlays (p. 21n.6, par. 2). Triffin's book (especially Chaps. I and II) is in fact a mine of information on the 'sharp contrasts' and 'divergences' between the two *theories:* (1) as he saw them (2) in 1940.

their points of tangency are also different. To hold otherwise is simply to confuse economics with geometry.

Let us take up specifically only two major problems, and Mrs. Robinson shall choose them. In her own 'debunking' operation, as she calls it,[4] she describes herself as having been interested mainly in the two problems of (1) welfare comparisons, and (2) the exploitation of labor. It is not too much to say that our conclusions with respect to both these subjects could hardly be farther apart; and the reason in both cases is that our assumptions—and therefore the theories—are different.

With respect to the first, perfect competition can be defended as a welfare ideal only under the assumptions (1) that products are homogeneous, and (2) that, at least for welfare purposes, people *want* homogeneous products in the sense that their market demand for variety is unimportant or 'irrational' and hence may be neglected. These are her 'assumptions' (the first explicit, the second implicit), and since quite different assumptions are made in monopolistic competition, the welfare ideal in this latter cannot be that of perfect competition.[5]

With respect to the second, Mrs. Robinson's conclusion that the 'hired factors' are exploited by entrepreneurs rests on a combination of the two assumptions (1) that within an industry the product is homogeneous, and (2) that the entrepreneur is an indivisible unit, one for each firm. Each of these assumptions is the reverse of what is assumed under monopolistic competition. The theories are therefore different, and that is why the conclusions on exploitation are different.[6]

Furthermore, although I hesitate to accuse Mrs. Robinson of a logical 'error,' I am bound to offer as a candidate for this designation her very general substitution, once it has been shown that 'hired factors' are exploited, of the particular factor labor

4. *Economic Journal*, December 1952, p. 925.

5. For further discussion see *Monopolistic Competition* (5th or later ed.), pp. 213-15, and Essay 5 above. Cf. also a recent article by Alex Hunter, 'Product Differentiation and Welfare Economics,' *Quarterly Journal of Economics*, November 1955.

6. These matters are discussed more in detail in *Monopolistic Competition*, Chap. VIII and (5th or later ed.) pp. 212-18; and above, pp. 193-6.

in place of the broader category of hired factors. Her analysis actually 'proves' (under her assumptions) that *hired factors* are exploited by *entrepreneurs;*[7] yet we never hear of such hired factors as rent receivers or interest receivers among the victims of exploitation. It is always labor. This is true of *Imperfect Competition* and also of the *Essay on Marxian Economics,* from which the following quotations are of interest: 'The modern theory of imperfect competition, although formally quite different from Marx's theory of exploitation, has a close affinity with it' (p. 4);[8] and 'Thus the share of labor in total output is ground between the upper and nether millstones of monopoly and monopsony' (p. 76). Furthermore, there is on page 80 a reference to the 'distribution of the product between labour and capital,' in relation to Marx and to the formula $\dfrac{e}{e-1}$, which looks suspiciously as though 'capital' (in this analysis a *hired factor*) might have replaced the indivisible entrepreneur as the exploiter of labor. I do hope that someone will not describe these propositions under the rubric, distressingly familiar in this area, of 'current doctrine,' with the implication that I am involved in them.[9] For so far as

7. Even though these latter make no more than 'normal' profits. I believe it to be widely thought that the issue of exploitation is merely definitional, in the sense that there is agreement that labor is paid less than the value of its marginal product in the firm and that Mrs. Robinson simply defines this as exploitation whereas I do not. This is flatly untrue. It is a part of Mrs. Robinson's doctrine that the entrepreneur receives correspondingly *more* than the value of his marginal product and *is thus the exploiter.* In my own theory, since nothing which could be called exploitation is indicated, there is naturally *neither* exploiter *nor* exploitee.

8. Jean Marchal seems to have followed Mrs. Robinson in this matter, including the (qualified) link with Marx. After summarizing her analysis, he asserts that 'it follows from the works of modern economists [sic] that in the market economy workers do not receive what is their right in strict commutative justice whenever there is imperfect competition. . . .' (*Les facteurs qui determinent le taux des salaires dans le monde moderne: du prix du travail au revenu du travailleur,' Revue Economique,* July 1950, p. 137. My translation. See also *American Economic Review,* September 1951, p. 558.

9. Jean Marchal's repeated references to 'modern economists' in this connection (see preceding footnote) does substantially this, in view of the close association in the minds of many between Mrs. Robinson's theory and my own.

I am able to see, the theory of monopolistic competition as such is 'neutral' with respect to exploitation; [10] it is unrelated to Marxian doctrines and its affinity with *Das Kapital* is *nil*.

To sum up this part of my comment, divergent conclusions as between the two theories, such as we have seen for welfare and exploitation, are a matter of *fact* and not of anyone's opinion. Putting 'errors' to one side, they result from differences in assumptions. This means that the theories are different—and *fundamentally*, for who among economists would wish to say that the two issues discussed are not among the most important in economic literature?

It remains to be pointed out that in the article under discussion, Mrs. Robinson has made major changes in her own assumptions. Some of these changes are:

(1) An 'industry,' defined earlier as a 'group of firms producing a single homogeneous commodity,' may now produce goods which are 'extremely remote substitutes for each other' (p. 579). A 'market,' clearly associated earlier with a 'commodity' and thus with an 'industry,' is now distinguished from an industry, and identified with 'a group of commodities which are close substitutes for each other.' But although the substitutes may be 'remote' in the one case, and are 'close' in the other, we no longer have a single *homogeneous* commodity in either industry or market. With this change the doctrine of (monopolistic) exploitation must be abandoned, since the argument requires a homogeneous product within the area ('industry') from which the indivisible entrepreneur is (logically) removed in order to measure his marginal product. It should be added that these difficulties were indicated as early as 1937 in my article, 'Monopolistic or Imperfect Competition?' [11] Yet in Mrs. Robinson's *Essay on Marxian Economics,* in 1942, 'labor' is still being exploited.[12]

10. Actually it opens up the possibility that monopoly incomes may be attributed to *any* factor, and in particular to organized labor through 'collective bargaining.' (See Essay 12 above, esp. pp. 261-6.) In this sense particular groups of laborers, far from being exploited, may be able to engage in monopolistic exploitation (of consumers) on their own account.

11. *Quarterly Journal of Economics,* August 1937 (later Chap. IX of *Monopolistic Competition*).

12. Was the effort ever made to 'grasp' the difference here?

(2) Product differentiation, which formerly played no part in her theory at all, and was *rejected* in her discussion of my own [13] is now one of the 'main vehicles of competition' (p. 584).

(3) Among other 'main vehicles,' seven in all, only one is lower price, so that six out of the seven are nonprice. None of these latter was a part of the original theory.[14]

(4) There is an 'apology' for the neglect of oligopoly and for the resulting 'fudge' in the demand curve. Here Mrs. Robinson now explains her omission by saying that she 'could not solve' the problem. But the real explanation is surely to be found in what she said in 1933, and it is highly significant. What she said then (*Imperfect Competition*, p. 21) was that it was 'not to her purpose.'

One might comment finally, that, in view of the great emphasis on 'geometry' in her earlier treatment, one of the most surprising changes in her present position lies in the statement that 'an individual demand curve (for a particular product produced by a particular firm) is a mere smudge, to which it is vain to attribute elegant geometrical properties' (p. 585).

Mrs. Robinson's 'revisit' to imperfect competition, if such it be, seems to have left it in something of a shambles. Should we not say that, instead of revisiting imperfect competition, she changed her itinerary and paid a rather extended visit to monopolistic competition—and *without even telling anyone where she was going?*

13. See above, p. 26n.50.

14. See above, p. 29. One who has not been fooled as to who it is Mrs. Robinson is 'visiting' at this point is Sidney Weintraub ('Concepts of Competition and Monopoly,' *American Economic Review*, May 1955, p. 470).

It should be noted here that what Mrs. Robinson omitted earlier (including oligopoly) and *now moves into the center of the stage* also escaped the attention of Mr. Harrod in his 1934 evaluation of the 'principal points of significance for economic theory' of the *two* theories. (See above, p. 285n.13.)

Index

Date Due

FEB 0 4 2007			